DESIGNING YOUR CLIENT'S HOUSE

DESIGNING YOUR CLIENT'S HOUSE

by Alfredo De Vido, FAIA

WHITNEY LIBRARY OF DESIGN
an imprint of Watson-Guptill Publications/New York

To C, R, and T

ACKNOWLEDGMENTS

I would like to thank the architects whose work appears in this book. Not only did they design the outstanding houses shown here, they also generously provided drawings, photographs, and detailed information on their designing and working processes.

Thanks also to Barbara Wood who patiently edited and clarified my rough drafts. Stephen A. Kliment, FAIA, Senior Editor of the Whitney Library of Design, served as my chief advisor. The book could not have materialized without his steady help and encouragement. Susan Davis, Editor, was patiently helpful in shepherding the book through to publication. Jay Anning contributed greatly to the quality of the book design.

Special thanks to my wife and co-worker, Catherine, who provided thoughtful comments on the text and typed the manuscript.

A final word of gratitude is due to the clients who commissioned these fine houses. Their enlightened outlook and patience are responsible for much of the quality in this work.

Paperback Edition
First Printing 1990

Copyright © 1983 by Whitney Library of Design

First published in 1983 by Whitney Library of Design,
an imprint of Watson-Guptill Publications,
a division of Billboard Publications, Inc.,
1515 Broadway, New York, N.Y. 10036

Library of Congress Catalog Card Number: 82-24805
ISBN 0-8230-7142-1
ISBN 0-8230-1307-3 (pbk.)

Distributed in the United Kingdom by Phiadon Press Ltd.,
Musterlin House, Jordan Hill Road, Oxford OX2 8DP

Manufactured in the U.S.A.

1 2 3 4 5 6 7 / 95 94 93 92 91 90

Edited by Stephen A. Kliment and Susan Davis
Designed by Jay Anning
Graphic production by Hector Campbell
Set in 9 point Helvetica Light

FOREWORD

BY WALTER F. WAGNER, JR.

For the past 18 years or so, as editor of *Architectural Record*, I have written many editorials urging more architects to get more involved in the design of houses. As I wrote to *Record's* architect readers just a few months ago: "I think it is important for architects to do houses—whenever they have a chance and *surely* whenever they are asked—because houses offer an ideal opportunity for architects to show people what architecture is about in a way and at a scale that everyone can understand and relate to. Houses are the form of architecture closest to people. When people understand about good design—whether they want the contemporary design that most architects want to do for them, or perhaps a remodeling of a worthwhile older house, or even (damn it) a *good* in-scale properly detailed version of Colonial—everyone benefits. Architects get to use their talent and skills; and the home owner gets a better house and lives, as the saying goes, 'happily ever after.' "

There are a lot of reasons why more architects have not been more involved in house design.

For one thing, there is a perception by many potential homebuyers that getting involved with an architect for the design of a custom house will add appreciably to the cost of the house. As the song goes, "it ain't necessarily so." There are of course a lot of expensive custom houses built—but in general they represent what a client who could afford an expensive house wanted and was willing to pay for. And there are, indeed, some architects who are interested only in doing expensive "showcase" houses.

But there are many other architects—young and not so young—who enjoy doing houses and enjoy the challenge of trying to create for the client family something special within very limited budgets. In support of the argument that a great house need not be expensive: Over the years, an extraordinary percentage of design awards have been won by vacation or second houses—typically built on relatively small budgets. One theory explaining this is that the client is less concerned with "status" in a vacation house and is willing to give the architect more freedom to explore new ideas. But I favor the theory that the limited budgets of second homes provide a constraint that leads to an essential simplicity, careful development of a single design idea, and attention to detail and detailing that sets these houses apart.

There is also the question in the public mind about architect's fees. I have always argued that a good architect can cover most of the fee by helping a client avoid expensive mistakes, setting cost-saving priorities, and designing for efficient construction. At any rate, many people I've talked to about retaining an architect are surprised to learn that in general architects hope to make about as much money as their clients earn—unless of course their client is a lawyer or a doctor, in which case they do not expect to earn nearly as much.

Looking at it from the other side, many architects are reluctant to undertake house design because "we can't make any money doing houses"—primarily because there is so much client contact involved and so many decisions to be made (from site selection to selection of door knobs) for a job of relatively limited budget (and therefore relatively limited fee).

One final constraint on architect involvement in house design: More than a few architects (including some first rate designers) do not really know how to design and detail a house so that a homebuilder can build it efficiently—and thus at a reasonable cost. For years, I have been urging architects interested in housing design to "take a good local homebuilder out to lunch." What I meant was that most architects have a lot they can learn about designing and detailing a house so that a builder, studying the plans to prepare a bid, understands exactly what is required, understands exactly what can be built to "builder standard" and what parts of the job will require special attention to detail, and understands exactly what finishes and special equipment he is expected to supply. Uncertainties make builders nervous—and when they are nervous about a job they tend to add extras just "to cover contingencies."

Well, if my best advice to architects up to now has been to take that homebuilder out to lunch, my best advice now is to read this book. Architect (and now author) Al De Vido clearly knows what he is talking about. He should. He has designed "somewhere between 125 and 150" houses that have been completed by homebuilders from the East Coast to California. He is steadily designing houses—though his practice includes commercial and institutional work as well. And he clearly enjoys doing houses, knows how to make a living doing it, and knows how to work with builders.

CONTENTS

His advice on cost-saving techniques and on designing to builder standard should be must reading for every architect. If you don't know why studs are pre-cut to 7 feet 10½ inches or what's magic about 3 feet 4 inches, you really need to read this book. If you can't get your house design on four or five sheets of drawing paper, you must read this book—because you are almost surely doing something wrong and wasting your client's money. To illustrate his advice and counsel, De Vido has chosen over 40 houses—some his, most by other good architects including some fine young architects who are just beginning to make their mark in the custom-house market. The houses are described not just in design terms, but against a box score of considerations that affect cost: site work, grids and modules, materials, construction techniques, interiors, heating and cooling, plumbing, lighting, special design treatments—and, again most significantly, management and documents.

I hope this book enjoys a very wide sale—not just because I wish its author well, or because I think it will be of real help to architects, but because I think it can result in better houses for a lot of families. Living in a dumb and ordinary house must be like being married to someone who is a boring conversationalist. You get used to it—but you miss a lot every day. Having a really good house (not an expensive house, not a luxurious house, but a good house) is one of life's great pleasures. Making good houses requires a very special teamwork among client and architect and builder. And this book should do much to make that teamwork more effective.

Let us hope that as a result of this book, a lot more families (and a lot more architects) live happily ever after.

INTRODUCTION

DESIGN ALONE IS NOT ENOUGH

Good design is every architect's goal. Professional success, however, is built on more than aesthetic skill. Unless you take into account the needs and life-styles of your clients, you are designing in the abstract. Your houses must incorporate quality materials and efficient layouts that are compatible with your clients' activities and preferences. And because it is the clients' money you are spending, you must accomplish all this within their budgets.

Costs are now more important than ever. In the face of the dramatic rise in housing costs—materials, labor, and financing—over the past few years, architects, builders and consumers alike are carefully examining ways of holding expenses down. Individuals can't control mortgage interest rates or prices; thus they turn increasingly to you, the architect, to effect savings in the design. It is not just people with unlimited resources who consult architects when they decide to build. Your client is just as likely to be a single person or a young couple on a limited budget who want to build a starter house. It's important to them that part of the expertise for which they are paying includes the architect's knowledge of how they can build for a reasonable price. Good design can cost a lot. As the houses in this book demonstrate, however, there are techniques you can use to make good design affordable, in accordance with your clients' needs.

HOW THE CLIENT AFFECTS THE PROJECT AND ITS COST

The starting point for determining the scope and cost of a house is the client's program. It may be only a statement of the number of rooms needed, or it may include detailed requirements such as square footage, room sizes, materials to be used, and ideas for the layout; it will probably include a cost ceiling. If your clients are builders, they will have very specific ideas about many aspects of the job. They may not be aware of some time- and cost-saving techniques, however, such as value engineering.

Your first job is to determine whether the program and its cost ceiling are realistic for the type of house the client wants. Any estimates you make at this point will not be binding, of course, but rough calculations will establish the range within which you will be working. Don't reject this first estimate because it is more than what the client has said can be spent. You may discover that the client has "tested" you with a low ceiling

and can actually afford to pay more. In any case, your relationship with a client will be better if you are straightforward about costs from the beginning. Before you proceed with the design, you must know whether the client will compromise on the program or on the budget if the two are at first incompatible. The first chapter of this book will show you the questions you need to ask to make this determination.

Your first estimate will be based on your knowledge of what materials and labor cost. A realistic estimate also takes the time factor into account—the cost of a house will increase by the rate of inflation during the construction period. Never base a first estimate on the lowest bid of your last job; costs have almost certainly risen since then, and each project must be considered independently.

It is you who must take responsibility for keeping the program and budget in line. Resist additions, alterations, and substitutions of materials that the client requests when they will affect costs. Many architects feel that denying the client's wishes will make them appear less than competent or difficult to work with. They therefore incorporate all client suggestions into their design, hoping that they can somehow manage to conjure up a balanced budget in the end or that the client will come up with the additional money. It is better to help the client keep costs down.

Be on guard: programs amended and expanded may cause the project to balloon beyond recognition—and beyond the means of the client. Don't revise the budget for every minor change, however. Inform the client as you go along of changes that will affect expenses. Then provide a formal update of the estimate about halfway through the design phase—perhaps at the model stage, if you are making one—and again when the project is ready to be turned over to a contractor.

If you think the contractors' bid will be out of line with the original budget because the scope of the project has increased since the outset, prepare the client by suggesting that the extra bedroom or more expensive building material be a bid alternate. Keep all such estimates clearly separate, and the client can then choose to do without or pay more.

THE ARCHITECT'S ROLE

Exercising an influence on your clients by keeping them informed of how changes will affect the budget is only part of the picture, however. Just as frequently, it is the architect who must be checked in his or her pursuit of originality; beware of decisions and ideas of your own that will result in a brokgn budget. If you feel that a particular feature is essential to produce a distinctive design, but will cost extra, discuss it honestly with the client.

Important factors in costs are materials and construction techniques. In these areas it is best to stick to the tried-and-true. "Original" details not only may not work, but the contractor may place a premium on their fabrication and installation. Ask yourself if the detail you want to use is really essential to the design concept. If so, research it thoroughly in advance so that you know what it will really cost and you will be certain it will work.

Focus on a rich organization of space, light, texture, and color to make your design statement. Limiting yourself to a few details and techniques and keeping to "builder's standards" (see Chapter 2) for executing them will hold costs down. Develop a system of design, such as modular units, and take the time to explain it to your clients and to builders. Many of the houses described in this book are effective and original designs that have successfully incorporated such systems.

WORKING WITH THE CONTRACTOR

After you and the client have agreed on a design, it is the contractor who must transform your plans into reality. You must make it possible to do so within or near the specified budget. This can be done in a variety of ways.

To begin with, gear your designs to the materials-handling and fabrication techniques available to house builders. Keep abreast of building techniques and materials costs by talking to builders and lumber-yard personnel. If you are knowledgeable about the constuction industry, you may be able to take advantage of timing to save money—building during slow economic periods, for instance, or when seasonal fluctuations lower the cost of materials.

Your rapport with the contractor is as important as your relationship with your client. Never insist that a contractor follow your techniques rigidly; it is the quality of the result that should be important. Don't make a contractor rip out something different from your specifications if it has been done in an equally acceptable way. Not only can you prevent cost overruns this way, but develop-

ing a good reputation among contractors is likely to result in lower bids and better negotiated contracts. Contractors who know that an architect won't insist on needless reworking will not have to build these costs into their estimates.

Communicate with the contractor clearly and concisely. For ordinary construction, develop a shorthand method of making your drawings. Avoid a multiplicity of details; standardize to a few typical sections. This way the contractor won't have to supervise the installation of every detail personally. Keep notes simple and direct. Avoid stylistic flourishes in drawing. Make everything clear and neat, with consistent line weights and materials indications. A reliable contractor is able to build well from an outline spec that points out the materials and quality level and a drawing that shows where the walls and openings are. Examine the drawings in this book and note the absence of nonessential information. How you communicate will be affected by the kind of contract the client has with the contractor—negotiated or bid.

WHAT TO DO IF PRECAUTIONS FAIL

Despite your careful attention to the foregoing factors, the bids for a project may still be higher than what the client can afford. This is not uncommon; on the average, only about one in four bids is within the original budget. When high bids occur, you have several options, the least satisfactory of which is to abandon the project. Alternatively, you might be able to get the client to raise the amount of money available, or you might be able to negotiate with the contractor to get a better price. If these two avenues fail, there is always the possibility of reworking the design with the client and submitting the changed plans for rebidding.

CHOOSING CONSULTANTS

The work of consultants can also affect the expense of a house, so choose them carefully. Seek a structural engineer who knows house-building techniques rather than one who specializes in larger buildings. Structural notes can be integrated with your architectural drawings. The structural engineer may be willing to red-mark a print and then give the completed job a final check for an hourly fee.

It is even more essential that mechanical consultants be familiar with house design. Systems used in residences are quite simple and do not require the sophistication that

those in a large building do. If you can find consultants who are familiar with residential installations, use them. If not, consider working with a contractor. Many are trained engineers and will combine practicality with professionalism. Pay them a fee for consultation so that you won't compromise yourself when awarding the contract.

IS IT POSSIBLE TO MAKE MONEY DOING HOUSES?

One of your goals is to make a living from your work. Fees for designing houses vary widely, from 45 cents per square foot for plans to 25 percent of the cost of construction. A reasonable median is 10 to 15 percent. Consider converting the amount of your fee into a lump sum if you think the client may be suspicious of your incentive to keep expenditures down when you will make more money by increasing them.

It is not unreasonable to set a goal of a 20 percent margin on direct costs. There are many ways of computing costs; the important thing is to be honest with yourself. Be realistic about what your work really costs. If you determine that the hours available for the job, based on your fee, seem impossibly low, you can ask for a higher amount. The least satisfactory option is to work at a loss. The key to profitability is to work efficiently; this book will show you how.

Other aspects of the design process that you should keep in mind because they affect your time—and therefore your costs—are conformance to building codes, zoning ordinances, environmental impact requirements, and labor union practices. Many towns have design review boards. Submissions to them can be time-consuming, not to mention frustrating, because they may be prejudiced against certain stylistic features. Investigate these prior to negotiating a fee so that you can include the time and cost in your estimates.

THE CHALLENGE OF PROJECT CONTROL

Creating a good design for a house while working within programmatic budget restrictions is a precarious balancing act. The processes described in this book have produced examples of responsive houses with a prevailing sense of quality, demonstrating that good design need not be unbuildable.

CHAPTER 1

BEFORE YOU DESIGN: WHAT YOU NEED TO KNOW

Your clients will probably approach you with specific ideas about the house they want you to design, a description of the site, and a budget. This is all right for a start, but to create a distinctive design you should probe beyond the bare facts given to you. The clients have most likely spent years dreaming about and planning their house, and understanding their thought process will be to your advantage.

KNOW THE PROGRAM

Clients prepare to varying degrees for the initial meeting with an architect. Some may present a simple list of rooms. Others may describe the overall appearance they want, give ideas for decorating, and specify materials and spatial relationships. They may reveal detailed plans that they have developed over the years. You need to know as much as they can tell you, so if they are vague, you must be prepared to draw them out; if their preferences are overly detailed, point out that the budget may not allow you to incorporate everything they want in your design.

If the clients have clippings from magazines, ask to borrow them. You needn't try to assemble a pastiche from the collection, but the clippings will provide an overview of the clients' aesthetic preferences. If you have a brochure of your own, encourage them to browse through it and indicate their "likes" and "dislikes." Your job will be easier if you know what features of your designs are appealing. Some clients may react so well to an existing design of yours (or someone else's) that they want you to replicate it. Explain that their program and site require something tailored to their personal needs rather than a carbon copy of another design.

Ask for a written program, emphasizing that it needn't be a polished essay. You'll be lucky if you get something like the one below, which was drawn up for an actual project. This is a particularly good example, because it describes design criteria but avoids specific solutions.

TYPICAL PROGRAM

Clients: Stuart and Deborah Minton
Property: Copake, New York

HOUSE PLANS

Square Feet: Not too large, 1,500–2,000 square feet

Size:
- Living room
- Large eat-in kitchen (to also serve as dining room; separate work area; floating island)
- Library/den/studio
- Master bedroom with bath
- Two additional bedrooms with shared bath
- One guest bath/powder room
- Fireplaces
- Basement/garage

Floor Plan:
- Two stories
- Bedrooms private, away from living spaces
- Large 2-story living area
- Well-defined entry space
- Fireplace to service more than one room
- Easy traffic flow

Space Utilization:
- Extremely important to have generous work space (kitchen) and storage (closets, kitchen and bath cabinets) plus closet in entry area

General Considerations:
- Rooms should receive bright sun
- Sense of outdoors
- No violation of site, sense of belonging
- Year-round house with look and feel of vacation home, that is, informality and minimal maintenance
- Usable exterior spaces for outdoor activities—deck (enclosed area too), barbecue, etc.
- Planning with possibility of pool at later date
- Pitched roof
- Play of structural elements to give liveliness
- Energy efficiency—good insulation, windows
- Large open spaces that still enable feeling of coziness, warmth—nothing overpowering

GENERAL CHARACTER
- Comfortably informal house, wedded to site. Two stories
- Large basement with 8-foot ceiling; good light
- Low maintenance inside and out. Minimum of painting and upkeep
- Feeling of space important, well related to the outdoors, but sense of sheltered en-

closure also important

- A natural wood house with a variety of spaces inside and out
- Out of sight of neighboring houses and road, but perhaps glimpse of rooftop or chimney from the road
- Garage as part of basement
- Country elegance; a retreat; informal, warm, gracious
- Interior furnishings: comfortable sofas and chairs, antique library tables, desks (auction/flea market finds). Interesting pottery, prints, etc.
- Provincial accents mixed with some modern but not cold pieces
- Charming, not contrived or self-conscious, planned casualness

THE MAIN APPROACH
- Turning in at drive, house blocked from view to be seen toward end with front door conspicuous and conventionally located
- Road should make use of "birch drive" as much as possible
- Ample parking area
- Warm and inviting entrance at end of drive; visitors made to feel welcome

ENTRANCES
- Inviting front door convenient to guest parking
- Comfortable entrance hall/greeting area with coat closet and guest bath convenient to kitchen, living room and private areas (bedrooms upstairs)
- Kitchen door near driveway for groceries
- Various doors to decks and garden as appropriate
- A "mud room" entrance through basement
- Access to living level from basement probably best near kitchen or into kitchen itself

KITCHEN
- Large kitchen with separate eating area
- Family social center
- Sunshine important
- Enjoy cooking so *very* generous counterspace, work island and cabinets
- Easy working layout/good refrigerator-stove-sink relationship
- Would like to be able to delegate dinner preparation so several (three) people should be able to work independently without crowding each other
- Space for dishwasher a must
- Entrance to living room through closed doorway

- Access to deck (or possibly enclosed outside eating area)
- Phone in kitchen—place to sit, take notes

DINING AREA OF KITCHEN
- Separated from kitchen work space; generous space for table (maybe large round one to seat eight and buffet (long French library table)
- Good lighting from outdoors, more intimate indoor lighting at night
- Aside from breakfast and lunch, see kitchen table as place to read newspaper in morning, write shopping lists, peruse cookbooks, etc., but in evening this will be our "formal" dining area
- Would like to be able to put very comfortable, slightly oversized upholstered dining chairs around this table

LIVING ROOM
- Spacious living room but comfortably secure when alone with a good book
- Large fireplace as focal point
- Roughly visualize three areas in this room: a central seating area around fireplace (not necessarily on top of it) and two areas flanking this (additional seating, gaming area, etc.)
- Would like to be able to convert one of these side areas into dining area if we have a large group, which won't be often

DINING ROOM
- No need for one as we see it now, but perhaps have option to add on one day
- Expect kitchen area with living room alternative to serve our needs adequately

STUDY
- A library with large desk, sofa, and comfortable reading chair
- Can be small but not confining
- Would like fireplace if possible
- A retreat

FIREPLACES
- Would like large fireplace in living room
- Since costs will probably prohibit us from two chimneys, would like this fireplace to service another room
- If den/study is not practical, maybe dining area of kitchen would be nice

BEDROOMS
- Master: Large with private bath, dressing area. Would like morning sun. Sitting area with writing table, phone, two closets
- Guest: Two guest bedrooms with shared

bath. Rooms need not be large but comfortably sized with reading areas or maybe window seats. One room will probably have twin beds so should be a little larger than other

BATHS
- Need not be large or fancy, but must be functional, convenient with good lighting and storage space for towels, linens, medicines extra
- Would like master bath to be largest

OTHER CONSIDERATIONS
- If master bedroom on same floor as guest, would like enough hall area to be separate
- Adjacent bedrooms should be separated by closet walls or bathrooms to muffle sounds or ensure privacy
- Should library double as a guest room replacing one of the two additional bedrooms above (would prefer not, but costs may leave no choice)
- Guest room double as workroom (again prefer not; hopefully basement can handle this)

STORAGE
- Very generous and as convenient as possible—"space for everything and everything in its place": coat closets, utility closets, kitchen/dining storage areas, liquor closet, bar, place for folding chairs, tables, games, etc.
- Woodbox for fireplace (or part of)
- Linen closet
- Clothes closet (two in master; one in each additional)
- Storage room (in basement)
- Lawnmowers, etc., in garage

BASEMENT
- If not practical on kitchen level, fine down here as long as easily accessible to kitchen
- In addition should have space for workshop (furniture stripping, plant transplanting, painting studio area), possible shower (if pool later). Maybe sauna, deep freeze, mud room

GROUNDS
- Cutting garden (English garden style—highly planned, but not manicured looking)
- Vegetable/herb garden
- Future pool or poolhouse. If so should have easy access to a basement entrance and basement shower

Lacking such a program, ask questions to find out as much as you can about the clients' professions and activities. Ascertain how and when they plan to use the spaces they have requested to see whether usage will match the function of each room. The answers to your questions will provide clues to what spaces can be combined, made smaller, or eliminated if a budget crunch develops.

At an early stage, suggest that narrowly specialized rooms be eliminated by incorporating their functions into other spaces. Work toward determining which areas can be expanded to accommodate multiple functions; enlarge a kitchen to include dining space, for instance. These are the areas that you should make visually important—in effect, where you should spend the available money.

KNOWING THE CLIENT

Getting to know the client is important for your understanding of the program. Try to fathom the clients' intangible goals. Do they want you to create an environment that provides comfort and satisfaction and expresses their personality, or are they more interested in status and prestige? Working with those whose motives are straightforward and who have clear ideas of what they want will be easy; you will have more trouble with those whose ambitions are confused or unformulated.

Find out how clients have come to you. Who referred you, or which of your projects they have seen? It is useful to know whether your recommendations have been unqualified and enthusiastic. Knowing the clients' degree of confidence in your ability will suggest how you should approach them. If the clients have interviewed other architects, find out who they are. If another architect has worked on the project previously, make sure that his or her services have been terminated properly.

Your understanding of the client will help you make some decisions. You should know, for example, how they feel about maintenance; some building materials require more upkeep than others. A client who is willing to participate actively in a solar heating system will enable you to save money by eliminating some automatic features. Know before you plan whether the clients prefer to save money or time. By the same token, try to determine whether a client prefers to economize on building costs

or in the long run with mechanical systems that are initially more expensive.

Create a proper mental atmosphere for decision making. Architects want to be regarded as wise and sensitive professionals, but you cannot expect clients to submit to your judgment completely. They will generally defer to your technical expertise, but they will also want to participate in the design process. Encourage this desire and use it creatively; the involvement of an intelligent, alert client will enrich a design and its layers of meaning.

Don't be stubborn when a client's needs conflict with aesthetic considerations. To achieve distinguished results that fit the program, meet the budget, and look good aesthetically, you must maintain control over the design, but total inflexibility on your part can destroy the critical relationship with the client.

As you get to know your clients better, you will discover what design factors might give their house its special character. Providing shelter, heat, light, and safety is basic; the keys to designing a unique house, however, are the details that symbolize the people who live there.

KNOWING THE BUILDER

If your clients are builders, you will need to know, in addition to the general program specifications, how many houses will be built from the model and how much flexibility you must provide to allow for customer modification. You should also find out who will make any changes a customer might request. If that job falls to the job superintendent, see if the builder will agree to consult you first (for an hourly fee), so that you can ensure the aesthetic success of the project. Ask about materials and color options; find out if customers will be permitted to choose cheap or inharmonious materials that will be out of place with the rest of the project.

Control is equally essential when you work with builders, but it is harder to negotiate. Most builders think the architect's role during construction is that of a watchdog, but they don't think they need watching. Work at developing a good relationship with the builders you deal with, so that you can work together rather than at cross purposes.

KNOWING THE SITE

Clients will undoubtedly understand that you need to know about the site in order to de-

sign their house. The factors besides location and acreage that must be taken into consideration are topography, vegetation, subsoil conditions, climate, and view.

Every site has a microclimate composed of sun orientation, temperature and humidity, wind velocity, and prevailing wind direction, all of which can affect the placement of the house, the choice of a heating and cooling system, and the building materials used. Take advantage of a site that has good sun exposure, for example, by incorporating passive heating and cooling features. A south-facing slope looking out on a view would present an opportunity to use sun apertures and collectors. Design with climate, not in spite of it; doing so will inevitably result in better, more livable spaces.

The topography of the site is important as well. A steeply sloping lot presents different problems—and potential solutions—from a relatively flat one. The presence of a view may be a paramount consideration, even overshadowing solar elements. Nevertheless, try to accommodate both. It may be possible to include a view to the north while catching the sun through clerestories to the south. Rocky sites present special problems, particularly with foundations and the placement of septic systems. Rock excavation is expensive and frequently beyond the expertise of builders who specialize in houses.

The composition of the soil and the kinds of plants and trees growing on the site can affect design decisions as well. Drainage and soil conditions may determine the placement of subterranean drainage pipes and catch basins. Bad soil conditions can necessitate elaborate septic systems. Drinking water may require wells hundreds of feet deep, drilled through rock. All these factors can substantially increase the cost of a house.

Intangible features of a site—noise from nearby houses or thoroughfares and privacy—are important primarily in relation to the clients' attitudes about them. Some prefer total privacy; others don't care. Privacy can be achieved with design techniques in a house on a lot that really isn't private—by placing openings high enough to admit light while blocking vision from the outside, or by planning small private courts, or by landscaping. Physical isolation presents other problems. Access to a site for people, vehicles, and utilities is a factor in construction costs. Find out early about water supply, power-line connections, and unusual septic conditions.

Finally, familiarize yourself with the laws, covenants, and restrictions governing the lot and the house. Ask about minimum area requirements and height limitations, and find out if there is a design review board that may be biased against certain styles, such as flat roofs. You may discover that your client owns a lot with a condition attached that the developer build the house you design. Find out if the building inspector is particularly tough to deal with.

DISCOVERING THE BUDGET

Your clients are about to pay the biggest bill of their lives. They know a house isn't built cheaply, but they expect to get the most for their money—and they are often wildly unrealistic about what that is. Discuss costs frankly with them from the start to make sure they understand what their budget will allow them to buy.

Budget for inflation. If you don't, the contractor will, and even a detailed and careful estimate from your office will not be accurate. Beware of clients who try to put more money into their house by cutting your fee. It may help to point out that compensating you properly will provide the incentive for finding inexpensive and inventive solutions and will ensure that you remain on the scene to guide the contractor. If you think you're dealing with a chiseler, consider refusing the job. It's likely to get worse rather than better, your best efforts notwithstanding.

Ascertain if there is any "stretch" in the client's budget. Some clients think—often with good reason—that architects always exceed their budgets, so they conceal the real amount of money they have available for the project. This will become apparent if they seem uninterested when you recommend economy or wonder if a change will cost only a little extra. Stick to your goal of remaining within their budget, however, and if it looks as though they are willing to increase the ceiling, discuss it frankly.

Use the questions in the following three checklists to guide you in your meetings with clients.

QUESTIONS FOR THE CLIENT

- What rooms does the client want? Which ones are essential? Which are most important? Which could be combined? Which could be eliminated if necessary?
- Has the client considered total square footage?

- What activities will take place in individual spaces?
- What key words describe the client's vision of the house? Snug, cozy? Spacious? Striking? Unpretentious? Natural-looking? Impressive?
- Is the client fussy and demanding about workmanship, or will builder's standards be adequate?
- Does the client prefer an open one-story plan or a series of clearly separated spaces?
- Is the client interested in solar energy and design?
- What furniture, art, and equipment must be accommodated? What are future needs for these items?
- Will the clients spend a lot of time outdoors or remain in the house and enjoy it from within? Do insects bother them? Do they like gardening?
- Is the client planning for resale? Is it realistic to design for unknown future inhabitants?
- How much maintenance is the client willing to put up with?
- Does the client like broad expanses of glass without mullions or smaller units that break up the walls and provide more enclosure? Does the client object to insect screens?
- How does the client feel about light, both natural and artificial? Which is preferable: a high level of lighting or subdued, restful levels? Are there specific activities that will require more light at times?
- Are there medical problems to be considered, such as difficulty climbing stairs?
- Is there some historical style, such as Colonial or Mission, that the client is enthusiastic about? A style the client doesn't like at all?
- Does the client want a detail-oriented house with lots of nooks and crannies and idiosyncratic twists, or a simple, straightforward plan?

QUESTIONS FOR BUILDERS

- How many units will be built, based on how many models?
- Will the models fit multiple site variations or client preferences, or both?
- What is the need for variations within each model? Can these be designed in a modular fashion so that the builder can suggest increases or decreases in size that are economical and reflect the design concept?

- How will you get paid: for the initial model or for subsequent replications? How long will you have to wait for payment if sales lag because of economic conditions?
- How many types of terrain must be accommodated? Does the number of models requested adequately cover the kinds of terrain? Should allowance be made for hidden site problems such as rock?
- Has consideration been given to zero-lot-line grouping of units or other site groupings?
- Will projected square footages fit easily within the buildable lot areas? If not, can variances be obtained from the community?
- What aspects of the design does the builder consider expensive? Should plans be simple? One story or two? What materials does the builder consider expensive?
- Has market research been done on what models and styles sell well? Is there need for special kinds of models—a stripped-down, low-budget economy model, for instance, or a small model designed specifically for later additions?
- If changes are made to accommodate specific custom requests, who will make them? Will you be consulted? How will you get paid for this consultation?
- Does the builder understand your role during the construction phase? Will the builder maintain proper liaison with you at that time?

QUESTIONS ABOUT THE SITE

- What are the microclimatic conditions—sun, wind, temperature, humidity—of the site?
- Are there slopes and subsurface conditions to be taken into account?
- Is solar orientation possible and/or required?
- Is there a view to take advantage of—or an unsightly one to avoid?
- Will a long access road be required?
- If a well is needed, how deep does it have to be? Will it be necessary to drill through rock? Should it be drilled with a rotary drill or "punched" with an up-and-down one?
- Is drainage adequate so that you can avoid building subsoil drainage systems?
- How far away are existing utility connections?
- Are any erosion problems likely once you have cleared the lot to build the house?
- Are there any ecological problems, such as contamination of nearby lakes and

streams because of septic effluent?
- Is there a likelihood of trapped ground water at any level that will cause problems with a projected basement?

QUESTIONS ABOUT THE BUDGET

- Is the client's budget flexible?
- Has inflation been considered?
- Will the schedule affect costs?
- Has the client figured the cost of financing, and is it available?
- Will site conditions, such as the need for a well or long access road, affect costs? Have large items been budgeted separately? What about utility costs?
- Has the client balanced first costs against operating costs of mechanical systems?
- What is included in the budget: just "bricks and mortar," or site development and utility costs as well? Have fees for lawyer, surveyor, and architect been budgeted separately?
- Is your fee to be settled initially, or will it be a part of a flexible building budget?
- Where is the client's money coming from? Is most of it from the bank, and will that affect the contractor's payment schedule? Is any of the "up-front" money, such as your fee, to come from the bank? Does the client know that banks will lend money on a percentage of the total project, including fees and land?
- Is the land paid for?
- Are there any special procurement procedures for building the house, such as the client's having a friend in the lumber business or a relative who is a plumber?

CHAPTER 2

COST-SAVING TECHNIQUES: A COMPENDIUM

Decisions that affect costs, both conceptual and practical, must be made in all phases of the complex process of designing a house. Architects must synthesize their selections into economical and well-designed houses. This chapter outlines the broad categories of decision making and proposes some possible options.

SITE WORK

Site demands vary, from those for an earth-sheltered home carefully related to topography, soil conditions, and orientation, to those for a flat suburban lot with overhead utilities and few possible orientations. No matter what the site, it is useful to keep the following ideas in mind.

Take Advantage of the Natural Landscape. Study the landscape before deciding where to place the house. Try to visualize how the house would fit into tree and shrub cover or a natural meadow. Select the best views in collaboration with the client, being sure to consider near views, such as a fine stand of plants, as well as panoramic ones.

Ground cover frequently indicates subsoil conditions; analyzing it can prevent future problems, such as a wet basement or crawl space. You may want to recommend hiring a landscape architect early in the design process to suggest the best placement of the access road and ways to preserve plants. A landscape architect may also have suggestions for additional planting to complement existing vegetation.

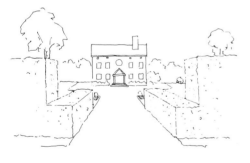

Your client may prefer something more formal.

Contract Separately for Landscaping and Driveways. Most house builders are not interested in doing landscape work because they do not have the proper equipment. If you include this type of work in your contract, the builder will ask another contractor for a price and add a markup to cover administrative time. Instead, suggest that the owner do the work or that you handle it.

Make It Clear That Extensive Site Work Is Not Generally Part of the Architect's Estimate and Fee Structure. When offering an early estimate of probable costs for a house, be sure the client understands that you have not included any site work other than basic excavation and backfill. Subsurface problems such as rock or water are extra to fix. If you suspect the presence of either of these, suggest that a trial excavation be made in the probable house location. Well and septic costs can be very high; make some inquiries among local contractors to gauge their probable impact on your budget.

Consider Grading Factors. Bulldozers can move mountains fairly economically unless rock is present, but extensive earth moving is not recommended unless there are other cost-saving factors involved, such as making foundations easier to install. Consider it, however, if it will mean fewer problems with site drainage, or provide frost cover for utilities, or make it easier to install the septic system. If there is an offensive view or noise problem, one solution is a berm, which can also become an attractive landscape feature.

Budget Separately for Decks and Driveways. A large deck or a long driveway can eat up significant hunks of the budget; a deck can cost 10 to 20 percent of the equivalent enclosed space. Be sure to allocate money for these separately from the budget for the house. Paved driveways built to street standards are frequently unnecessary (consult a local paving contractor for recommended installation procedures). Do not use a standard paving spec. The types of subbase, oil treatment, and gravel toppings vary from place to place. Using local techniques will save money.

Make the Construction Access the Final Road. Using the road as construction access will help compact the subbase and will reveal any drainage problems prior to final surfacing.

GRIDS AND MODULES

Using grids and modules can save money by avoiding waste of materials. Of equal importance, however, is their value in facilitating communications. In the office, a planning grid can make a rough sketch easily understood, and it can be translated into working drawings quickly. Once clients understand the system, they will realize that small dimensional changes are difficult, which will make your work easier; clients will also appreciate that simplifying construction with a module will save them money. For builders, the grid or module is a quick check on dimensions. Contractors can pick up potential errors in drawings before they are built. In short, grids and modules are helpful to all involved.

Planning Grids. Use a grid or module that makes good practical sense. A fairly common size is 4 feet, the width of many building

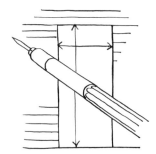

Nobody likes to work in fractional dimensions.

materials such as plywood and sheetrock. Other sizes may be more suitable for your working patterns. Consider 3 feet 4 inches, which combines to a 10-foot unit. It is almost exactly a meter, which will help you work with the metric measuring system as it becomes increasingly common.

Vertical Modules. The precut stud is an important component of American houses. It comes in 2-x-4 and 2-x-6 sizes and is 7 feet 8½ inches long. Normal house-building practice calls for a horizontal 2X member at the bottom of these studs and two horizontal 2X members at the top. These 2-x-4 or 2-x-6 members, which are actually 1½ x 3½ inches or 1½ x 5½ inches, add 4½ inches to the length of the studs for a total of 8 feet 1 inch. When the thickness of the finish on rough floors and ceilings is deducted, the clear ceiling height works out to 8 feet, an American standard.

Within this vertical setup, the heights of lintels for doors and windows are standard. Their undersides are generally set at 6 feet 10½ inches above the rough floor, so that stock doors (6 feet 8 inches) and their frames will fit under them. The tops of windows are usually set under the same lintel heights as well.

The height of the floor joists must also be figured in addition to this 8-foot-1-inch grid. If the joists are 2-x-8s, add 7½ inches (the actual height of the members) plus ½ inch for the subfloor; the overall floor-to-floor height is thus 8 feet 9 inches. If the floor joists are 2-x-10s, the floor-to-floor height is 8 feet 11 inches—and so on. Establishing these vertical modules around the building will help the contractor even if you have designed a multistory open space.

Round Off Dimensions. Carpenters cannot work to tolerances smaller than ¼ inch because of normal shrinkage and variances in materials sizes. Keep this in mind if you are designing a planning grid for which dimensions work out to eighths of an inch. Rounding off dimensions will also save time and eliminate the frustration of combining eighths with quarters and halves.

Work with Stock Sizes. Sheet materials such as plywood and sheetrock generally require cutting. A carefully worked-out plan that does not require them to be cut at the corners will save some money, but not a lot. Of greater importance is using stock window and door sizes, which should be incorporated into whatever module you decide to work with. Provide the rough openings given in the window and door catalogs in your dimensioning. Remember also that lintels must be supported on each side, either by so-called jack studs in wood construction or by piers in masonry construction.

It is possible to deviate from stock sizes, but too many departures from standard practice will result in cost overruns. Use nonstandard sizes only when you think the resultant design benefit will be worth the extra money.

Use Modules with Masonry Too. Although wood construction is widely used, you may be called upon to design with masonry. In some areas of the country, such as the South, masonry buildings are mandatory because of termite and rotting problems. The most important modular consideration in masonry construction is the size of the concrete masonry unit plus its joints, both horizontal and vertical. All dimensioning should be worked out to full or half masonry units.

Masonry modules can be integrated within a standard planning module, such as the previously recommended 3 feet 4 inches, which will accommodate five 8-inch masonry units. It is also possible to integrate the vertical module when using brick or block veneer by adjusting the foundation support for the veneer.

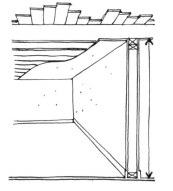

Top: Carpenters will assume standard lintel heights unless told otherwise.

Above: The use of precut studs will save a lot of cutting.

Look at Prefab Ideas. The use of prefab panels is not widespread, but some large manufacturers make use of them. Although they are not generally available at this time, it is likely that fabrication of wall elements, ceiling and floor panels, and kitchen, bath, and stair elements will increase. At present, large-scale units such as wall and ceiling panels are not often used in individual houses because the equipment needed to handle them is not generally available to the average house builder.

Integrate Nonrectilinear Concepts with Your Module. Using a planned grid can actually help in laying out angles and curves. If you have decided to use them, bear in mind that fabrication of skewed or curved walls and fitting materials to them is more expensive than with straight walls. Once you decide that the intended effect of these unusual elements is worth the money, it is imperative to give the builder an easy way to lay them out.

For curves, locate center joints on module line intersections, giving the radius of the curve. Keep the end of the radius within the module as well.

For skew walls, work out the angles so that the ends of the wall land on the intersection of module lines.

If you've decided to work with an overall geometric grid such as octagons or diamonds, consider laying it out on a slab with score marks (as Frank Lloyd Wright frequently did) and centering the walls on the modular pattern. Be sure to show the overall pattern on your drawings so that the contractor can see what you want.

Last, and most important, be sure to sit down with the contractor before the job is bid and explain the concept of your module. Without some introductory comments from you, the drawings may seem too complex, which the contractor may reflect in a very high bid.

MATERIALS

The choice of materials can affect costs more than almost any other budget factor. A finish material may cost only a dollar more than another per square foot, but when that is multiplied by the area to be covered, the total amount can be significant.

Try to set an overall quality level that corresponds to the budget. For instance, plywood exterior siding is not in keeping with expensive tile in the interior. Avoid commit-

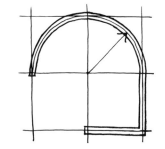 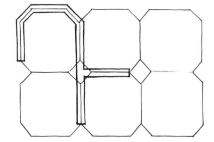

Top: Prefab panels can be combined with more traditional materials.

Left: Curves and angles must be made comprehensible in the field.

Above: Try working with a scored pattern in the concrete.

ting yourself to higher quality standards than your budget will permit. Discuss materials options with your client early in the design process. It is far easier to make changes at that stage than later, when the client may have a certain set of finishes in mind.

Here are some of the more common options.

Pick Concrete and Masonry Items to Fit the Job. Consult an engineer to determine what strength concrete and what type of block to specify. Investigate the appearance of the concrete masonry units that are produced locally.

Colored concrete without a finish overlay is an inexpensive option. It is possible to add an integral color mix to the concrete or to paint it with epoxy. Masonry without a finish is usually a cost saver, but there is the potential of damage to it from other trades. For instance, a block wall that will have a poured concrete slab above will certainly get drips all over it unless the contractor is alerted and takes necessary precautions.

Consider Carpentry Materials and Finishes First. Limited by good structural practice, there are many opportunities to save in selecting carpentry materials. Start with the species of framing lumber. Douglas fir has good strength characteristics but costs more than hemlock fir, which in turn costs more than yellow pine. Check the costs and properties of lumber options; Yellow pine, for instance, though inexpensive, can warp and twist.

Think about the thickness of common materials such as plywood sheathing and sheetrock. A thickness of ½ inch is usual, but not always necessary on framing that is 16 inches on center.

Finish materials are generally expensive. The choice of a finish for the outside of the house is most important, for both cost and appearance. The selection is enormous, and prices vary widely. Question the manufacturer if you want to use something new. For instance:

· How long has this material been in use?
· Where can examples be seen?
· Does it discolor or dent easily?
· Are any special tools needed to install it?
· Are any lawsuits pending concerning it?
· Is it available locally?
· Can small additional quantities be ordered if the first order isn't enough?
· Can contractors understand its applications easily?

A common material can be transformed into something more elegant with trim embellishment. For instance, the addition of battens on top of textured plywood can alter its appearance significantly.

Materials not commonly used for house construction are another possibility. For instance, corrugated fiberglass can be used to cover an atrium or sunroom in an attractive manner. Prefabricated lattice, commonly available at most lumber yards, creates an interesting texture over another inexpensive finish material.

Avoid Custom Doors, Windows, and Glass. Use stock units as much as possible. Not only are they cheaper than custom or homemade units, but you'll also have the manufacturer's guarantee to back you up if anything goes wrong. Don't economize falsely on these items; doors and windows are among the few parts of a house that actually move, so they're ideal places to emphasize quality. Exterior doors frequently warp unless they are metal. Again, don't skimp on quality here.

If you want to use a big piece of glass for aesthetic effect, check with an engineer for wind loads and mounting details. Be aware that large sheets of glass require special handling equipment such as pneumatic suction cups and that with the special handling will inevitably come higher costs.

Separate Specialties from the Rest of the Job. Specialty items include mainly hardware, stoves, special windows and skylights, furniture, appliances, and special equipment. Find out if your client is particularly sensitive to this sort of detail. Lever handles, for instance, can cost five times as much as ordinary knobs. Before you specify something, know its cost. If you want something unusual it's frequently better to call it out on the drawings as "owner-supplied" or "not in contract." Not only will this eliminate potential confusion as to the source of the item, it will alert the client to the additional expense.

CONSTRUCTION TECHNIQUES

"Builder's standard" is a phrase repeated often in this book; it simply means not asking builders to do something that they do not already know how to do. These standards vary from region to region; talking to local contractors to find out how they normally do things—and then following those practices—will certainly stretch your building budget.

Don't be afraid to teach the builder some-

Top: Stock units give carpenters a feeling of confidence.

Above: Consider buying specialty items such as fancy doors separately.

thing, however, if you think that you can save money by doing so. For instance, 24-inch-on-center framing for floors and roof with glued/nailed plywood is economical, but if the contractor doesn't like the idea, the bid won't indicate any savings. Explaining the idea to the contractor first can prevent unnecessary overruns.

Size Foundations Properly. Don't over-engineer foundations. Six-inch blocks are sometimes adequate for residential applications. You might use different foundation techniques such as pouring footings and floor in one operation in warmer climates. Substituting an all-wood foundation for masonry foundations is gaining acceptance, but be prepared for builder resistance.

Simplify Structural Systems and Finishes. The recommendations contained in a project of the National Association of Home-builders Research Foundation, sponsored by the Department of Housing and Urban Development, represent a whole sequence of planning, engineering, and construction techniques that complement one another. This system is called OVE—Optimum Value Engineering—and you can realize significant savings by using some of the techniques it includes.

Some of them, such as eliminating cross bridging between joists, will find ready acceptance with all but the most conservative of builders, whereas others will probably encounter stiff resistance. The elimination of wood sills atop foundations, for example, means that builders must have the mason make a level top on the foundation. Still other recommendations, such as lowering the customary 8-foot ceiling height to 7 feet 6 inches, may run into client resistance.

In addition to looking at OVE recommendations, keep abreast of the findings of other house research organizations, such as NAHB and Small Homes Council.

Try to question whether you need the usual trim items, such as window surrounds and baseboards, unless they are part of your design. To get yourself into the right frame of mind, try computing the entire square footage of all surfaces in a modest 2,000-square-foot house; it will probably be 20,000 to 25,000 square feet. Small increases in square-foot costs will therefore have a substantial overall impact.

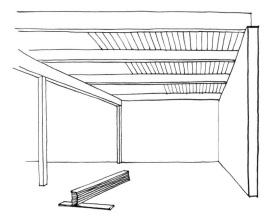

A simple structure is basic to building economy.

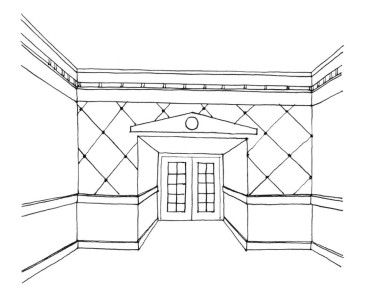

Top: *Texture, pattern, and color should not be ignored.*

Above: *Trim is practical and can also be decorative.*

INTERIORS

Interiors can be the result of the placement of walls; they can also be transformed into more than mere enclosures by the use of color, texture, pattern, and trim. Most of these items can be applied rather inexpensively, yet they have a substantial effect on the overall aesthetic quality of a house.

Use Color as an Inexpensive Device.
Painting the various surfaces of a room can have a lot of design impact for very little cost. White paint on all surfaces can be a good solution, provided that the spaces have enough shape, view, and light to succeed on those terms alone. Color in selected areas, however, can enhance any space.

Explore Texture and Pattern as Accents.
Pick out a particular surface to accent the room. A wood board ceiling or wallpaper in selected spots can effectively accent an otherwise ordinary space.

Use Trim as a Decorative Feature. The use of trim is a historically important method of decorating space that fell into disfavor with the early modernists, who emphasized plain surfaces. As an accent in a room, however, it is relatively inexpensive and can be aesthetically satisfying.

THERMAL COMFORT AND PLUMBING

The amount of heating and cooling required in a house varies in different regions of the country. Choosing the right system or combination of systems to fit the budget for a project requires judgment and care, because an elaborate mechanical system can take as much as 20 to 30 percent of a house budget.

Consider Solar Systems. In designing domestic heating and cooling systems, find out first if there is sufficent money in the budget and sufficient client interest to justify using passive or active solar systems. An investment in these features can pay for itself quickly, and it has the added benefit of conserving the world's shrinking resources. Solar engineers are increasingly knowledgeable, and the forecasting technology of systems performance is good, particularly with the advent of inexpensive mini-and micro-computers. If you do not have the interest, time, and money to learn these techniques yourself, consult the local solar energy society. Beware of consultants who use a lot of hard-to-understand jargon; solar work is based on a few simple rules of physics, and it is not as complex as some would have you believe.

If possible, hire an engineer who will also be able to work out your backup system and tie the two systems together. In large metropolitan areas, it is possible to find engineers who are capable of this. If you are unable to locate one, consider working with a knowledgeable contractor without compromising your impartiality in selecting the lowest qualified bidder for the whole job.

Avoid Systems That Are Hard to Fix. Anything mechanical will inevitably break down. Some questions you might ask potential equipment suppliers are:
·   What can go wrong with this system?
·   Who is qualified to fix it?
·   How many dealers and installations are in this area?
Avoid sophisticated control devices unless your client knows how to operate them and can ascertain what might be wrong if they malfunction.

Keep Abreast of Energy Developments. Systems such as heat exchangers, photovoltaic devices, higher-efficiency furnaces, and the like are undergoing rapid development as the country tries to adjust to escalating energy prices. Although house systems are relatively simple, some knowledge of these developments is essential. A subscription to an energy journal or periodic conversations with an engineer or contractor are essential to keep informed.

Be Aware of Where the Costs Really Are. Although it is certainly true that stacked plumbing saves money, fixture selection is far more important. Sit down with a sales representative from a plumbing manufacturer and ask how the catalog is laid out with regard to prices; the most expensive fixtures are probably shown first and the least expensive last. The most expensive can cost 10 to 20 times more than the cheapest. Caution your clients about this when selecting the fixtures.

The costs of heating and cooling systems will probably lie in the choice of equipment, again, rather than in the layout of ducts or piping required for distribution.

Talk to the Local Utility Company. Many utilities are underutilized, because of conservation in commercial and industrial energy use, and may offer package deals for all-electric houses that meet certain specifi-

Top: The lining up of trim around the room can be a useful ordering device.

Above: The sun will be with us for billions of years.

cations. In addition, many utilities have a consumer education program that you may want to take advantage of; for instance, they may offer deals for houses with domestic hot water solar panels or heat pumps.

Inform Your Clients of Initial Versus Operating Costs and Tax Benefits. Some of the cheapest systems to install are also the most expensive to operate. Get some idea of the comparative operating costs of the different systems; these change frequently because of changes in government subsidies and rate regulations.

Some energy-conservation and passive/active solar features are eligible for tax credits. Calculating these is beyond the scope of normal architectural services; suggest that clients speak to an accountant.

LIGHTING

Residential lighting systems range from table and floor lamps to elaborate built-in fixtures. The simple provision of wall convenience outlets is economical. Some consideration should be given to more elaborate systems, but discuss their cost with the client, because lighting fixtures and wiring can be expensive.

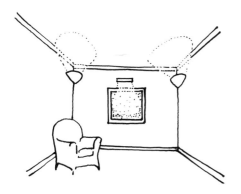

Artificial lighting comes in many forms.

Find Out How Much Light Is Required and Where. Ascertain this from the client by direct questioning. Caution that a lot of artificial light is costly to install and operate. Work out a minimal system that will enable circulation around the house in safety and illuminate rooms from the entrance door. Beyond this, only certain areas require a great deal of light, such as kitchens, bathroom vanity areas, and home workshops. Lighting standards have been reduced because of the high cost of energy; it is no longer considered necessary to have sufficient light to read by in a hallway, for instance.

Integrate Natural and Artificial Sources. Room orientation can determine the amount of natural light that enters. Bedrooms need less artificial light if they are illuminated by the rising sun, for instance. A skylight or other natural light source in high-illumination areas such as a kitchen can reduce the number of fixtures required as well as curtail energy usage.

Consider Low-Voltage Systems, Conservation Devices, and Other Than Incandescent Lighting. The installation of low-voltage control systems and conservation devices, such as automatic turnoff systems, will save on operating costs. Various sources of illumination, such as mercury and sodium vapor fixtures and improved fluorescent bulbs, have undergone rapid development recently and need not have an industrial or commercial stigma when used in the home. The initial cost/operating expense tradeoff must be reviewed individually. If you propose an unusual lighting source, such as mercury vapor, be sure your client sees an actual installation and approves the quality of the light.

Don't Be Profligate with the Number of Outlets. Electricians routinely count the number of light switches, fixtures, and convenience outlets on the drawings and multiply that number by a flat figure to cover their installation costs. To this they add the cost of fixtures, devices, and service into the house. Alert your clients to this method of calculation before responding to a request for "plenty of convenience outlets."

Recommend Energy-Efficient Appliances and Fixtures. Heaters for domestic hot water can consume 30 to 40 percent of the total electrical usage in a house. Recommend investigating conservation features in this vital

appliance as well as in kitchen and laundry equipment and lighting fixtures.

Check Electrical Codes. Electrical underwriters, who generally have to sign off an installation before anyone can move into a house, are increasingly mindful of electrical hazards that endanger life and property. As a result, electrical codes are updated frequently. Avoid using stock specifications; they may result in a request for contract extras. As simple a phrase as "per code" somewhere in your specifications will cover the minimum safe installation. You can then specify higher-quality items if you or your client wants to.

MANAGEMENT AND DOCUMENTS

There's some truth in the adage that contractors figure house costs by weighing the drawings; however, it is necessary to protect the interests of your client with sufficiently detailed drawings to ensure that intended materials get installed properly. It is also important that you manage the job efficiently.

Find the Right Contractor. Builders can be located through other architects who have built houses in the area or through realtors. If you've had experience in an area, a good builder who may be busy for a particular job may recommend others he or she considers qualified.

Once you get a list of potential builders, ask them for one or two recommendations and try to see an example of their work. It is important for you to find a builder whom you trust and who seems sympathetic to what you are doing. A good way to gauge this is by interviewing the builder yourself. Ask the following questions:
- Have you worked with architects before?
- Do you mind working with them?
- Have you built houses in a similar style to this?
- How do you normally get paid—monthly or in accordance with the bank's schedule of payments?
- Are there any special details that you like to have spelled out?
- Do you have any questions concerning architectural drawings in general? For instance, do you work easily with a detailed set, or do you prefer a simpler set supplemented by frequent field consultations with the architect?
- Do you have any preference for the method of installation of the various materials?

- Will you have any problem with unusual features, such as angles or curves or solar installations?
- Are you willing to give a lump-sum bid, or do you always work on another basis like cost plus a markup?
- Are you competitive with other builders, or is most of your work referrals without tight budgets?

Provide Only What the Contractor Needs to Know. The amount of information required to construct a house is enormous; however, it is not necessary to put all this information on your contract documents. If you've selected builders on the basis of their qualifications, it's reasonable to assume that they will know their craft. It is also reasonable to assume that you will not have to give instructions about basic construction techniques. Remember always that it is the end result you are interested in and accountable for. This is not to say that knowledge of builder's techniques is unnecessary—on the contrary, it is essential that you know their job in order to prepare your work better. There is no need for you to draw endless repetitive details for joints and corners that a builder will do routinely.

Here are some suggestions:
- Dimension plans to the studs and use actual sizes of these members. In the case of masonry construction, show dimensions to the masonry unit rather than to any finish on it. Builders generally need to know this information first; the finish is applied later.
- Show rough openings for windows and doors.
- Show typical details and label them as such. If there are unusual details, show them and label them as well.
- Use schedules on the drawings for room finishes, lighting fixtures, doors and windows, and hardware. Key them to the plans in some simple and clear manner. An alternative is to put them directly on the plans within an ellipse or some other graphic device.
- Structure must be shown clearly. Draw structural plans directly on the floor plans for a simple house, or draw separate framing plans. For the latter, ⅛-inch plans may suffice to complement the ¼-inch scale plans.
- Label details clearly. Those marked "typical," for example, will indicate to the con-

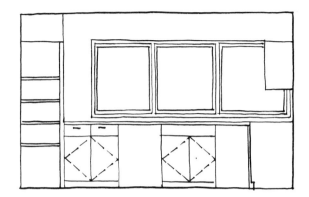

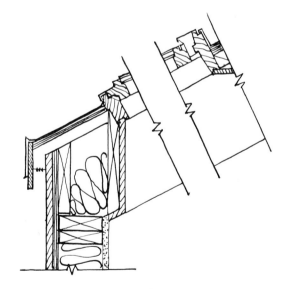

Top: Cabinetwork is nonstructural and must be shown separately.

Above: It's better to have typical details and adjust the house to them.

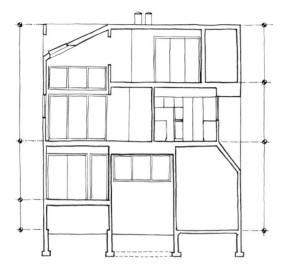

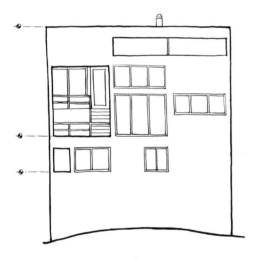

Top: Call out levels on sections to the top of rough structure.

Bottom: Levels on elevations should be to the top of rough structure or bottoms of structural lintels.

tractor that all instances of that detail are the same.

- Draw interior elevations for areas such as kitchen and baths or where there is extensive millwork. Dimension heights directly on them.
- Show larger-scale drawings at 3 inches = 1 foot, or half size if the detail requires it. Although this large scale is necessary only when millwork profiles are unusual, the contractor will appreciate the bigger scale to send to the lumber yard or millwork shop.
- Draw sections through the entire house at the same scale as the floor plans. Dimension all floor-to-floor heights, ridge levels, lintel heights, and bottoms of footings to give the builder required vertical dimensions to complement the plan dimensions.
- A full wall section through typical walls may be useful for some designs. They can be drawn at ¾-inch scale and show heights of windows and material relations. An alternative is to draw the wall sections at 1½-inch scale and section out unnecessary areas to show complicated detail areas, such as windows, in a clearer way than the ¾-inch section.
- Key sections directly to the plans and elevations.
- Consider showing exterior elevations at a smaller scale, such as ⅛ inch. If vertical and horizontal dimensions are shown on plans and sections, there is little need for large-scale elevations.
- Provide a foundation plan at the same scale as the floor plan. General contractors usually subcontract masonry work, and a separate plan can be sent directly to the mason. Show bottoms of footings, sizes of footings, and tops of foundation walls.
- Heating and air conditioning, plumbing, and electrical work, like masonry, are also frequently subcontracted. Organize them on one sheet that the general contractor can send out separately. If electrical work is shown directly on the floor plans and plumbing fixture selection on a schedule or in the specifications, separate drawings are not necessary. It is generally not essential to draw each of these trades on a separate plan.

Use a Standard Preprinted Sheet. The most common sheet size is 24 x 36 inches, which is easily handled in the field. Printers have stock paper rolls of this size for reproduction. Consider having these preprinted on blue-line graph paper. Include all necessary general title block information, such as the firm name, address, telephone number, and any required borders. The blue lines will enable you to letter on the sheet without additional guidelines, and they will disappear in the reproduction process.

Put Specifications Directly on the Drawings. If you use an abbreviated specification style, you can put all essential specifications directly on your drawings by typing them on pressure-sensitive sheets, cutting out sections, and taping them after typing or by using a wide-carriage typewriter or lettering machine. In general, avoid long, thick specifications.

Minimize the Number of Drawings; Organize Them. Draw no more than is necessary. A concise set of documents will help convince contractors that you've given some thought to making their job easier. Because densely packed sheets may make it difficult to locate the various kinds of materials, highlight them with a system of bold titles, using pressure-sensitive lettering or a lettering machine.

Organize the drawings carefully. When doing so, put all plans on one sheet, if possible. Sections and elevations complement each other and can be placed together on another sheet. Details, interior elevations, and schedules can follow.

Standardize Lettering and Drawing Conventions. Establish office standards for lettering size and style and for drawing conventions. A lack of uniformity will only confuse contractors.

If Your Design Is Complex, Build a Model. A model will help you explain your design to clients and contractors; it will also aid you and your staff. Models need not be detailed or carefully constructed; a simple chipboard or balsa model will do the job. A scale of ⅛ inch is frequently sufficient.

Explain Your Contract Documents to the Client and Contractor. A short explanation of what you did and why and what the purpose of each drawing is will help everyone understand the general thinking behind your layouts.

Meet with the Contractors Shortly After They've Examined the Drawings. In addition to your prebid conversations, a meeting at bidding time will give you a chance to answer any questions the contractor has about the documents or design. It will usually result in a lower bid, since unanswered questions are frequently priced out higher in a bid.

After Award, Outline Your Construction Observation Schedule for the Builder. Tell the builder when you think it will be necessary for you to see the job, and explain why you want to see certain stages of completion. It's a good idea to schedule these meetings when you can discuss the next phase before it is started. Encourage builders to ask questions, and let them know when they can expect to reach you in the office. It's frustrating for the builder to have a question and find the architect unavailable.

Enlist the Builder as a Part of Your Team. Builders are practical people who frequently have experience that architects lack. Try to make them contributors to the success of your buildings by asking them to suggest ways of improving details. Their suggestions will often help you avoid future problems.

Answer Construction Questions Quickly; Keep Your Clients Advised. It's important to answer construction questions immediately and to supplement your answers with sketches if necessary. If the contract amount will be affected by a clarification, negotiate a price, secure your client's approval, and confirm everything in writing. Insist that all construction questions, changes, and decisions be channeled through your office. Both client and contractor will generally welcome the procedure.

Process Requests for Payment Immediately. House builders are generally small-business owners who are undercapitalized in relation to the amount of money they are responsible for. They will want to get the monthly discount from their materials suppliers and to pay their subcontractors quickly. Be alert to certain kinds of job delays such as the failure of subcontractors to show up. It may be that the general contractor has not yet paid for the previous phase of work and a question may be in order.

At Job Completion, Prepare a "Punch List" of Uncompleted or Unsatisfactory Items. The contractor will want to receive the final payment as soon as possible, because it will frequently represent the profit margin. You should prepare your punch list as soon as it is requested, review it with your client, and forward it to the contractor. If

Simple scale models help to avoid confusion.

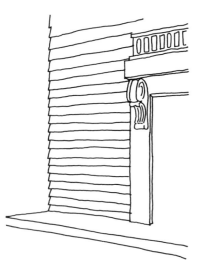

Maybe a traditional doorway will look good in a simple facade.

A few special details can add great distinction to a space.

there are one or two items at the end that cannot be completed expeditiously because of delays in materials shipments or other problems, it's reasonable to withhold only the amount of money necessary to cover those items.

SPECIAL DESIGN TREATMENTS

Many features can be incorporated into the design of a low-budget house to give it a special atmosphere. These include decorative appliqués that suggest richness, elements that "refer" to previous architectural eras, and simple tradeoffs, where the budget permits, of a small area of luxury finishes to be contrasted with a more economical palette. Some other possibilities follow.

Consider Treating Some Spaces in a Special Way. When the budget is limited, it is impossible to use luxury finishes everywhere. Find out from the client what areas are most important, and design accordingly. In addition to allocating more space to those areas, you can accent them with a special feature such as a fireplace or a stove; or treat them in a color or texture different from the others; or organize the plan so that other spaces feed into or radiate from it.

Contrast Public and Private Areas. Public and private areas can be differentiated by plan organization or by level changes. An unusual door, such as a ship's door, will heighten the sense of entering a private domain. You can make public areas more inviting by opening them to the outside or by lowering them, or by using warm materials that invite relaxation.

Consolidate Usages to Eliminate Superfluous Space. This possibility is usually determined in the program stage, but it can also be determined in the design stage. Plan arrangements are possible that will divide what otherwise is a simple space. Differentiation of use within the same space is also possible with changes in colors or materials. A simple change in floor material, for instance, immediately conveys the idea of a different use.

Find Out Which of the Client's Wants Are the Most Important. Spaces can convey qualities such as warmth, intimacy, grandeur, or playfulness. Find out what qualities your clients are searching for, and try to design elements that will fill the bill. For instance, an inglenook in an otherwise ordinary space will provide an inviting sense

of intimacy; a tall space with some free-standing columns will convey monumentality; an oddly shaped or skew window will connote playfulness.

Consider Meaningful Patterns and Symbols. The use of an eclectic column or homey latticework can give a house scale and relate it to the client's sense of what a home should be; most people have definite ideas about this. A simple device such as a front porch with columns supporting the roof establishes an intermediate zone between outside and inside that conveys a sense of invitation and welcome. Latticework provides some separation and privacy, yet is decorative. Wallpaper or a printed pattern on floors or walls is inexpensive yet distinctive.

Work with Vernacular Forms. In a region that has a strong local building tradition, consider incorporating some aspect of it into your design. Often there are good practical reasons for such traditions, and builders will probably reflect your response to them with lower prices. The house will also achieve a better "fit" into the neighborhood.

Create a Presence Larger Than the Actual House Size. Overscaling design elements such as the chimney or windows can suggest a larger structure than actually exists. Other options are combining the house walls with exterior walls by using pattern and color and stretching the facade with landscape features. A large bay window or an interesting grouping of windows will also make a house seem larger.

Accent Special Features Such as Handmade or "Found" Items. These features can give a house a sense of uniqueness, yet they cost little. Small details such as post brackets or kitchen counter inlays mean much to the client, as does careful placement of an object they own, be it a treasured piece of furniture or an architectural fragment they've collected.

Use Elements That Characterize the Inhabitants. Individual elements such as window seats, unusual stairways, or balconies will give an intimate scale to a house. Don't repeat them, since repetition of this kind of element will cause a loss of effectiveness.

Emphasize Human Scale. Thick walls, with hollows or niches for seating or displaying objects, and columns or balustrades that define a path suggest human use. Think of the traditional Swiss chalet with the exterior porches and carved balustrades; without these scale-giving railings, there is no sense of human activity.

Provide Places That Demand Daily Participation by Occupants. On the Greek islands, residents paint their dwellings white and scrub their stairs frequently. Brass knockers in Georgian London and brass vent plates on Park Avenue in New York need polishing often; their luster testifies to the care and pride of the occupants. Flower boxes, planters, polished brass doorknobs—all encourage owner participation in a house.

Plan for Future Additions and Modifications. An old Chinese proverb states, "House completed, life over." This suggests that the inhabitants of a house will want to make modifications to it, whether the design allows for them or not. Recognize this by providing an open-ended design that will permit change. In a simple form, alterations can be as minor as new window curtains or slipcovers on a favorite chair. A more complex modification is a roof extension without sidewalls left for completion at a later date, with or without the aid of the architect. The drawings could specify future additions. A master plan for landscaping or furnishing will provide years of enjoyment to the occupants, who can complete their home as money permits.

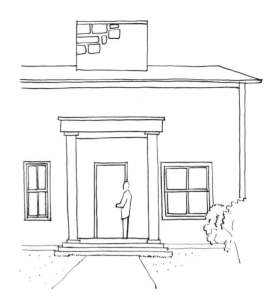

An extra large window will change the scale.

Perhaps the client owns an architectural fragment that can be put to good use.

CHAPTER 3

EFFECTIVE HOUSES AND HOW TO DESIGN THEM

The projects that follow illustrate how the techniques and ideas described in the preceding chapter can be incorporated into house designs. The examples cover a wide range of locations, styles, and client needs and wants. Most are new, but several are restorations or major additions to existing structures. They fit varying climatic demands and were constructed to suit differing sites. The main criterion for including each house was the combination of program response on cost-saving ideas with good design. Some of the ideas depend on economies of scale (such as a house designed for a client as part of a multiple-house development) or on the owner's participation in construction, sometimes known as "sweat equity."

HOW TO USE THIS CHAPTER

A brief introduction to each project highlights the site and program demands, the way the project was designed and managed, and any special design tradeoffs or features and their effect on cost. This general description is followed by the pertinent data: project, architects' names, areas, date completed, and cost. Costs do not include land, fees, furniture, or landscaping, unless otherwise stated. The third section is a detailed "box score," which lists specifics of the design treatment and its cost-saving features. The same format is used for all houses, even if the architect did not emphasize certain categories. Drawings and photographs supplement the descriptions and box scores.

The work of twenty-three architects has been presented here. The concern has been to vary the types of projects and the geographic locations.

When an architect is represented by more than one project, a summary of the unique approach, how it is used, and how it affects costs precedes the individual projects. When an architect has chosen to depart from that approach in a particular project in order to emphasize a design feature—a view, a detail, an arrangement of doors or windows—there is an explanation of why the decision was made. At times the approach did not apply or did not work in a project; such cases are explained.

The box score includes information about work done to the site and whether this was a factor in the budget. If grids or modules were an important feature of the house, they are described. Materials and construction techniques are listed and other options discussed.

Interior treatments and furnishings are difficult subjects to treat adequately in a book of this scope. These are very real concerns of the architect who has worked hard to get the house itself built within the budget. All too often there is little or no money left for the furnishings or built-ins (such as cabinets, seating, or tables) that will make the house a meaningful environment. The box score notes imaginative solutions to this problem.

Thermal comfort, plumbing, and lighting are also analyzed. Plumbing is basic. Its cost implications are important, but the range of cost-saving solutions is not large. Some practical approaches were discussed in the preceding chapter.

Heating and cooling systems provide greater scope for innovative, affordable design, but decisions concerning them relate to operating costs as much as or more than to installation costs. This subject is especially important in houses oriented toward solar energy.

Lighting can be done "per code" with minimal cost or in an elaborate, expensive way. The box score notes unusual lighting schemes.

Some cost-saving design approaches depend on special management practices, such as close coordination with the contractor. These intangibles are more difficult to demonstrate than the less abstract facets of a project, but where applicable, they are mentioned. For some projects there are samples of contract documents, which can be major cost-savers, not only because they can reduce office production time, but also because they can make the intent of the architect unmistakably clear to the contractor.

Finally, the last item in the box score focuses on the details of the design that make it effective. Some of these are simple devices; others are more elaborate and expensive but were deliberate creative choices of the architect. The tradeoffs are explained.

The forty-three houses included here are proof that saving money and creating a good design are not incompatible goals. The nine categories of cost-saving ideas include many options and their various combinations. There are so many different design solutions that there is no excuse for citing program and budget limitations as a reason for poor design.

LEUNG, HEMMLER, CAMAYD, ARCHITECTS
SCRANTON, PA

Architects achieve special impact despite limited materials and basic techniques

After drawing out their clients' ideas and wishes and identifying the peculiarities of the program, Leung, Hemmler, Camayd, Architects use the Construction Specifications Institute (CSI) format as a basis for outlining specifications requirements or preferences that will reduce costs. With inexpensive materials and simple techniques, they use this basic palette to arrange the design elements of houses into meaningful and attractive wholes.

They explain to their clients that expensive materials and techniques would necessitate settling for less space and restricting imaginative design options. Clients' building dollars are used more effectively for such design details as grouping elements (doors, windows, plumbing, wiring), applying color, and treating walls in various ways.

This cost-saving approach depends on the designer's creativity. Its major drawback is that the designer may not know where to stop in the effort to impart creative meaning to simple materials and techniques. For example, House 1 has an arcade of simple painted columns that increase the apparent size of the house; the architects had to resist the urge to embellish the columns for that additional ounce of impact. Similarly, the row of trees planted to give rhythm to the landscaping could easily have gotten out of hand if the architects had ignored the cost of maintaining the planting.

Frequent cost estimates are essential in an approach like this one if the total of such creative decisions is not to exceed the budget. Selecting the most effective grouping of elements and using the least expensive means to achieve the effect requires self-discipline. Color is an obvious example, one that these architects use effectively.

DIVISION 1: GENERAL CONDITIONS
Avoid requisitions for bid or performance bonds.

Keep insurance requirements to a minimum.

DIVISION 2: SITE WORK
Keep general site work and excavation to a minimum. Avoid blasting whenever possible.

Keep landscaping to a minimum and covered by owner under separate contract.

Use gravel and modified road surfaces in lieu of other more expensive treatments.

Use crawl spaces whenever possible and full basements only when necessary or convenient.

DIVISION 3: CONCRETE WORK
Limit the use of concrete to footings only.

Use concrete masonry unit (CMU) foundation walls.

DIVISION 4: MASONRY
Avoid labor-intensive masonry construction.

Use cinder blocks in lieu of more expensive concrete blocks.

Avoid masonry chimney and fireplaces.

DIVISION 5: METALS
Use standard-size steel members
Avoid exposing steel structures whenever necessary, since they demand careful finishes.

DIVISION 6: CARPENTRY
Use stock sizes, construction-grade lumber (spruce) for all rough framing.

Whenever necessary, use builtup wood beams instead of steel.

29

Use plywood exterior siding in lieu of tongue-and-groove redwood or cedar.

Use 2 x 4 at 16'' on center with 4'' batt insulation; or 2 x 6 at 2'0'' with 6'' batt insulation.

Use treated lumber for exterior decking.

Use white pine for all interior and exterior trim.

Stairs made up of construction-grade plywood or particle board in lieu of oak or better lumber.

Use standard cabinetry in bathroom and kitchen. Improve its appearance through the use of color (plastic laminate) and better hardware.

Avoid all custom millwork.

DIVISION 7: THERMAL AND MOISTURE PROTECTION

Use lightweight (235-pound) asphalt shingles whenever possible.

Introduce color(s) to improve their appearance.

Use standard residential aluminum gutters and downspouts.

Use 1'' or 2'' rigid insulation combined with 4'' fiberglass batts to prevent infiltration.

DIVISION 8: DOORS, WINDOWS, AND GLASS

Use standard-size prefabricated doors and windows.

Use ⅝''-thick double-insulated glass whenever custom work is specified.

Use average- to better-grade hardware throughout the home.

Use prehung, standard-size doors throughout interiors.

Improve appearance with color or better veneers when budget allows.

DIVISION 9: FINISHES

Use gypsum board at walls and ceilings in lieu of plaster throughout interiors.

Use economy-grade carpet of simple design and durable quality.

Use standard hardwood flooring with a clear polyurethane finish.

Use quarry tile in kitchen and bathrooms in lieu of more expensive, luxurious materials.

Use vinyl asbestos tile (VAT) flooring with special design or color combinations. Wide use of color enhances simple interior finishes.

DIVISION 10: SPECIALITIES

Use prefabricated fireplace units with insulated stainless-steel chimneys.

Use better-quality hardware for doors, cabinetry, and builtin furniture if the budget allows it.

Use better-quality bathroom accessories if the budget allows it.

Avoid expensive kitchen appliances and unnecessary gadgets.

DIVISION 15A: PLUMBING

Keep all plumbing simple.

Avoid expensive plumbing fixtures. Use prefabricated shower/tubs whenever possible.

DIVISION 15B: HVAC

Avoid air conditioning if at all possible.

Select efficient yet economical heating system. Electric baseboard has least initial expense.

Other possibilities include hydronic gas- or oil-fired systems with a built-in coil for domestic hot water. These systems have a higher initial price tag but reduce monthly energy bills.

DIVISION 16: ELECTRICAL

Avoid expensive service installations.

Limit underground service to a minimum.

Reduce distance between meter and electrical panel.

Make use of low-priced lighting fixtures. Industrial fixtures are generally painted to enhance their appearance.

HOUSE 1
LEUNG, HEMMLER, CAMAYD, ARCHITECTS

Screen walls, changes in color and texture expand scale of simple house

The client for this ski house 40 miles north of Scranton, Pennsylvania, requested a small three-bedroom house on a site facing the mountains. The main ground-floor rooms were to focus on the view; a relatively blank facade would be presented to the road.

The architects planned the house as an L with living room, dining room, and kitchen in one leg, master bedroom in the other. Both legs have bedroom lofts above. The one above the living room is open to increase the sense of space in both rooms.

The architects' principal task was to work within a limited program and budget. Their choices centered on scale-increasing devices that make this small house and its main features look larger. For example, the entrance looks bigger than it really is because of the change in color and the square glass feature overhead. The grouped windows on the two entrance sides provide a larger scale through color and a change in texture.

PROJECT: Faber House, Pennsylvania
ARCHITECTS: Leung, Hemmler, Camayd, Architects; Scranton, PA
AREAS: 1,850 square feet on 2 acres
DATE COMPLETED: October 1980
COST: $76,600

SITE WORK

The existing site was left in its natural state. Some formal shrubbery was planted in front of the house to direct attention to the entrance. The driveway and paths, which were kept to a minimum, are gravel.

GRIDS AND MODULES

No overall modular system was used, but window and door heights were stock, which governed their placement in the facades.

MATERIALS

Textured plywood, stucco, and asphalt shingles on the exterior were designed to complement each other through their colors. Sheetrock and carpeting were used inside. All materials are inexpensive; some additional costs were incurred, however, in special areas such as the entry, which is tiled.

CONSTRUCTION TECHNIQUES

Builder's standards were followed. This important term means that construction was done according to a typical builder's typical procedures. Conventional wood-frame or masonry walls were erected, and stock windows were "popped in" and trimmed out, concealing wiring and ducts.

The costly alternative would have been to build the house virtually as a cabinet, with pieces of glass, often large, installed in custom-made frames with minimal clearances and trimmed all around with flexible extruded gaskets. To avoid interior wood trim, sheetrock is returned around window jambs and trimmed with J-beads.

The white arcade tacked onto the overhang increases the apparent size of the house in the rear.

Even higher cost penalties arise when wiring, instead of being concealed, becomes a decorative hi-tech element, so that all junctions must be ground and aligned. None of this can be done quickly, because the builder must take extra care at every step of the way.

In the Faber house, although builder's standards were observed, care was taken to control the size and placement of trim, both inside and out. The pipe rails used indoors cost more than alternatives, but their connection to walls and posts is standard.

INTERIORS

Sheetrock and carpet were used throughout, except in the entry, kitchen, and baths. Furniture was kept to a minimum and tightly grouped to enhance the sense of spaciousness. Pipe rails suggest large space despite the fact that these rooms are not large at all. Had the architects used sheetrock to close off the bedroom loft, this already small house would have seemed even smaller.

THERMAL COMFORT AND PLUMBING

Electric baseboard heating is inexpensive to install and allows good control in individual rooms, but it costs more to operate. The decision to use it was justified because this is a vacation dwelling that is not in constant use. Prefab fireplaces in the living room and master bedroom supplement the heat. Plumbing is grouped and stacked.

LIGHTING

"High-Hats" (recessed downlights) and track lighting permit flexibility. Natural lighting from many directions decreases the need for artificial light during the day.

MANAGEMENT AND DOCUMENTS

Drawings and specs consisted of ¼-inch-scale plans, elevations, and sections and outline specs. The contractor was interested in the job, worked with enthusiasm, and did not balk at nonstandard details. (The importance of developing such a relationship is discussed elsewhere in this book.) There was close communication between contractor and architects.

The change of color around the grouped windows, the accent on the entrance, and the cornice details are rich effects achieved with modest materials.

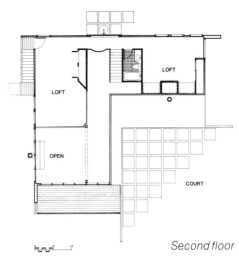

Second floor

Ground floor

SPECIAL DESIGN TREATMENTS

Several design features increase the apparent scale and create a special "feel." The solid-seeming stucco walls impart a sense of importance and large scale to the entrance facades. This is accented by the exaggeration of the entrance feature to two stories through a change in color and material; it ends richly at the top with another change in color.

Stopping the stucco walls short of the walls of the "sheds" behind creates the effect of a cornice. Stock windows are grouped and accented for greater impact.

At the rear, the house is made to seem larger because of the arcade of columns that appear to enlarge the interior in a formal way by means of the overhang of the roof and in a horizontal way by extending the columns beyond the sides of the L.

Color is used effectively inside and out. The stucco is painted tan, the siding gray, the roof reddish, and the arcade beige. The group of four windows in front and the square over the entry are green. The intent was to make the scale-manipulating features stand out boldly in colors that contrast with the quiet tan stucco and gray siding of the basic house.

Within, the main design device is openness created through the use of light pipe rails and an open loft.

Above left: Light from many sources and the open loft seem to expand the small interior space.

Top and above: An L is a basic plan type that is simple yet provides privacy in each of its wings.

33

HOUSE 2
LEUNG, HEMMLER, CAMAYD, ARCHITECTS

House is located among tract split-level and ranch houses

The clients wanted their house to be different from their neighbors' conventionally styled houses. They had been struck by the interiors that they were beginning to see in housing magazines, and their friendship with one of the architects convinced them that they could have a well-designed house resembling these despite their restricted budget.

The program was that of the typical American family: formal living and dining area, kitchen with adjacent informal living space, master bedroom and two children's bedrooms, one multipurpose bath, and a guest powder room. A garage was eliminated early because of site restrictions and budget limitations. A screened porch for alfresco dining was an addition.

PROJECT: Hobbs house, Peckville, PA
ARCHITECTS: Leung, Hemmler, Camayd, Architects; Scranton, PA
AREAS: 1,905 square feet on 12,960-square-foot site
DATE COMPLETED: 1980
COST: $50,000

SITE WORK
The site is the uppermost lot in a mountainside development of new houses, most of which are conventional American fare: brick and aluminum or stucco boxes with hip or gable roofs. Scattered about, however, are several architect-designed homes. The Hobbs house is approached from the street above; behind, to the south, stretches a view of the urbanized valley below, toward which the land slopes sharply. Site work consisted of connections to existing utilities.

GRIDS AND MODULES
None.

MATERIALS
Exterior walls are stucco with textured plywood in recessed areas. Wide wood trim was provided around stock wood windows.

CONSTRUCTION TECHNIQUES
Builder's standards were followed throughout.

INTERIORS
The street entry is from the high point of the hill, on the bedroom level. A major cost saving was achieved by placing the living spaces where the basement would ordinarily be, thereby saving exterior finish on the side dug into the hill. A basementlike feeling is avoided, however, because the foyer overlooks the two-story dining porch directly ahead, and to the left is an overlook of the entire volume of the house.
A gently pitched stair links the foyer with the area below. Directly ahead is the fireplace, with a stainless-steel chimney, and to the left are recessed clerestory windows. On the right, the bedroom parapet curves to reveal the two-story wraparound glass and corner porch. The tight and functional kitchen opens to the living area and dining porch beyond. All these spatial connections open the lower level to the light and air above.

THERMAL COMFORT AND PLUMBING
Heating is with electric baseboard units; no air conditioning is provided.

LIGHTING
Builder's standard lighting was installed: convenience outlets per code, minimal recessed lights in corridors, plus bath and kitchen lighting.

MANAGEMENT AND DOCUMENTS
Documents consisted of five 24-x-36-inch sheets, with ¼-inch-scale plans, elevations, and interior elevations, plus an electrical plan. The house was conventionally bid, and the contract was awarded to the lowest qualified bidder. The owners did their own painting inside and out. A relative of the owners furnished and applied much of the wood trim.

SPECIAL DESIGN TREATMENTS
Outside, the red roof is accentuated by a green stripe, which surrounds the windows. The street facade is simple and has few windows. The entry porch is balanced by a square window over the porch that is centered on the floor plane to reveal the double-story height of the living room. The south elevation is more open and inviting. There, punched-out windows in the stucco wall suggest a Tuscan villa. A terrace linking the dining and corner porches provides a variety of outdoor living spaces.

Top: The one-story street facade is accented by a column at the entrance, a horizontal colored stripe, and window surrounds.

Left: Projecting second-story bedrooms and kitchen enliven the rear facade under a uniform roof line.

Below: An *I* plan has been enlarged and enriched by projections, add-ons, and internal curves.

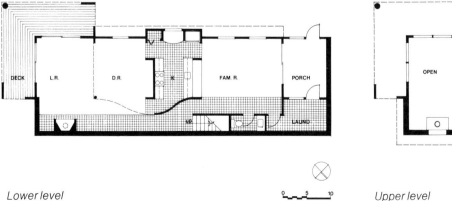

Lower level

Upper level

Above: A traditional column accents the covered deck.

Right: The curved parapet opens the entry into the living room; the reverse curve below permits access to kitchen and family room.

NAGLE, HARTRAY & ASSOCIATES
CHICAGO, IL

Regional traditions and practices spur architects to adaptable designs

Faced with the problem of working with contractors in a wide geographical area ranging from Chicago, Illinois, to Colorado and Texas, these architects tailor their efforts to the local talent. By doing so, they can take advantage of available skills and resultant economies. If only one good contractor is available in a particular area, they begin working with him as early as the design stage and continue through construction, thereby ensuring a sympathetic interpretation of their design intent. Where there is more competition among contractors, the architects take competitive bids. In these cases they ask for a price on the complete job, but also request a breakdown of payments on a separate form. When the bids are submitted, they can tell if subcontractors' prices are too high or too low and resolve misunderstandings about the scopes of subcontracts before awarding the contract.

The architects adjust to regional differences also in the overall form and detailing of their houses. Their design for a house in a wooded area differs in both materials and form from one in the mountains, where cold and snow are important considerations.

HOUSE 3
NAGLE, HARTRAY & ASSOCIATES

Simple octagonal form offers construction economies

The clients for this second home, an active family with four children, had chosen a well-wooded site overlooking the rocky shore of Lake Michigan. They wanted a generous social area, three bedrooms, including bunk rooms for the children and a master bedroom/guest room suite, and a separate quiet space with a view.

The architects conceived an octagonal shape with a treetop observatory. They took a sketch of their idea—plans, elevations, and sections—to the site, where the clients examined it and said, "We like it—don't change anything." The architects then had to figure out how to execute their idea within the client's budget.

The plan is arranged in three levels: the three bedrooms below, a raised second level that serves as the main living and eating area, and above this an observatory. All levels are connected with an interior circular stair. Decks extend in two directions from the raised main floor; fireplaces are located on the first two levels.

Project: Family lighthouse, Wisconsin
Architects: Nagle, Hartray & Associates; Chicago, IL; Job Captain: William Sitton
Areas: 2,300 square feet on 5 acres
DATE COMPLETED: 1980
COST: $125,000

SITE WORK

The house was placed in a handsomely wooded lot with as little damage to existing growth as possible. In order to raise the main living area above the bedrooms for a better view of the surrounding landscape, the architects built a small berm on the entrance side. The berm also shortens the run of stairs to the entrance deck on the second floor. The lot is deep, so a long gravel driveway was required.

GRIDS AND MODULES

The symmetrical octagonal plan constitutes a repetitive module.

MATERIALS

The entire house is clad with 1-x-8-inch tongue-and-groove stained cedar siding, smooth-surface V-groove over 15-pound building paper, and ½-inch plywood on 2-x-6-inch studs, 16 inches on center. Interior walls, floors, and ceilings are varnished clear fir. Birch doors and cabinetry and pine frames and trim are inexpensive materials that local carpenters are used to handling. A wood-shingle roof and a stucco chimney complete the exterior materials. All windows and doors are good-quality wood stock units.

Also contributing to the economical materials list are stovewood fronts rather than masonry on the prefabricated fireplaces, recycled bowling alley countertops, recycled door hardware, and rope railings.

CONSTRUCTION TECHNIQUES

The overall frame of the house consists of studs, beams, and rafters, all 16 inches on center, with a system of 4-x-10-inch exposed tie beams and 6-x-6-inch posts that hold the walls of the lofty main living space together. These tie beams are necessary because the octagon has no ridge beam. They keep the exterior walls from spreading and act as wind bracing for the otherwise unbraced volume. Concrete grade beams are tied to lower-level shear walls for wind resistance.

The uniformity of the interior finishes made them easy to detail and therefore easy to build—the carpenters knew that all situations were similar.

Little sitework was required for the tall house in its surrounding of trees. Good views remain into and above the treetops.

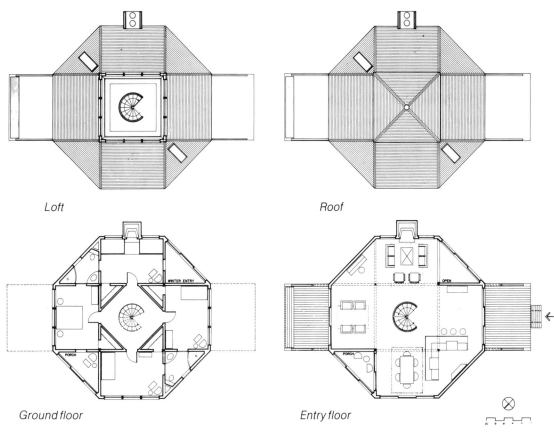

Loft

Roof

Ground floor

Entry floor

Spaces within plans of this shape can be difficult to organize because of the acute angles in some corners. Cutting materials can be costly. However, the architects have planned the spaces well to minimize awkward junctures, and the repetition of elements over the four quadrants resulted in economy.

INTERIORS

Cabinlike details were used: ship's openings for closet doors, for example, raised 7 inches from the floor with rounded corners and curtains rather than doors. The central spiral stair provides a strong visual focus for the center of the house.

THERMAL COMFORT AND PLUMBING

Electric baseboard heat and simple plumbing fixtures were specified. Electric heat is the most economical to install, but it can be expensive to operate if local utility rates are high. In second homes like this one, however, its use can be justified by the flexibility it affords in the selection of which spaces are to be heated and at what temperature. For example, in the winter when guest rooms are not fully utilized, they can be closed off and left unheated. No air conditioning was provided.

Baths were limited to two, which were simply fitted with shower, w.c., and basin. Hose bibbs are located on the exterior immediately adjacent to the baths, and the kitchen is located above one of them, thereby shortening plumbing runs.

LIGHTING

Lighting was held to a minimum. Many fixtures are simply exposed light bulbs behind a valance.

MANAGEMENT AND DOCUMENTS

For this project the architects used 24-x-36-inch sheets, with specifications written directly on them. Plans, elevations, and sections were drawn at ¼ inch = 1 foot, and ⅛-inch framing plans were provided. They used schedules for electric heating, outlets and switches, electrical fixtures, doors, finishes, and hardware.

SPECIAL DESIGN TREATMENTS

Having come up with the strong scheme for this house, which echoes nearby lighthouses, the architects detailed it simply to bring it in near budget. The design suggests a rugged tree house well suited to its use as a vacation hideaway.

Right: The section indicates the tension rods that support the balconies and the organizing central stair.

Below: Natural materials unify this faceted space. The exposed posts and free-standing beams are functional as well as decorative.

North elevation   Section

HOUSE 4
NAGLE, HARTRAY & ASSOCIATES

Design for mountain house reflects regional traditions

This house is built at an elevation of 11,000 feet in a remote part of Colorado where snow can accumulate to a depth of 10 feet. The couple who own it needed bedrooms and activity space for four older chilgen, gathering space for entertaining, a master bedroom suite, and an apartment for year-round tenants.

There were few builders in the area, so the architects selected one early in the design process to maintain budgetary control and had him bid out the job to his subcontractors. The contractor was thus available from the beginning to make recommendations concerning the most economical local materials and customary construction techniques.

The plan is well integrated with the site. The entry at midlevel leads to the living, kitchen, and dining areas, which catch a view of the mountains. This level also contains a garage and south-facing porch as well as stairs to the upper and lower levels. The upper level is interesting in that it includes a studio apartment with its own private entrance, as well as the master bedroom remote from the other sleeping quarters. On the lower level two bunk rooms are grouped around a common social room that opens directly to grade and the view.

PROJECT: Mountain house, Crested Butte, CO
ARCHITECTS: Nagle, Hartray & Associates; Chicago, IL
Job Captain: Brian Robertson
AREAS: 2,911 square feet on ½ acre
DATE COMPLETED: 1981
COST: $150,000

SITE WORK

Mountain sites in Colorado tend to be beautiful in all seasons without additional landscaping, so the architects chose to position the house with minimal disturbance to the site, working with existing contours. A stabilized road permits vehicular access.

GRIDS AND MODULES

The building's plan is symmetrical—rooms are organized on two axes, the entrance and a central wall perpendicular to the entrance that provides structural bracing. This geometry enabled the contractor to understand the overall concept and to frame major walls and floors quickly.

MATERIALS

Natural local cedar lap siding, wood shingles, oak floors and ceilings, pine trim, and birch doors and cabinetry are used. These are easy for Rocky Mountain carpenters to work with and build the house in an unpretentious and economical way.

CONSTRUCTION TECHNIQUES

Wind load was a major consideration, so the architects organized the house around plywood-sheathed shear walls to withstand these stresses. Exterior walls are 2-x-6-inch studs at 24 inches on center with 2-x-12-inch floor and roof joists over the short spans. The outside walls and central shear walls are sheathed with plywood to provide resistance to lateral forces and are finished inside with ½-inch sheetrock, outside with siding.

Both rigid and batt insulation were used to develop very high R values, an essential provision in this cold climate where winter temperatures can reach well below zero.

INTERIORS

Materials and techniques are directly detailed. Thus, walls and ceilings join without reveals, and where dissimilar materials meet, such as at the junction of walls and oak floors, wood trim strips of sufficient width are provided to avoid time-consuming and costly fitting of materials. Similar detailing is used where stock windows and doors meet interior finishes.

THERMAL COMFORT AND PLUMBING

An important factor in the economy of the house is the stacked plumbing and the electric heat without ductwork. Baths and kitchens are clustered tightly on all three levels, permitting relatively straight waste, vent, and supply piping. Electrical resistance heating is the most economical to install in the Rockies. It is also economical to operate because hydroelectric power is inexpensive.

Efficient passive solar features are important in the operation of this house. The building is symmetrical, but the windows are not. There are a few north-facing windows, but most face south, as do the greenhouse and deck.

LIGHTING

Natural light is generously distributed in the rooms that are used often during the day, such as the living and dining areas. Bunk rooms and bedrooms have enough windows to provide daylight and cross ventilation, supplemented with recessed and table lighting for nighttime use.

MANAGEMENT AND DOCUMENTS

Close liaison with a selected contractor enabled the architects to simplify details and supervision. Working drawings consisted of ¼-inch plans, sections, and elevations; ½-inch kitchen and bath elevations; ¼-inch structural plans; and typical wall sections and structural details. No material specificaitions were provided other than general structural notes. Materials were listed on schedules and by notation on the sections and interior elevations.

The number of window sizes was limited, and they were organized in an orderly fashion. This aided the contractor, because he could arrange the wall structure on upper floors in a line with that of the lower floors.

SPECIAL DESIGN TREATMENTS

The house borrows from the local vernacular in the arrangement of short spans with high central roof and slanted side spaces—a configuration seen in houses throughout the mountains. This traditional arrangement is the key to the simplicity and economy of other elements, such as framing, materials selection, and detailing.

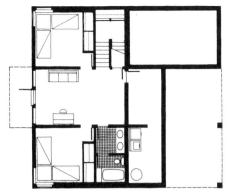

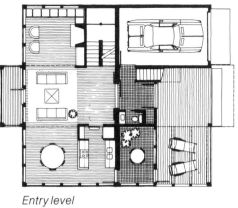

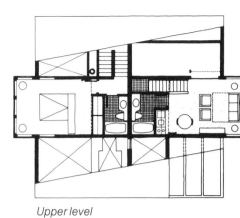

Ground level

Entry level

Upper level

Clockwise from top: The location of the bracing walls was an important factor in organizing the spaces; trim in the interiors was limited to those joints requiring closure, such as around doors and windows or at the juncture of floors and walls; a gloss finish on the exposed trusses enlivens their decorative aspect.

43

JAMES COOTE
AUSTIN, TX

Careful analysis of program is key to economy

The architect writes, "Regardless of size or budget, a custom house affords the opportunity for precise tailoring to the client. To have an environment fitted to order, to one's idiosyncrasies and dreams, seems one of the few possible reasons for a client to endure involvement in its creation. Limited budgets require shrewd evaluation of alternatives, relentless editing, and some divination of what is truly significant for the client. Where the tolerances for success are so slim, a continuous dialog with the client seems indispensable, an effort to be realistic about costs and to define the budget without illusions, and to avoid an inflated program from the very beginning. All my projects seem to begin with the eternal tension between the physical context (the site, the neighborhood) and the programmatic requirements of the clients."

Coote believes that site development and landscaping are integral parts of his designs, especially for small or low-budget houses, and he is willing to limit the amount spent on the house itself in order to have reserves available for landscaping. Another important aspect of this architect's approach is the distinctive variation of interior spaces through what he calls "selective eccentricity"—dislocations of scale, exaggeration of details or alignments, use of special materials for significant elements, allusions to local or occasionally exotic precedents.

HOUSE 5
JAMES COOTE

House site chosen for its landscape potential

The site is in a small new subdivision adjacent to a large estate in the hill country outside Austin, Texas. The owners, one of whom is a landscape architect, chose it because of its landscaping possibilities. The two acres encompassed a narrow plateau at the street, a ravine with a dry stream, and a thick cedar forest beyond. There was an abundance of native plants. In addition, the site afforded views of the nearby hills and of the city through a gap in the hills.

The owners required separate zones that would include office and living spaces for the landscape architect and a separate realm for the other owner, a banker, and his son. They also wanted a communal place for cooking, eating, and entertaining. This tripartite arrangement can be read in the plan, but it is not expressed outside.

PROJECT: Peese-David house, Austin, TX
ARCHITECT: James Coote; Austin, TX
AREAS: 2,400 square feet on 2.3 acre
DATE COMPLETED: 1979
COST: $90,000

SITE WORK
The house was built on a plateau near the street to keep the driveway short, to avoid bridging an adjacent ravine, and to take full advantage of the view. The portion most exposed to the street was developed to enhance the emerging neighborhood and to display some of the professional skill of the landscape architect owner.

The architect's major contributions were to stretch the house along the edge of the ravine and to extend its volume with high walls and a grape arbor, as well as to create a generous gravel court, with enough space so that several cars can park, turn around, and exit forward, as if on a mini-estate. The house was turned skew to the street in order to suggest a country house rather than a regimented suburban house. The angle also lined the house up with the view of the distant city. Once the major site decisions were made, the owners developed a series of ornamental and vegetable gardens, a roof terrace, arbor, and dry stone walls, all of which amplify the basic concept and character of the design.

GRIDS AND MODULES
The house is not modular.

MATERIALS
Most of the materials are standard inexpensive items available locally, although the house does rely for its effect on a few costly touches: the fragment of exterior stonework, the special chimney, four large sliding glass doors, high-quality wood windows, fossilized cut limestone around the fireplace, and ceramic tile and marble counters in the bathrooms.

Otherwise, inexpensive terracotta pavers gain distinction by being set diagonally. The stucco exterior is tinted a soft rose peach, accented by the deep blue green of the minimal exposed wood trim and doors.

CONSTRUCTION TECHNIQUES
Builder's standards were used.

INTERIORS
The architect focused his efforts on creating the sense of a much larger space than the 2,400 square feet that the budget allowed. His major device was to make spaces distinctively different from each other.

Private zones were placed one above the other: the lower area (office and living space for the landscape architect) is a room with a flat, heavily ribbed and planked ceiling and dark gray walls; the upper one is a suite of two rooms (a bedroom and a study/son's bedroom) with high white ceilings that follow the roof pitch. The lower zone is oriented toward the ravine. A third zone is a tall, two-story space entered from or overlooked by the two private zones.

A limestone fireplace alcove and a dining bay that is an extension of the main space give this "great hall" a more intimate scale. From there the two private volumes inserted within the larger shell of the house can be experienced. An unusually wide stair rising from the hall has walls painted different shades of peach and cream. The carpet is a strong terracotta color.

Devices such as the stair, the large dining bay, the cabinetwork that climbs high on the wall, and the standard-size french doors with little glass panes are examples of the architect's attempt to create an impression of greater size and variety.

There is no special cabinetwork or built-in furniture or trim. The whole interior is sheetrock, painted with nearly a dozen different colors. Throughout the house, paint colors were an all-important device for creating atmosphere and separating spaces.

The perforated screen to the right of the garage door lengthens the house. The fragments of stonework around the entrance distinguish and emphasize it with minimal cost premium.

THERMAL COMFORT AND PLUMBING

There are two air-conditioning zones and a ventilating wall fan. Combined with ample insulation and good orientation, these result in low operating costs. Plumbing for the two baths is stacked.

LIGHTING

Artificial lighting is provided by table and floor lamps. There are a few recessed downlights and fluorescents behind eggcrate grilles in the bathrooms.

MANAGEMENT AND DOCUMENTS

The architect tried to curtail fees by involving the owners in several ways: (1) they investigated local building regulations and codes; (2) they arranged for a mortgage; (3) they developed portions of the working drawings and specifications involving equipment and some materials; and (4) they actually drew up some of the schedules and proofread and typed the final copy of the specifications. In addition, they assumed major responsibility for supervision with the approval of the architect, who had known them for a long time.

SPECIAL DESIGN TREATMENTS

In addition to the landscape development that enhances the "country" siting, the design of the exterior was intended to create a presence much larger than the actual house size. This was done by overscaling the chimney and placing it noticeably on the front, by combining the garage doors and the adjacent garden screen by pattern and color, and by stretching the facade with walls on one end and a meandering arbor of exposed concrete columns and steel piping on the other. These large elements and the terracotta tile roof contrast with such small elements as the bathroom window and steel arbor of the roof terrace.

Another significant element is the entrance porch, made important by the use of local limestone at the exposed corner. A single oversized concrete column was left with Sonotube marks to emphasize the entrance further.

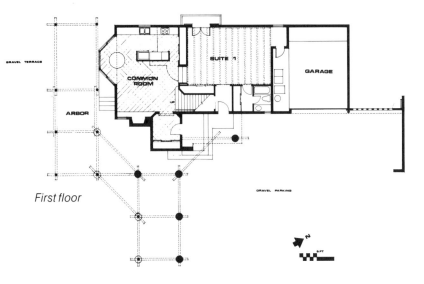

First floor

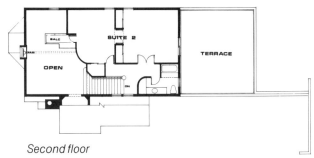

Second floor

Top: Regional traditions such as the tile roof relate the house to its locale. The roof is visually extended over the second-floor terrace with an arbor constructed of steel pipe. Heavy concrete columns with the formwork exposed are softened by planting.

Above: The arbor and extending walls are important parts of the plan.

Following page: A curved wall in the second-floor suite is revealed in the common room below as a canopy above the doors to the first-floor suite. These doors are glazed, providing a space-extending glimpse to the room beyond.

47

KELBAUGH & LEE
PRINCETON, NJ

Firm's designs stress energy-saving elements

The architects organize their houses according to the client's site, required spaces, square footage, and their interrelationships, but with an emphasis on passive heating and cooling methods. In preliminary talks with the client, they make known their belief that a smaller house, better built, is superior to a larger, poorly crafted house. Standard construction techniques and materials, including a great deal of natural wood, are employed. A list of bid alternatives gives the client the option of buying the job without some of the more luxurious finishes or the less cost-effective passive solar features. The firm incorporates many traditional elements in its designs, but with relatively inexpensive symbols of historical styles, such as traditional spatial organization or eclectic columns or porticos.

Some rooms are left unfinished until the owner can better afford to complete them properly. Economy in the use of space is important; if rooms are to be seldom used, the firm proposes minimum sizes for them, shifting the difference to rooms that are more important to the life-style of the occupants.

One-story house is built into a hill

The focus of this plan is the greenhouse/kitchen, which splits a heat-retaining Trombe wall into two sections. This central space, which is sunk two steps below the other rooms, acts as the circulation spine; virtually every other room empties into it. The greenhouse portion accommodates the owners' plant collection, but it also stores solar heat in its dark tile and concrete floor, dark blue back wall, and nine 55-gallon water drums. The 8-inch solid-block rear wall radiates warmth to the rooms behind it as well as back into the greenhouse. Its several windows allow warm air to circulate. The back rooms also receive solar heat from a south-facing glazed continuous roof projection, which allows the winter sun to shine on the massive rear wall cut into the hill. Direct sunlight enters every room.

PROJECT: Dehkan house, Newton, NJ
ARCHITECTS: Kelbaugh & Lee; Princeton, NJ
AREAS: 1,720 square feet plus partial basement on 23-acre site
DATE COMPLETED: 1977
COST: $105,000 plus excavation costs

SITE WORK

The house was inserted into the top of a small hill to conserve heat. This necessitated some blasting and earth moving, but the cost was justified because heat loss through the building skin was thereby minimized. The building was also better protected from the horticultural nursery on the large site.

GRIDS AND MODULES

There was no modular plan, but stock material sizes were used and the building was dimensioned to minimize the cutting of beams.

MATERIALS

Most of the materials are commonly used by builders. A typical wood frame, from the inside out, consists of ½-inch sheetrock, 3½-inch fiberglass batts or cellulosic fiber, ½-inch plywood sheathing, 1-inch Thermax insulation board, and 1-X-6-inch tongue-and-groove rough-sawn cedar siding.

The roof is constructed of ½-inch sheetrock, 9½ inches of fiberglass or cellulosic fiber, ½-inch plywood decking, and a 4-ply builtup roof. The north wall is an 8-inch solid-block wall with 4-inch polystyrene beadboard and Dryvit stucco.

Interior partitions are 2-x-4-inch wood studs with ½-inch sheetrock on either side; the cavities are filled with fiberglass or cellulosic fiber insulation as a sound barrier. The floor is a 4-inch concrete slab with ½-inch dark brown quarry tile throughout, except over the basement, which has a wood floor.

The superior thermal performance of special materials like Polystyrene beadboard and Dryvit stucco justified their use. The quarry-tile finish over concrete slabs was a bid alternate.

CONSTRUCTION TECHNIQUES

The conventional wood frame has ceiling rafters on economical 24-inch centers rather than the usual 16-inch ones. The circular fireplace appears to be custom, but is in fact built with standard manhole block.

The Trombe walls are made of 12-inch heavyweight concrete block whose cores are filled with grout. They were painted flat black with Nextel selective paint after the wall was treated with a masonry conditioner.

Glazing is 1-inch insulating glass held in aluminum frames with thermal breaks at contact points. Reflector shutters are installed in front of the greenhouse water drums only. They are made of 1-inch Thermax insulation board in a wood frame covered with Thermaply. They are operated manually from the outside.

The roof-aperture glazing is SDP Acrylite; Llumar-aluminized Mylar film is glued to the roof and to the underside of the roof monitor to bounce additional solar energy through the glazing. The contractor required special guidance from the architects in the use of aluminized Mylar and selective paints.

INTERIORS

Sheetrock walls were painted with light colors to reflect light onto the heat-absorbing surfaces. Double- and triple-glazed operable and fixed windows were left with a natural wood finish on the interior for easy maintenance.

Axonometric drawing shows the relationships of rooms and the fold-down thermal shutters.

Opposite page: On the south-facing exterior the different kinds of glazing are unified by concealment behind a long fascia / trellis, which also serves to visually extend the spaces behind.

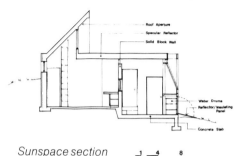

In the sunspace a plant shelf sits above 55-gallon water storage drums. Free-standing Venetian blinds provide sun control to the space.

Sunspace section

Living room section

Top: A section of the sunspace shows the relation of the roof aperture to the masonry wall behind.

Above: A section of the living room shows the use of reflecting and insulating shutters to block and reflect sunlight.

THERMAL COMFORT AND PLUMBING

The goal in this building was to cut energy consumption to the minimum. The client was willing to participate actively in the operation of the passive systems; therefore, all shutters, shades, and curtains are manually operated. The furnace is fired primarily with wood from the property.

The client opposed electric air conditioning, so in the summer cooling is accomplished by means of natural ventilation and good insulation. The backup heating system is a three-zone hydronic system with ¾-inch fin-tube baseboard radiators.

LIGHTING

Ceiling fixtures are recessed "cans" or surface-mounted tracks and fixtures. Convenience outlets were provided where required and per code. Continuous plugmold in the sunspace and kitchen is for the owners' use in tending plants.

MANAGEMENT AND DOCUMENTS

Drawings consisted of ¼-inch plans and elevations; framing, electrical, and mechanical plans; and 1½-inch wall sections. The architects supervised the construction. They issued a supplemental drawing for the special fireplace for modification of the flue support.

The owner acted as general contractor and was careful to maintain good relations with his subcontractors, a practice that resulted in efficient construction progress.

SPECIAL DESIGN TREATMENT

The uncomplicated linear design of the house straightforwardly reveals the solar heating elements, such as the water drums and manually operated shutters/reflectors for the water-drum wall.

HOUSE 7
KELBAUGH & LEE

Suburban house designed for energy efficiency is reconciled with surrounding traditional dwellings

The house is a one-story, two- or three-bed-room house spread east to west on five slightly different levels. It sits in the middle of a wooded 100-x-200-foot suburban lot, with 100 feet of frontage on a quiet street of neo-colonial houses. The longer dimension runs east to west, with high ground at the east end and a 5 to 10 percent slope to the west.

PROJECT: Sisko house, Metuchen, NJ
ARCHITECTS: Kelbaugh & Lee; Princeton, NJ
AREAS: 1,875 square feet heated, 625 square feet unheated, on a 20,000-square-foot lot
DATE COMPLETED: 1980
COST: $140,000 plus landscaping

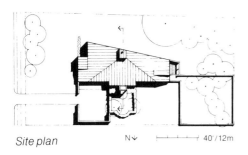

Site plan   N↓   ├─────┼─── 40'/12m

Formal landscaping devices help to define the main entrance on the side of the house.

SITE WORK

The building sits on an earthen podium that was created from cutting and filling the site. The extent of this podium was limited by the budgetary decision to avoid borrowed fill. Many trees were cut down, but the better specimens were saved. A small forecourt is formally planted to emphasize the axis of the house; the rest was left natural to minimize site improvement costs.

GRIDS AND MODULES:

None.

MATERIALS:

Materials used are basically economical. Walls consist of wood shingles over 1½-inch styro-foam over plywood sheathing with 3½ inches of cellulosic fiber pumped into the cavities and ½-inch sheetrock. The roof is asphalt shingles over plywood sheathing over 2-x-10-inch rafters with 9¼ inches of cellulosic fiber pumped into the cavities, and ½-inch sheetrock.

Some more expensive finish materials were used strategically to reinforce design concepts, such as quarry tile floors in the vestibule and semicircular foyer.

CONSTRUCTION TECHNIQUES:

Concrete block on concrete footings, 2-x-4-inch standard wood-frame 16-inch centers. Slab on grade, 2-x-10-inch wood beam roof, conventionally framed. No exposed structure.

THERMAL COMFORT AND PLUMBING

The bedrooms and living room are lined up along the south side of the house. Each has its own 60-square-foot unvented Trombe wall. A solarium at the southeast corner has a thermal-mass floor and wall, which also draws warm air into the living room during the day. Bathrooms, closets, and kitchen—the less frequently occupied rooms—are placed on the north side to act as a buffer zone for the other rooms.

The forced-hot-air auxiliary furnace can redistribute excess solar heat from the south to the north without being fired. The bathrooms have several electric infrared lamps for quick, short-term heat.

Summer cooling is achieved by shading from trees and awnings at each Trombe wall, by cross-ventilation, and by induced ventilation through the large cupola, which contains a 42-inch fan. The fan shares the cupola with a metal chimney from a wood-burning stove.

The solar hot-water preheater forms the roof of the portico, actively marking entry while passively heating water. It is of the "breadbox" type, a 40-gallon tank covered in selective foil, quadruple-glazed with Teflon and glass layers. All plumbing is grouped on the north wall.

LIGHTING

Skylights are introduced in the roof to allow natural daylight to penetrate to the deeper areas of the plan. Artificial lighting is provided along the south wall to dramatize the texture of the Trombe wall.

MANAGEMENT AND DOCUMENTS

The architects provided the following bid alternates:

ALTERNATES

1. Delete deck in its entirety including: footings, railings, and finishes. Substitute temporary wood steps at rear door.

2. Substitute 300-pound fiberglass roof shingles over ⅝" plyscore for corrugated asphalt roofing in all locations. Consult architect for detail.

3. Substitute ½" gravel for brick and concrete sidewalk and circle.

4. Standard insulating glass with ½" airspace for large panes (large light salon to be 3/16" glass and other lights to be ⅛" glass.

On the bid form, the architects left space for noting whether alternate 2 was an "add" or a "subtract," since the specified roofing was an unusual item.

Right: On the south elevation an entire wall is skewed to face the sun directly. The pitched roof slopes to provide a spatial climax at the center of the living room where the hearth is located. The sun penetrates the high semi-circular window.

Below: The axonometric drawing shows the relation of levels to the sloping site and the entry sequence from the gravel parking area.

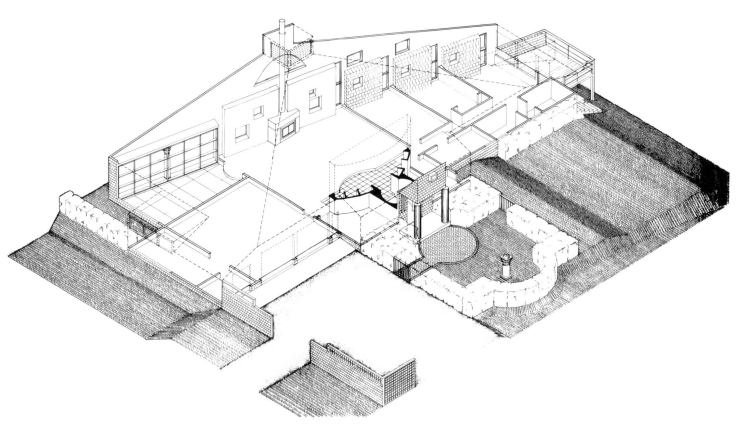

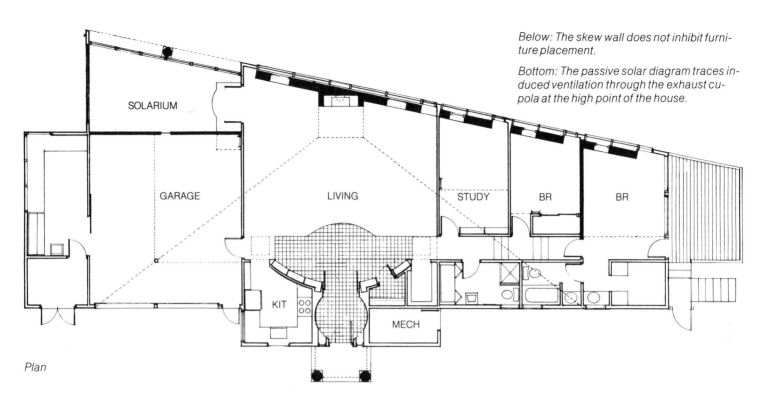

SOLARIUM

GARAGE

LIVING

STUDY

BR

BR

KIT

MECH

Plan

Below: The skew wall does not inhibit furniture placement.

Bottom: The passive solar diagram traces induced ventilation through the exhaust cupola at the high point of the house.

Above: The entry introduces curves to accent its ceremonial importance. This is achieved economically with the use of different materials, a one-step level change, and a wall of bookshelves.

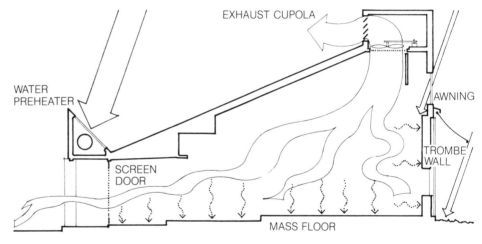

EXHAUST CUPOLA

WATER PREHEATER

SCREEN DOOR

MASS FLOOR

AWNING

TROMBE WALL

Passive solar diagram, summer

SPECIAL DESIGN TREATMENTS:

The owner requested a single major living-entertaining space; the architects designed it to occupy the tall center portion of the house. The preparation of food and dining were not high priorities, so a very small kitchen was provided. The dining area is in the large living space.

The entire house could not be turned on the small lot, so the skew wall on the south side solves the problem of facing the sun with the major heat-gathering elements. The entrance, defined by a curving wall of books, is oriented on an axis with the fireplace.

Augmenting the solar concerns that helped shape the plan are some shingle-style elements: the curved window in the living room, the random window sizes and placement, and the asymmetrical hip roof. These elements reconcile the house with the surrounding dwellings, all of which are mostly traditional in character.

ERROL BARRON / MICHAEL TOUPS ARCHITECTS
NEW ORLEANS, LA

Architects' aim is expanded discourse between architect, owner, contractor

Barron and Toups believe that little discussed but important ingredients in budget-wise, need-fitting house building are the negotiations and discourse among owner, architect, and contractor. The most important of these relationships is that between owner and architect, who must work closely to achieve a house of distinction. To this end, Barron and Toups are willing to spend more than the average amount of time with clients to encourage their cooperation and participation in the design process, hoping that they will become enthusiastic about it.

In negotiations the architects try to maintain a neutral stance with all parties. They believe that the architect must be able to work with detachment and that the owner must have confidence in the architect and the builder. Probably no residential project should be undertaken, they feel, when this climate of trust does not exist.

They strive for a simple set of construction documents and supplement them with perspectives and annotated three-dimensional drawings. Good and cooperative builders are essential to this practice.

The architects believe that flexibility is necessary on the construction site and that the architect must be able to think quickly of alternatives consistent with the intent of the house design but within the contractor's abilities and limitations. So that contractors can anticipate the intent of drawings and thereby save time and money, Barron and Toups deal with contractors as equals on the team, rather than as instruction-following laborers.

HOUSE 8
ERROL BARRON/MICHAEL TOUPS ARCHITECTS

Contemporary New Orleans house fits into established neighborhood

The building site was an urban lot in an area in New Orleans dominated by large, two-story pedimented houses. Guided by this vernacular architecture, the architects evolved a pedimented design of their own. The pediments are held away from the house to form a sunscreen in the rear and porches at the front and rear. The backs of the pediments are painted orange, so that they reflect warm light into the rooms behind them.

The plan is similar to that of conventional New Orleans houses: an L shape providing a rear porch and a side gallery. The living room and gallery are arranged around a central axis extending from the front to the rear of the site. Upstairs quarters are arranged around a center stair lighted by a north-facing clerestory at the peak of the roof. The master bedroom is situated along the back wall of the house and has a roof deck over the kitchen extension. Using conventional configuration makes economical sense—if architects deviate from certain plan types that are familiar to local contractors; the scheme is regarded as "unusual" and may result in higher prices.

PROJECT: Stafford house, New Orleans, LA
ARCHITECTS: Errol Barron/Michael Toups Architects; New Orleans, LA
AREAS: 3,900 square feet on 6,750-square-foot lot
DATE COMPLETED: 1980
COST: $175,000

SITE WORK

The location of the house on the lot was mandated by the narrowness of the plot and the required setbacks. Utility connections were made to public services in the street.

GRIDS AND MODULES

A 4-foot module was used with standard doors and windows. The heights of these units were set to constant reference points. The horizontal dimensions were marked by ledges, offsets in the sheetrock, duct chases, and changes of paint color to emphasize the modular method.

MATERIALS

The frame is wood, with stucco over plywood. Interior walls are sheetrock; the first floor is Mexican tile on a plywood subfloor. Floors elsewhere wood with carpeting.

CONSTRUCTION TECHNIQUES

The house is raised in a conventional New Orleans manner. The 2- × -12-inch joists placed on concrete blocks elevate the house above the damp soil, permitting access to pipes and air-conditioning equipment hung beneath the house. Detailing for all walls and the roof is standard.

INTERIORS

Bedrooms on the second level were conceived as boxes slung from one wall to the other with a void between. This void is the two-story-high space of the living room and an upstairs sitting/family room. The two bedroom boxes span from wall to wall, overhanging the gallery and entry on the front and, in a more generous way, a rear gallery, which is the center of family activity during hot summer months. This simple scheme is well in keeping with local traditions.

An exterior view of the entrance establishes the bulk and shape of the house in the context of the neighborhood.

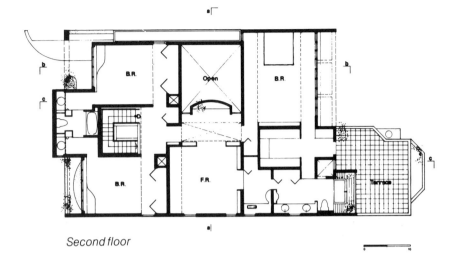

Second floor

Left and below: The traditional L shape of the ground plan provides a sheltered porch at the rear, which is covered by the master bedroom on the second level. A dramatic top-lighted area in the center of the house opens up the second floor over the living room.

Bottom left: The high skylight, which introduces light to the second-floor balcony, and the two-story first-floor living room can be seen in the short section.

Bottom right: The long section indicates the raising of the main floor over the New Orleans ground—a traditional practice in this hot, damp climate—and the free-standing second-floor exterior screens, which diffuse the intense sunlight.

Right: The dramatic living room is accented by a curved bay on the balcony above.

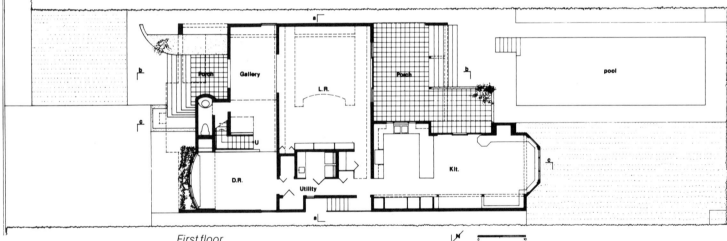

First floor

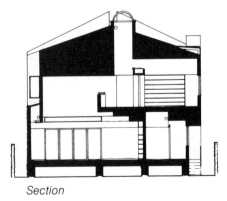

Section

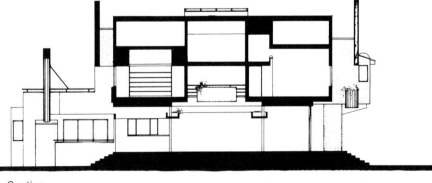

Section

This view of the entrance hall shows the care with which the architect located the intersecting wall and ceiling planes. The underside of the stairs and a higher ceiling are highlighted with color, further emphasizing the vertical planes.

THERMAL COMFORT AND PLUMBING

Although solar panels were considered for both the hot-water system and the pool heater, both were rejected because of their high initial cost. The house emphasizes passive cooling techniques; an attic fan to draw air through the house on cool summer evenings, high ceilings indirectly lighted, and deep overhangs on the porches.

LIGHTING

Because of the intense heat of the New Orleans sun, especially during the summer, the main living rooms of the house are lighted indirectly. Light enters the living room from four sides, but always screened by deep overhangs or by indirect skylights. The result is a light and airy effect achieved without direct sunlight.

MANAGEMENT AND DOCUMENTS

Simple documents and close liaison with the contractor enabled the architects to add some of the more complex features of the house at a lower cost than if they had been detailed at the beginning. Builders generally feel that if details are not familiar, they are difficult and therefore expensive to build. Many times it is possible in the field to show a contractor how a special structure or trim can be incorporated without scaring him with elaborately detailed drawings.

The original design came in substantially over budget; 500 square feet were eliminated from the upper level of the house to cut costs.

SPECIAL DESIGN TREATMENTS

The owner did not want a traditional house, but the architects incorporated such traditional New Orleans amenities as shaded overhangs of cool, indirectly lighted spaces and an airy sense of volume. The emphasis on wall rather than roof, however, ran somewhat contrary to local patterns. To relate the house visually to its neighbors, the architects established the basic volume of the house and then recessed all openings into the skin of the structure.

HOUSE 9
ERROL BARRON/MICHAEL TOUPS ARCHITECTS

Beach pilings shape house form

The clients for this beach house wanted a comfortable vacation home that would be suitable for their eventual retirement. They requested three to four bedrooms and three baths, all relatively small, with a dining room, kitchen, living area, and adequate porches from which to enjoy the beachfront view.

The site is a sliver of land running at right angles to the beach along a row of rather undistinguished beach houses, all on pilings. The architects wanted the house to be open toward the water and closed toward the road. Setback requirements mandated that the house be near the road, however. To afford protection from traffic during the day, bedrooms, bathrooms, kitchen, and dining room were placed between the living room and the road. The living room was given extra height and prominence. Most glass areas face the ocean.

The budget for this project was conventional, based on the houses around it. The design differs from them in its organization and fenestration; however, it borrows forms from the nineteenth-century beach houses around it, such as the steep roof, high profile, and vertical facades.

In order to adhere to the limited budget, the architects kept bedroom and bathroom sizes minimal and made ceilings a standard 8-foot height throughout, except in the living room, which has a 16-foot ceiling, and in the dining room and kitchen, where the ceilings are sloped. They achieved a closer relationship between inside and outside spaces by cutting into the form of the house to make one of the main porches.

PROJECT: Gibson house, Navarre Beach, FL
ARCHITECTS: Errol Barron/Michael Toups Architects; New Orleans, LA
AREAS: 2,600 square feet without porches on ¼ acre
DATE COMPLETED: 1982
COST: $145,000

SITE WORK
The Department of Natural Resources required that the site be left undisturbed. Native sea oats were planted at the front entrance of the house.

GRIDS AND MODULES
A standard 12-foot dimension was used throughout.

MATERIALS
Board-and-batten siding was used with standard anodized aluminum windows and a built-up asphalt roof. The siding was stained to match the color of the surrounding vegetation. Interiors are sheetrock with 1-x-4-inch wood trim. A tile kitchen counter was installed at the owners' request.

CONSTRUCTION TECHNIQUES
In negotiations with the local builder, the architects learned what details were familiar to him. They reserved special details requiring more imagination and coordination for particular items, such as handrails and the front entry.

The only nonconventional construction item was a drop in the level of the front porch below that of the living room so that the deck handrail did not obstruct the view from the living room. Conventional wood-frame construction was used throughout, but shear walls were located every 12 feet perpendicular to the axis to resist wind.

The 12-foot module was established by pilings driven into the ground and ending 20 feet above. The house hangs between these pilings, because of its height and because of the strong winds prevalent in Florida. The house is structured somewhat like a tree—pilings extend from below grade to the roof. The architects selected this method over others because it provides greater structural stability. A more conventional method is to build a house platform on top of the pilings.

INTERIORS
The interior arrangement of the rooms was based on the fine view toward sea and beach. Public spaces such as gallery, living and dining rooms, and kitchen were given priority over bedrooms rarely used in the daytime. Linking the master bedrooms and living room by means of a book-lined gallery adjacent to the covered porch is an important feature.

The living room, which is the central space, was painted white and supplied with carefully placed windows and a pattern of partially exposed joists on the ceiling. The color scheme for the rest of the house consists of colors from the surrounding landscape.

The shear walls described under Construction Techniques were sheathed with 1-x-4-inch tongue-and-groove siding as a decorative feature. Openings in the these walls are not square but are beveled to indicate their structural purpose.

THERMAL COMFORT AND PLUMBING
Standard residential heating, cooling, and plumbing systems were used.

LIGHTING
Large expanses of glass are set back under deep porches or have lowered screens to help diffuse the strong beach sunlight.

MANAGEMENT AND DOCUMENTS
Documents and specs consisted of ¼-inch-scale plans, typical elevations and sections, with a minimum of details. The drawings were left sketchy; the architects worked with the contractor to develop details as the job progressed. This procedure is more time-consuming, but allows for adjustment as the house takes shape. The architect must make decisions quickly on site and draw three-dimensionally what is intended. Close communication between architect and contractor was required.

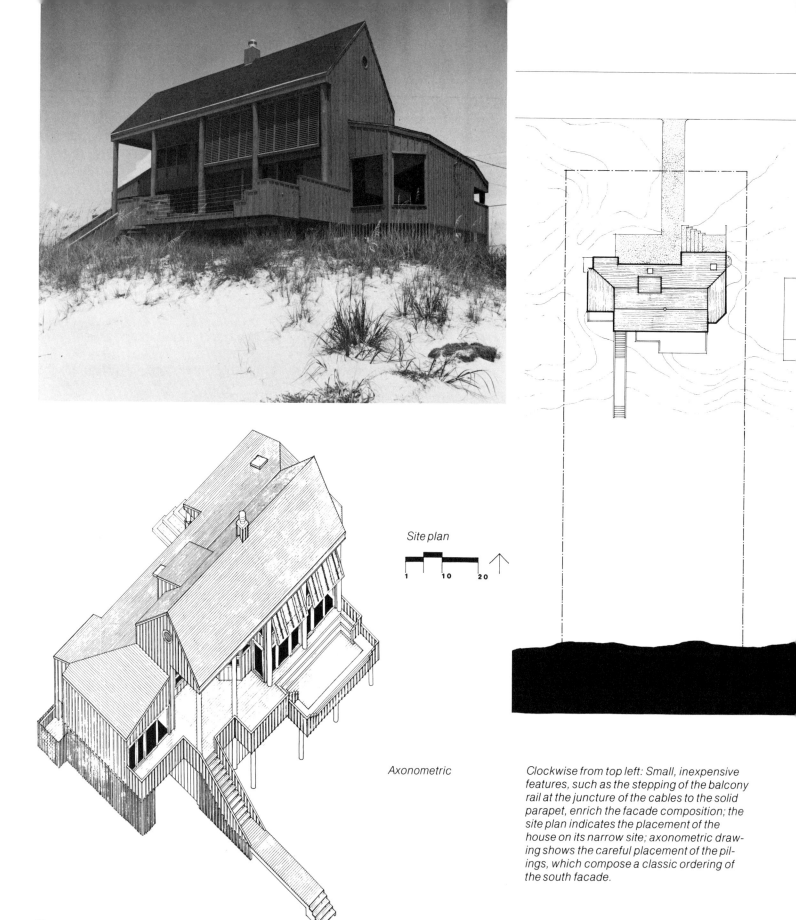

Site plan

1 10 20

Axonometric

Clockwise from top left: Small, inexpensive features, such as the stepping of the balcony rail at the juncture of the cables to the solid parapet, enrich the facade composition; the site plan indicates the placement of the house on its narrow site; axonometric drawing shows the careful placement of the pilings, which compose a classic ordering of the south facade.

SPECIAL DESIGN TREATMENTS

The owners came to Barron/Toups knowing little about the architectural process. The firm had been recommended by a friend of a relative, and things went very well at first. The clients were pleased with the design, which came in on budget, and the contractor whom the architects helped them select appeared to be excellent. During construction, however, the owner and contractor began to make changes without fully understanding their impact on the design. This resulted in details that are inconsistent with the basic approach. The architects note that a tight construction schedule and the client's desire to occupy the house before summer were largely responsible for this deviation from normal procedure.

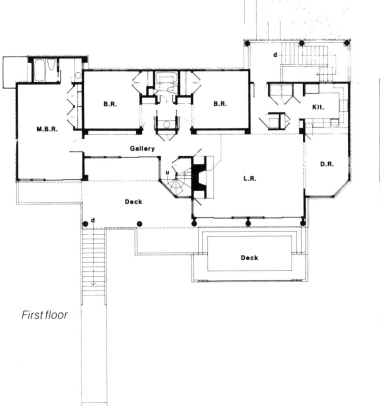

First floor

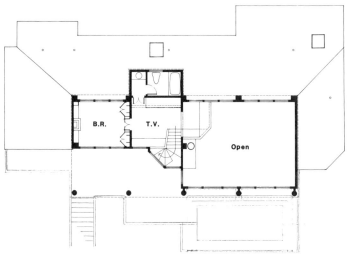

Second floor

Above and right: First-floor plan shows three bedrooms grouped on the street side opposite the living and dining rooms and decks, which face the sun and the view to the south.

Distinctive detailing emphasizes the importance of the central living space. Note the partially exposed joists in the ceiling.

Shear walls are expressed by beveling the tops of openings through them, providing a decorative accent. Note the contrasting trim.

FRANK LLOYD WRIGHT
(1867-1959)

Dean of the American house summarizes design principles

Frank Lloyd Wright's work is well known to architects, builders, and many laypeople. Not as well known, perhaps, is the summary of design ideas for the Zimmerman house, built in 1951 in New Hampshire, which he prepared for publication in House & Home magazine.*

Wright evolved his design approach over the course of the seventy-odd years he practiced. He did this house in a mature period, when he was able to look back on a long and productive career and summarize some of the ideas he had worked out. At that point in his life, he was very interested in the small house and how to make it suitable for the average American, as well as in extending public interest in good architecture. His ideas from that article follow.

32 SIMPLE AND BASIC DESIGN IDEAS TO MAKE A SMALL HOUSE LOOK BIGGER—OUTSIDE

1. Stress the horizontals: (a) Stretch the roof line. (b) Keep the fascia in one straight line, except for a good reason. (c) Define a strong middle line.
2. (a) Don't waste a big overhang on the north, and (b) don't feel you must use the same roof pitch on both sides.
3. Keep the roof line low.
4. Don't build a whole wall and punch holes in it for your windows. Build your wall only to sill height and then rest your windows in structural courses above it.
5. Scale an entrance to its wall. Don't put a dinky, too-small doorway in a big surface.
6. Don't stick a toy chimney in a big expanse of roof or it will look like an afterthought.

TO MAKE A SMALL HOUSE LOOK BIGGER—INSIDE

7. Dramatize a high ceiling by emphasizing a below-standard ceiling line to fool the eye.
8. Use a dropped ceiling in the hall to make the living room ceiling seem higher by contrast.
9. Make the room seem wider by placing an important design element—like brick window columns—at right angles to the room.
10. Use a glass gable without an overhang to let the sun play changing patterns on the ceiling.

11. Plan built-ins around the walls to free center space and make a narrow room work like a wider one.
12. Break up the open plan by letting it flow around corners, so you can't see all the dining area from the living room or all the open kitchen from the dining room.

TO MAKE A SMALL HOUSE WORK BETTER—OUTSIDE

13. Make the terrace seem a part of the living room. For example: (a) Carry your planting through the glass. (b) Carry your floor line through the wall. (c) Use ceiling-high glass to let people see your ceiling run right past the wall. (d) Continue the ceiling pattern out onto the overhang.
14. Miter the glass in corner windows to make the corner disappear.
15. Provide a driveway big enough for off-street parking.
16. Don't landscape the grounds for expensive maintenance.
17. Give the house privacy from the street—by planting, by facing glass areas toward the rear, by setting the house back.
18. Raise the planting boxes so the gardener won't have to bend. Provide hose bibs in each box.
19. Make the terrace big enough to serve as an outdoor room, or it merely becomes a path.
20. Raise the terrace slightly to get good drainage and make lawn maintenance easier.

21. Face the house toward the sun and away from stormy winds, if it is built in cold country.

TO MAKE A SMALL HOUSE WORK BETTER—INSIDE

22. Put everything in the kitchen within easy reach. Store utensils and dishes used every day on open shelves so cupboard doors don't have to be opened over and over.
23. Make the kitchen tall so cooking odors can rise.
24. Keep the mess of the open kitchen out of sight.
25. Punch a hole in the roof of an inside bath; light it from above.
26. Give the owner a huge bathroom mirror, and light it evenly all around the border.
27. Make the low ceiling line do double duty as a lighting trough.
28. Use natural materials that call for little maintenance.
29. Use shelves for decoration.
30. Make even a small entrance hall long enough to give the living room some privacy. And make the coat closet big enough.
31. Put your kitchen at the heart of the house, even if it has to be an inside kitchen.
32. Pivot rooms around a huge fireplace—and hide the heater room behind it.

*"This Rich and Rhythmic House Expresses 32 Simple and Basic Design Ideas," *House & Home*, September 1956, pages 136–141.

HOUSE 10
FRANK LLOYD WRIGHT

Classic Wright house illustrates principles

The clients requested a two-bedroom house with master bedroom and living and dining spaces focused on their garden. Wright composed the house in accordance with the principles set forth on page 75.

PROJECT: Zimmerman house, Manchester, NH
ARCHITECT: Frank Lloyd Wright
AREAS: 1,400 square feet on 2 acres
DATE COMPLETED: 1951
COST: $42,000.

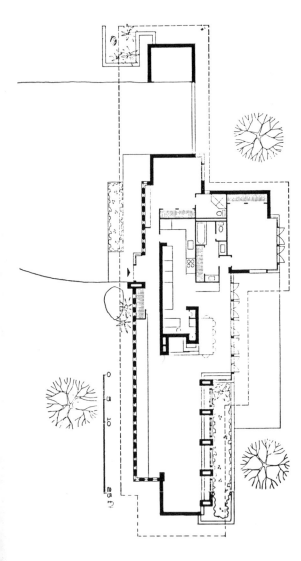

SITE WORK

Connections were made to water and sewer mains. A graveled entrance court to the carport and entry were built by the owner.

GRIDS AND MODULES

The following note is contained on sheet 1 of the drawings: "This house is planned upon a unit system of 4'0'' x 4'0''. Unless dimensioned otherwise, all masonry walls are located with one face on the unit or half-unit."

MATERIALS

The materials consist of common red brick, longleaf yellow pine framing, and red tidewater cypress board and batten for interior walls, sash, frames, casings, trim, and fascias. There is a 4-inch-thick concrete floor throughout, topped with red integral coloring steel troweled to a smooth surface. After they hardened, the concrete floors were treated with a glazing compound. Sloped roofs are No. 1 red cedar shingles. The flat roof is 4-ply.

CONSTRUCTION TECHNIQUES

Exterior walls are brick, either continuous to windowsills or in piers with windows or french doors in between. Continuous ribbon windows are set in precast concrete sills; heads and mullions are fixed. Walls and piers are set on reinforced grade beams 9 x 9 inches on a wider bed of crushed stone carried below the frost line. Roof construction is steel girders combined with 2-x-8-inch wood rafters 24 inches on center. The interior work space has a brick wall to one side; with the brick fireplace it provides bearing for the steel ridge beams.

INTERIORS

Interiors are natural materials with emphasis placed on horizontal details. For instance, the horizontal joints are raked out of the brickwork and the vertical ones are flush; interior board-and-batten walls are detailed with a combination of 9-inch-wide boards set with thinner 3-inch-wide boards, all horizontal.

The fireplace is sculpturally designed to provide a focus for the long living room. Wright specified that all interior woodwork have cracks and holes filled with beeswax and then coated with one coat of shellac followed by one coat of paste wax buffed to a finish. All interior hardware is bright brass; all doors have piano hinges. All ceilings are natural wood, detailed similarly to the walls, with the pattern shown on a reflected ceiling plan. Interior seating is builtin.

THERMAL COMFORT AND PLUMBING

Heating is with an oil-fired boiler providing hot water to 1 ½-inch wrought-iron pipes 18 inches on center buried in the slab. There are three circuits; one thermostat controls all. Supply piping to the fixtures is ¾ inch rather than the now customary ½ inch.

LIGHTING

Fluorescents are built into recessed troughs in the wood ceiling; troughs are provided as well in the deep overhangs.

MANAGEMENT AND DOCUMENTS

Nine 24-x-36-inch sheets were provided, consisting of a ⅛-inch plot plan, ¼-inch general structural and reflected ceiling plans, ¾-inch sections and work-space details, full- and quarter-full-size millwork details, and a sheet of mechanical and plumbing details, with a ¼-inch heating plan showing the floor piping layout. Supplementary sheets were issued to revise the elevations and roof framing. A supplementary foundation plan was also issued at a later date.

All specifications are hand-lettered on the drawings in outline form. An apprentice who remained on the job for a year furnished supplementary sketches as necessary. The client was financially responsible for the room and board of this apprentice. The architect's fee was 10 percent of cost.

SPECIAL DESIGN TREATMENTS

The clients were specifically interested in a good ambience for the playing of musical instruments; Wright planned the acoustical properties of the living room accordingly.

Opposite page: The long plan reinforces the low roof lines and provides vistas within the house. Privacy is aided by the linear separation of spaces.

Left: The mitered glass corners, deep overhangs, and rows of windows and doors are the result of Wright's interest in a close relationship between interior spaces and the landscape.

Below: Wright's love of ground-hugging low lines is evident in this view of the rear of the house.

Right and below: Interiors feature natural materials and a careful arrangement of joints. Note the contrast of the low corridor with the higher living room.

BAHR, VERMEER & HAECKER, ARCHITECTS
OMAHA, NB

Special program features or site characteristics are the keys to design solutions

When approached with a potential house commission, the architects ask clients to write down their ideas about what the house should *be*—not just what rooms and square footage they want, but how they would like to live, how they envision their ideal house. Using this approach, they have received some fresh and enlightening insights into their clients' expectations. These program ideas help the architects formulate designs through logic, as opposed to whim, stylization, or a desire to develop interesting forms. They begin with a general idea and work the specifics of the program into it. For example, a recent bachelor client requested an "open" house. Based on this clue, the architects proceeded to design a loft house with no interior doors.

Bahr, Vermeer & Haecker look for places where the client wants special emphasis and for characteristics of the site that may suggest areas to be dealt with in a sepcial way, such as a view, a large tree, an access road, or adjacent neighbors. Several details always warrant their particular attention: entries, circulation, fenestration, and an expression of the parts and pieces, such as beams and bay windows. They see the entry as an important demarcation of the passage from outside to inside, so they sometimes design a special door or mark the entry with a special light or covering. Circulation, the architects feel, must be efficient—hence the straight, short corridor, or circulation through a room, omitting hallways completely. Stairs offer the potential for special treatment as well. Doors and windows go far toward establishing the character of a house.

This firm develops the majority of its work without benefit of contractor input. Seldom do the architects bring in a contractor early to establish rapport or mutually explore solutions; they have found an abundance of good contractors in their area and do not feel pressured to work with any particular one, although they have developed a select list. Nor do they find it advantageous to negotiate with a single contractor in a competitive bidding market.

Making a profit on houses is difficult, especially since this firm does not specialize in houses. Bahr, Vermeer & Haecker work at an hourly rate, for a flat fee, or for a percentage of the cost of construction; they prefer an hourly fee with no limit. They avoid lump-sum fees if at all possible, but sometimes a client will insist. Whatever the arrangement, all reimbursable expenses are extra. Sometimes the firm gives an "estimated" total fee; hours and costs are estimated as conservatively as possible. When they work on a percentage basis, they use 15 percent for houses under $200,000; over $200,000 the percentage can be lower—maybe 12 to 14 percent. To stay within fees, they make a summary of projected time and monitor it weekly.

HOUSE 11
BAHR, VERMEER & HAECKER, ARCHITECTS

Economy of architect's compact house is reinforced by building in a group of five

Five young architects wanted to build their own houses, but they knew they couldn't afford to unless they built together. They purchased a 1.4-acre site with an existing house and drew a master plan for ten new houses with common public spaces. After each of the five designed his own house, the group sold the existing structure and the five remaining lots. With that money, they leveraged individual mortgage loans for construction. The owners of the remaining lots obtained their own financing and built their own houses, but within established design standards. The resulting project includes courtyards and other amenities that are available to all homeowners. The bank was willing to establish credit for "sweat equity." (In this kind of system, credit is given to the borrower for work he or she agrees to complete, such as painting, building decks, or installing hardware and skylights.)

The linear configuration of the plan of the Bowen house resulted in short corridors. The interior volume is visually increased by the exposed roof structure (in lieu of a conventional flat ceiling and attic). These features provide more usable space and allowed the owner to satisfy his space needs while spending less money.

The owner acted as general contractor: he took bids from subcontractors, selected craftsmen, purchased materials with trade discounts, and supervised construction.

PROJECT: Bowen house, Omaha, NB
ARCHITECTS: Bahr, Vermeer & Haecker, Architects; Gary Bowen, Project Architect
AREAS: 1,950 square feet on 1.4 acres shared with ten other houses
DATE COMPLETED: 1978
COST: $69,000, including land and fees

SITE WORK
Driveways were grouped and paved in brick. Utility connections were grouped to shorten runs. Other common areas such as green spaces were left natural. The shared site work was one of the more cost-effective aspects of this joint development (such costs can frequently account for 10 to 20 percent of a project's expense).

GRIDS AND MODULES
The width of this long, narrow house is 16 feet, an economical span for wood joists. The rafters are 2 feet on center; all walls below are on a rafter line.

MATERIALS
Exterior materials include cedar lap siding, asphalt shingles, and galvanized gutter downspouts. On the interior, floors are oak; walls are sheetrock; ceilings are stained fir decking and joists.

CONSTRUCTION TECHNIQUES
Conventional building techniques were used with several exceptions. The roof construction called for 2-x-8-inch rafters 24 inches on center tied together with rods 4 feet on center with 3-inch rigid insulation above the decking, because the architect wanted an exposed rafter roof. The long, unsupported roof would have required an unusually large ridge beam; the tie rods eliminated the need for this while performing the necessary structural job of holding the side walls together.

Other nonstandard details included the large two-story window in the living room and the fixed clerestory on the west side of the house. The two-story south window is steel, with small panes, approximately 1 foot high and 18 inches wide. This window and clerestory cover the 7-x-16-foot opening and expose the living room and another sitting room on the second floor to the south sun and a view of the city. Wood windows more conventionally framed would have blocked more of the light and the view.

For the fixed-glass clerestory, which marks the top of the stair on the second floor and allows head room, the architect specified an 8-x-8-foot sheet of ⅝-inch insulating glass to let light penetrate to the landing and into the void beyond directly over the kitchen. Although smaller conventional windows would have served, they would have lacked the dramatic impact of this large piece of glass.

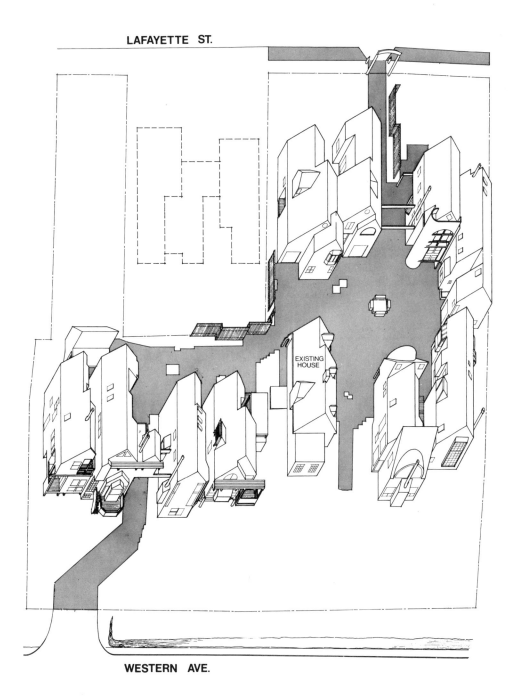

LAFAYETTE ST.

EXISTING
HOUSE

WESTERN AVE.

Left: Despite different and often assertive forms, the house groups convey a quiet sense of unity through the use of similar materials and careful siting.

Above: The axonometric drawing of the entire site reveals the similarity of the gable roofs and the various details, such as bay windows, semicircular windows, and other projecting elements.

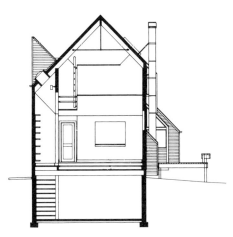

Section A

Above: Section A shows the gable roof and modulating add-ons, clerestories, and skylights.

Right: The plans indicate an economical arrangement of spaces within a long rectangle, with a series of add-on window seats, closets, a breakfast nook, and the fireplace.

INTERIORS

The most arresting feature in the interior of this house is the long-ridged exposed roof with its tie rods. Sisal matting is used where the architect wanted a soft floor finish.

THERMAL COMFORT AND PLUMBING

Warm-air heating is supplemented with a heat-circulating fireplace. A roof fan provides summer ventilation. Plumbing is stacked back to back in a single plumbing chase.

LIGHTING

Track lights or floor and area lamps are used. Some recessed fixtures were selected for bedrooms and baths.

MANAGEMENT AND DOCUMENTS

Nine 24-x-36-inch sheets contained ¼-inch-scale plans, elevations, and sections; ⅛-inch-scale mechanical, electrical, framing, and foundation plans; and ½-inch-scale typical wall sections and elevations of interior cabinetwork.

SPECIAL DESIGN TREATMENTS

The compact, narrow house features a light, open interior. Circulation paths have been minimized. The skylights and the large south window contribute to the airiness of the interior. The bedrooms and bathrooms are enclosed, but all other rooms share the long, tall interior volume. This expansive quality, the exposed roof structure, and the linear plan reflect the owner's memories of favorite places: warehouse loft apartments, Nebraska barns, and narrow London townhouses.

Upper floor

Ground floor

Above: The visual variety that can be obtained within a simple shape is evident in this view. Note the void to the area below, the glimpse of space in the add-on to the left, and the drafting studio tucked under the ridge above.

Left: The linear quality of the house is apparent in this view toward the kitchen and bedroom beyond.

73

LOUIS MACKALL AND PARTNER
BRANFORD, CT

Architect integrates construction and design

This architect's key cost-control technique is reducing the number of middlemen. In addition to doing all the designing and drawing for the projects shown here, he built most of the cabinetry, stairs, doors, and specialty items.

Mackall states: "I have for some time divided the work on a house into two parts. The first is that which a builder can feel comfortable bidding on, and hence building; the second is the oddball stuff. The former is put out to a selected list of contractors for bids. The latter is made in our shop or subcontracted to specific craftsmen with whom we have worked before and with whom we share a common body of skills, expectations, experience, motivation, and so on. Keeping the out-of-the-ordinary work close in this way makes three things happen. One: it gets done without hassle and subsequent ulcers. Two: the feedback results in changes that make the end product better. And three: close-up experience thus gained nourishes future work. The last consideration is tremendously important."

His approach makes sense, because most builders readily understand the basic techniques of house construction, but frequently have trouble with special items that architects specify. Although the architect in this instance does the work with his own hands, the approach can have equal validity when unusual parts of a house are contracted for separately on behalf of the owner. Understanding and trust between architect and client are important elements in this particular working process.

The importance of the curved roof to the design is made clear in the section drawing. The heavy beams supporting the second floor stop short of the exterior walls and reinforce the sheltering effect of the curved roof and its subtle juncture with the exterior walls.

HOUSE 12

LOUIS MACKALL AND PARTNER

Curved roof and custom millwork enrich simple plan

The Wierdsma house was built on Nantucket Island by a builder and the architect, who was also the cabinetmaker. The clients wanted their vacation house to include four bedrooms, three baths, a kitchen-dining area, a living room, and a screened-in porch, and they wanted to be able to enjoy the fine view toward the water. They planned to use the house during the summer and for occasional vacations in the winter.

A glass-roofed atrium divides the house into two parts. To the left of it is the living/kitchen/master bedroom unit, and a three-bedroom sleeping unit is on the right. The two areas are connected on the second story by a bridge.

A key factor of the program was the set of requirements made by the Historic Districts Commission, which had to review the house design to see that it was compatible with the island's aesthetic. The commission's rules determined exterior materials and eave detail and forced the architect to eliminate a center roof skylight and a triangular chimney originally planned for the house.

PROJECT: Wierdsma house, Nantucket, MA
ARCHITECT: Louis Mackall and Partner; Branford, CT
AREAS: 2,464 square feet on 8 acres
DATE COMPLETED: 1974
COST: $100,000

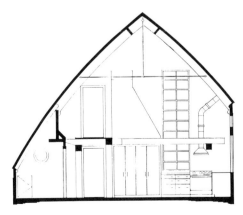

SITE WORK
None, other than required utilities and an access road.

GRIDS AND MODULES
A 2-foot module runs the length of the buildings.

MATERIALS
The roof consists of shingles over Homasote panels, which serve as the inside finish. Exterior walls are shingles over wood studs. The clients expressed a desire for heavy wood beams early in discussions with the architect. The finish for both floors is 2-inch Douglas fir decking, tongue and groove. The underside of the second floor serves as the ceiling of the first floor. The floor is finished with urethane on the first floor, painted on the second.

CONSTRUCTION TECHNIQUES
The most striking feature of the house is the curved roof, an example of which the architect had seen in an old house near his office. The rafters are cut from 3-x-12-inch joists; two pieces are joined to provide the necessary structural depth. The curve at top and bottom are gentle enough to allow cutting with a standard circular saw. Tie rods, which occur every other rafter, eliminate the need for collar beams, necessary to keep the exterior walls from spreading. The tie rods are also visually attractive.

The architect himself made all the doors and cabinets, as well as the railing stanchions, which are mortised into the rafters. They are paired at every other rafter, or 4 feet on center.

The fireplace was designed according to the rules of Count Rumford, an early fireplace designer who worked out guidelines for energy-efficient fireplaces that remain valid to this day.

The structural system for the two floors consists of 10-x-10-inch beams pinned to corresponding posts with two 24-x-⅝-inch steel rods. These are spaced 6 feet on center, and the posts are held back 4 feet from the exterior walls. Beams are then cut to taper up to the exterior walls, where they are fastened.

INTERIORS
Beams, cabinets, and first-floor beams, left natural, contrast with the white-painted walls and exposed roof structure. In all rooms except the baths, the 2-inch planking that is the floor structure also serves as the finished floor. Details such as the teak counters and brass inlay near the stove and cherry cabinet fronts reveal a hand-crafted look.

THERMAL COMFORT AND PLUMBING
The heating system is electric forced air.

LIGHTING
The peripheries of the living area and the porch are lighted with fixtures attached to the conduit, which also serves as the lower railing for the upstairs walkway. Bedrooms are lighted with duplex convenience outlets. One of these is switched, so that a floor or table lamp can be switched on or off from the door while another electrical fixture, such as a clock or radio, can remain permanently on.

MANAGEMENT AND DOCUMENTS
Plans consisted of eight 24-x-36-inch sheets, containing ¼-inch-scale plans and sections and an isometric of the structural system. Also provided were 1½-inch-and ¾-inch-scale wall sections and selected details. Most of the general construction was done by a local contractor; the architect-built details were installed later.

SPECIAL DESIGN TREATMENTS
The house reflects traditional New England architecture in its overall shape, exterior treatments, and hand-crafted details. Window frames are picture-framed on the exterior, with wide board surrounds painted to match the windows, and the juncture of curved roof with exterior walls is accented with a 12-inch piece of painted plywood. The curved rafters of the roof recall early shipbuilding techniques.

The simple shape and vernacular materials tie the house handsomely to the landscape.

The plans show the modular rhythm set up by the heavy post-and-beam system supporting the second floor. The plan is otherwise an economically arranged pair of rectangles, connected by a glassed-in atrium and second-floor bridges.

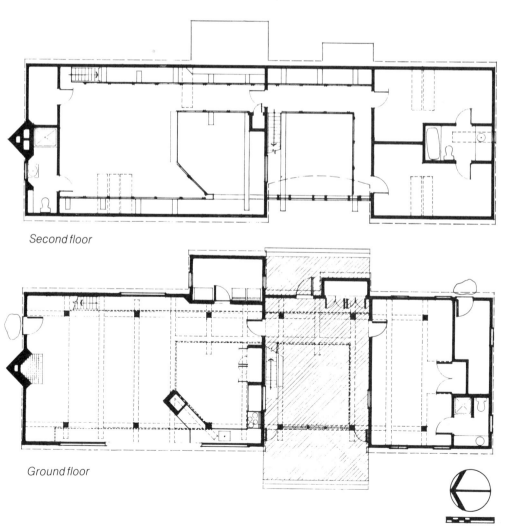

Second floor

Ground floor

Left: The second floor is like a platform within the house. The stanchionlike railings and metal tie rods provide a light structural counterpoint to the heavy structural beams.

Left: Light industrial windows, pipe railings, and an exposed vent pipe for the range hood contrast with the otherwise traditional materials.

Above: Details such as this handsome insert in the wood counter are the architect's own handiwork.

HOUSE 13
LOUIS MACKALL AND PARTNER

Architect cast masonry shingles for own house

The program for this house, an owner-built project, evolved during construction. The basic requirements were two bedrooms, a large living and dining room, a kitchen, a studio for Mrs. Mackall, and a basement shop/office for the architect. The Mackalls also wanted a close relationship between the house and the garden in the rear.

PROJECT: Mackall house, Guilford, CT
ARCHITECT: Louis Mackall and Partner; Branford, CT
AREAS: 2,300 square feet on 14 acres
DATE COMPLETED: 1975
COST: $64,000

Above right: Note the joining of the precast concrete panels and the window units set within them.

Right: Spaces are arranged along a retaining wall, behind which is the architect's shop and on top of which is a two-story dwelling. An office is located in a separate building along the wall.

SITE WORK
None, other than an unpaved driveway and utility connections. Landscaping consisted of clearing the trees in the immediate area of the house and digging two ponds where swamps previously existed.

GRIDS AND MODULES
Walls were laid out to fit the precast units on the exterior, 21 x 27 inches. Half-units were provided where required.

MATERIALS
Framing is conventional 2-x-4 studs, 16 inches on center. The outside finish is 21-x27-inch concrete panels screwed to 1-x-3-inch strapping nailed to the studs. The inside finish is cement stucco, scratch and brown coats only. The flooring, exterior doors, interior door frames, and other miscellaneous woodwork is red and white oak, purchased from a local sawmill.

Siding, door frames, window frames, exterior stairs, and miscellaneous trim are concrete. All concrete, including the slab but excluding the foundation, was mixed in a small mixer, borrowed from a local farmer for the duration of the job.

The roof finish is Neoprene-Hypalon over ½-inch plywood. Window catches are teak with brass reinforcements. Skylights are ¼-inch homemade plexiglass. The kitchen counter is teak and the sink soapstone. The main bathroom fixtures are secondhand, secured by the architect's wife from a building that was being torn down in Bridgeport.

CONSTRUCTION TECHNIQUES
Originally the architect wanted a stucco exterior, but he soon realized that would be expensive. He recalled a technique devised by Bernard Maybeck, a California architect of the early twentieth century, which consisted of dipping burlap bags in a frothy cement-stucco mixture and hanging them up to dry as shingles. Mackall adapted this technique and used concrete on the exterior, including door and window frames, stairs, walkway, and siding. These items were cast on site, either in fiberglass molds or in place in plywood forms.

INTERIORS
Curved wood shelves and cabinets that contrast with the cement stucco rely heavily on Mackall's skill as a cabinetmaker.

THERMAL COMFORT AND PLUMBING
Heating is from a wood/oil boiler to baseboard radiation on the ground floor only. During the winter, cordwood is regularly burned in a parlor stove. The upstairs is heated by convection. Screened upper parts of exterior doors allow ventilation like a dutch door, except that the upper door is hinged within the whole.

LIGHTING
There are some hanging fixtures in the main living areas; otherwise lighting is with floor and table lamps.

MANAGEMENT AND DOCUMENTS
Four 24-x-36-inch sheets showed ¼-inch plans, sections, elevations, and a site plan. The house was entirely owner-built.

SPECIAL DESIGN TREATMENTS
The house incorporates a unique vocabulary of handmade items: concrete shingles, curved windows/skylights, portholes, and cabinetwork. Privacy was important, and it determined the elevations, with natural light and air brought in from above to the bedrooms.

First floor

Second floor

Right: This specially fabricated plexiglass window is hinged at the top and is opened by the release of a locking bar at the bottom. It fits against a gasket on the sides. Plexiglass of this dimension is flexible enough to permit outward bending.

Below: Custom doors like this one were fabricated in the architect's shop.

ALFREDO DE VIDO ASSOCIATES, ARCHITECTS

NEW YORK, NY

Architect combines program response and energy conservation within modular framework

The clients for this firm have diverse programmatic, site, and budget needs. Client participation is felt to be an important factor in designs; it is the only way the building can reflect clients' needs accurately.

The firm also takes energy conservation (and the use of solar energy) into account on every project. At the simplest level, the structure is tightened through insulation, weatherstripping, airlock entries, and double glazing. At a more complex level, the flow of thermal energy through the building is controlled by natural passive means, such as direct heat gain, sunspace, siting, orientation of the building, and the use of Trombe walls (heavy masonry covered with glass, named after its French inventor) and thermal massing.

Of great importance in cost control is the method on which the following three projects were based, which calls for plan dimensions in equal segments of a 10-foot module. This system allows builders to put together one-of-a-kind houses at almost the speed of production houses. It does away with the time normally spent calculating heights, elevations, and spans by offering a consistent set of heights for such elements as doors and window lintels. Builders know that all dimensions are equal divisions of the same module, so the system reduces job-site mistakes and avoids costly redoing of incorrect work. Builders can make site corrections even in cases of dimensional error on a drawing. Those who have worked with such a system claim that jobs based on it can be explained quickly to carpenters and subcontractors.

Interior spaces are also broken down into multiples or divisions of 10 feet. Curved or circular partitions are dimensioned from points within the module (see plan). Angled walls are easily laid out in plan; roof lines in elevations are also determined by the basic grid.

The system makes multilevel spaces simpler to lay out. Window headers, for example, are always 6 feet 10½ inches above an imaginary second-story floor. That dimension in turn is predetermined by the basic vertical module, which combines precut stud dimensions with the floor-beam thickness.

Another money-saving feature of the system is the use of stock materials such as windows, precut studs (the basis for the vertical module), and standard sheathing and siding.

Using such a modular system can save builders 10 to 15 percent in construction costs, according to users.

HOUSE 14
ALFREDO DE VIDO ASSOCIATES, ARCHITECTS

Cube form increases apparent space and size of activity areas

The clients requested a small house with vertically grouped rooms to take advantage of an interesting view up the Hudson River. Living areas were to include a master bedroom remote from two others for visiting children and a living-dining area occupying the center of the house.

The architect's solution was to organize the rooms and other spaces within a cube. The enclosure is punctured where it reveals the river view and where the entry of sunlight is desirable. Outdoor deck areas and covered entranceways are all contained within the cube. The cube is economical because it is compact and requires the least amount of outside wall area to enclose the same volume and because it allows for tight planning of such elements as foundation and roof.

Interior spaces are simply detailed and furnished; there are no chair rails, picture rails, or multiple interior cornices. The house has 6-inch walls and 12-inch roof planes, as well as triple glazing for heat conservation. It is heated and cooled with a heat pump.

Given the initial concept of a cubical form, which the client endorsed at an early meeting, the architect's principal task was to arrange the client's activities and space requirements in a richly organized whole.

PROJECT: Sametz house, Philipstown, NY
ARCHITECTS: Alfredo De Vido Associates, Architects; New York, NY
AREAS: 1,675 square feet on 1 acre
DATE COMPLETED: 1980
COST: $82,000

SITE WORK

Trees between the house and the view were cleared and the area planted with ground cover and rough grass to avoid maintenance time and expense. Access roads and walks are gravel.

GRIDS AND MODULES

The module is essential to this design. The activities and vertical free space or voids are organized three-dimensionally within the strict discipline of the cube, making small rooms look bigger. The grid enabled the contractor to see at once where all walls and openings were, once the system was explained.

MATERIALS

The principle of homogeneity increases the apparent size and simplifies the potentially complex relationships of small areas. Rough cut cedar siding was used on the exterior. All interiors are clad in sheetrock, except for the important living/dining/master bedroom grouping, which has wood ceiling accents.

Floors are carpeted (an economical way to finish a floor), except where important areas needed an accent—the entry, for example, which is tiled. A cost-saving option would have been to finish the floor in concrete for later tiling.

The lattice of columns and free-standing beams combined with the recesses increased the apparent size of the house.

1 Master BR
2 Bath
3 Library
4 Deck
5 Open to below

Master bedroom level

1 Living
2 Kitchen
3 Deck

Living / kitchen level

1 Vestibule
2 BR
3 Study / BR
4 Bath
5 Open to below

Entry level

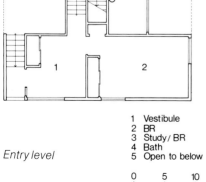

0   5   10

Left: Organizing spaces around a central stair within a cube provides the opportunity for views in at least two directions from every space.

Above: Axonometric drawing shows recesses into the cubical mass of the house.

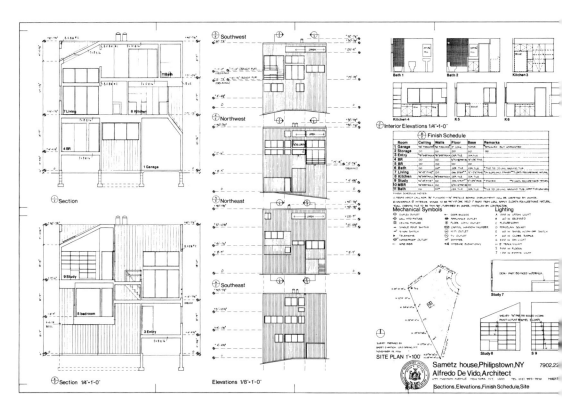

Sametz house, Philipstown, NY   7902.22
Alfredo De Vido, Architect
Sections, Elevations, Finish Schedule, Site

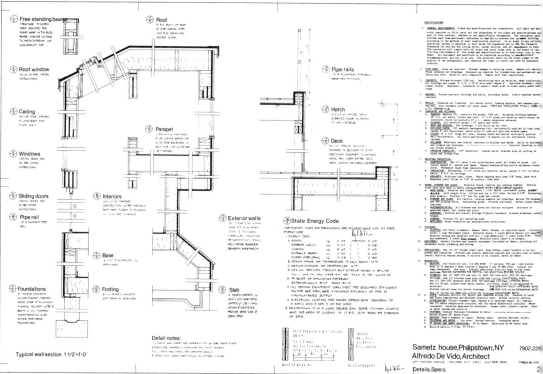

Typical wall section 1 1/2"=1'-0"

Sametz house, Philipstown, NY   7902.22
Alfredo De Vido, Architect
Details, Specs

CONSTRUCTION TECHNIQUES

All walls were built with stock precut 2-x-6 (exterior) and 2-x-4 (interior) studs and normal plates and headers, within which lintels were set at a uniform height of 6 feet 10½ inches. The combination of stock materials and the modular approach enabled the builder to erect the framing rapidly. Other details are builder's standard; for example, windows were set in rough openings and trimmed after the finish was applied. Window openings are trimless.

INTERIORS

Light, movable furniture is combined with a few built-ins to keep the spaces open and to increase their apparent size. The contractor-fabricated built-ins include beds, living-room seating, a coffee table, and assorted tables and desks. These proved to be less expensive, less space-consuming, and more attractive than most available movable furniture.

THERMAL COMFORT AND PLUMBING

Insulated R-19 exterior walls and R-23 ceilings were combined with triple-glazing to produce a tight, well-insulated skin for this exposed site. The heat pump provides year-round comfort conditioning and is economical to operate. Its initial cost was higher than that of other systems considered, but it was selected because of the exposed site and the strong wind that blows from the Hudson Valley.

LIGHTING

Daylight from many directions illuminates major areas uniformly, eliminating the need for day-time artificial light. Recesses in this multistory design permit light from the skylights to reach lower levels. Artificial lighting is built in and flexibly switched. This provides operating econo-mies (lights can be switched on in groups instead of all at once) that offset the higher installa-tion cost.

Opposite page and below: The working draw-ings, on three 24-x-36-inch sheets, include all essential information. They helped con-vince the contractor that the house would be economical to build.

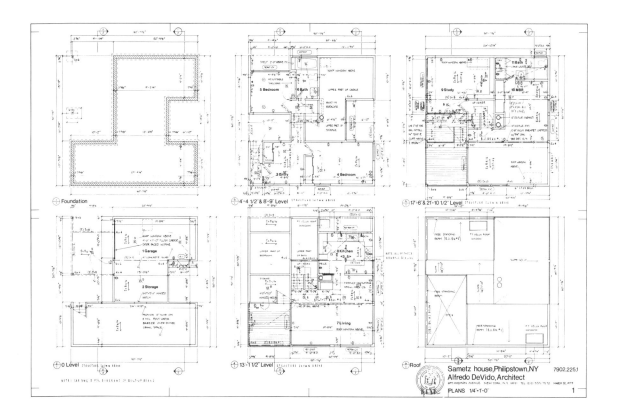

Sametz house, Philipstown, NY
Alfredo DeVido, Architect

Above: A light enclosure frames the view and reveals the relationships of elements within the cost-saving modular system.

Right: Open room plans make the interior seem larger. The built-in coffee table and couch have an uncluttered look and allow more floor space. The change in ceiling material emphasizes the importance of this space, despite the overall use of economical materials.

MANAGEMENT AND DOCUMENTS

The three drawings reproduced here represent the entire set of contract documents. They were done in the context of the modular system, which the architect explains to contractors at the initial prebid meeting. This enables the builder to understand the job readily and is reflected in job costs. Details are typical, meaning that the same details (such as those shown on sheet 3) are to be used in all parts of the project.

SPECIAL DESIGN TREATMENTS

The smaller spaces borrow from the larger cube, which increases their apparent size. Cutouts appear to enlarge the area of exterior walls. This admittedly raised the price of the house, but the expense was justified by the heightened visual interest and the wind-sheltered exterior areas that resulted. Freestanding beams complete the cube in a natural, economical way.

HOUSE 15
ALFREDO DE VIDO ASSOCIATES, ARCHITECTS

House built from published plans is adjusted for site and owner

An architectural rendering of a house in project form designed by this firm caught the eye of an editor who felt the plan and style could be adapted to his family's needs as a vacation house. "It was exactly what we wanted: unassuming yet architectural, modest in size yet large enough for the family, friends, and shared interests in crafts that were overflowing our New York City brownstone," he said. The family found some land in a seaside community on Long Island and worked with the architect to modify the design to suit their specific needs.

The plan was enlarged to meet the town's square footage requirements. To enlarge the studio, overhead space in the adjacent garage was redesigned as a skylight loft. Provision was made to add domestic solar hot water collectors.

PROJECT: Gropp house, Quoque, NY
ARCHITECT: Alfredo De Vido Associates, Architects; New York, NY
AREAS: 2,020 square feet on 1 acre
DATE COMPLETED: 1978
COST: $70,000

SITE WORK
Besides a gravel driveway to the house, a septic system and well were required. The site was generally left in its natural wooded state.

GRIDS AND MODULES
The house was built according to the architect's plan module. In this case the contractor, who was familiar with the system because he had already built several houses for the architect, worked smoothly in the construction phase and rarely had to call the architect about routine dimensional questions.

MATERIALS
Walls consist of shiplap cedar siding over 15-pound building paper on ½-inch plywood on 6-inch studs, fully insulated. Interiors are ½-inch sheetrock over a 6-mil vapor barrier to keep moisture out of the wall cavity. The roof is heavy asphalt shingles on ½-inch plywood on the structure, fully insulated. A vent strip at eaves and ridge allows air circulation to prevent condensation buildup. Quarry tile floors provide thin thermal mass.

CONSTRUCTION TECHNIQUES
The frame is builder's standard, plus the additional insulation and vapor barriers that are required in a well-insulated house. A passive solar house generally costs 10 percent more to build than a conventional house because of the additional costs of materials—south-facing glass, insulation, and thermal mass—and labor. The savings in energy costs, however, can balance the initial expenditure over a period of time called the payback period. (See Thermal Comfort and Plumbing.)

INTERIORS
The architect used the shape and the relationship of the spaces to create drama in the interior. The living area is one large space open vertically to the cedar-lined ceiling that rises above the second-floor balcony hall to the peak of the saltbox shape. This technique of visually borrowing space from another area costs little, but it pays dividends in making small spaces look larger. Natural quarry tile floors also serve as the base for the seating and a display shelf for favorite objects. Materials were chosen to be compatible with nature.

THERMAL COMFORT AND PLUMBING
Large areas of glass are oriented south and southwest for the best passive solar benefit. Another thermal feature is the exterior panels that close like barn doors over the glass. In addition to the privacy and protection they provide when the house is not in use, the owners saw them as a way to help control heat gain and loss. The panels are constructed of the same cedar boards that sheathe the exterior walls.

A solar domestic hot water system was provided. In general, the incorporation of solar apertures, extra insulation, and thermal mass is advisable if the payback is less than five to seven years. This depends on local, state, and federal tax credits for such installation, as well as interest rates. Savings can be substantial.

LIGHTING
Track lights are wall-mounted in the living space; recessed lights are used in selected areas such as kitchens and baths. A ceiling-hung lamp highlights artwork, and a standing lamp is a sculptural object.

MANAGEMENT AND DOCUMENTS
Modifications were made to the plans. The architect worked with a contractor who had built previous houses for him, thereby lessening construction supervision time.

SPECIAL DESIGN TREATMENTS
The simplicity of this design, which attracted the owners when they saw the first drawing, is derived from the architectural traditions of eastern Long Island.

Right: The broad fascia ties both building units together into a more unified whole.

Below: Opposing gable roofs and a recess at the front door contribute to an inviting street facade.

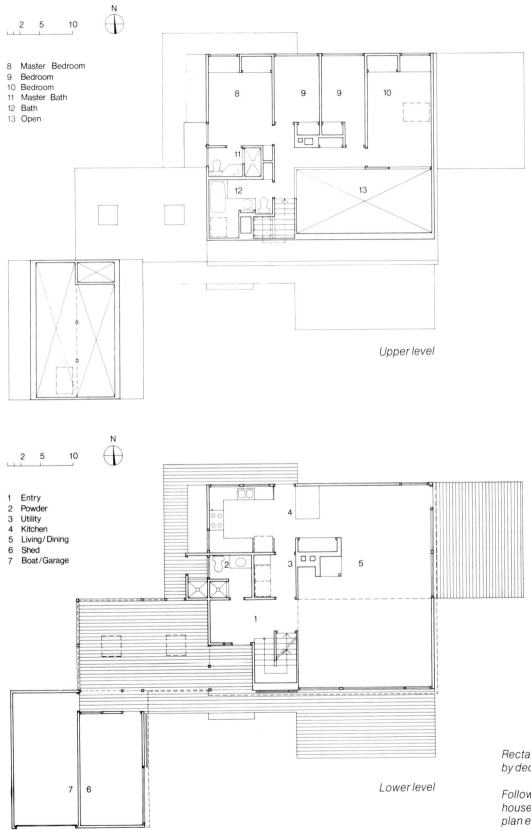

2 5 10

N

8 Master Bedroom
9 Bedroom
10 Bedroom
11 Master Bath
12 Bath
13 Open

8   9   9   10

11

12   13

Upper level

2 5 10

N

1 Entry
2 Powder
3 Utility
4 Kitchen
5 Living/Dining
6 Shed
7 Boat/Garage

4

2   3   5

1

7 6

Lower level

*Rectangular building outlines are connected
by decks and the screened porch.*

*Following page: A simple saltbox exterior
houses a multistory space within. The open
plan extends the spaces visually.*

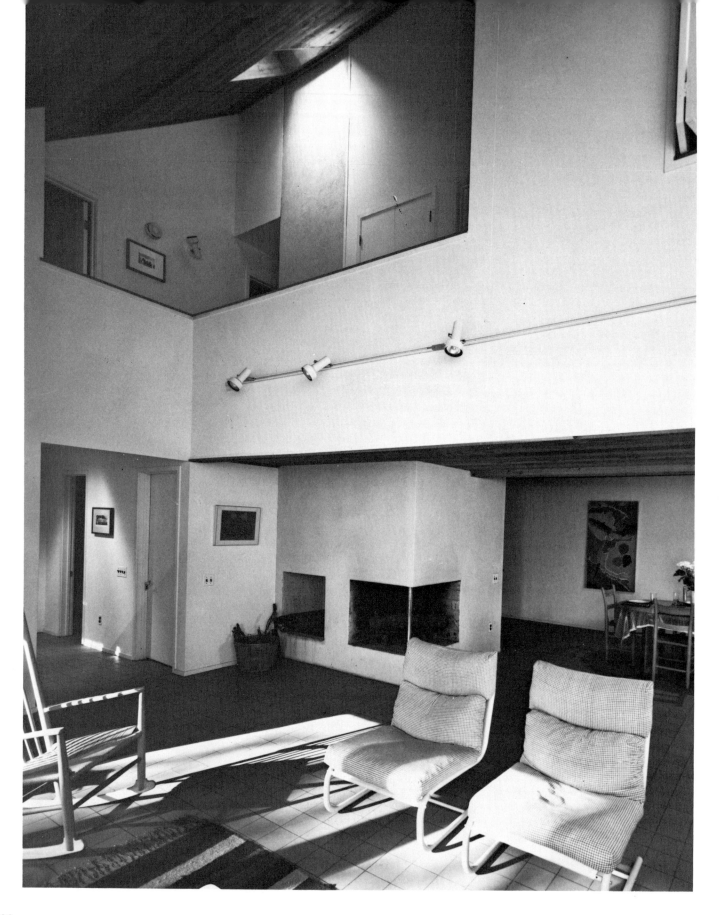

HOUSE 16
ALFREDO DE VIDO ASSOCIATES, ARCHITECTS

House that emphasizes daylight incorporates means of controlling it

This house was designed for a suburban wooded lot and provides a series of spaces to capture views of the surrounding landscape. The owners requested a three-bedroom house with provisions for a family room and a potential fourth bedroom on the lowest level. That level and an adjacent swimming pool were to remain unfinished until funds were available. The clients wanted well-lit spaces for drama and visual interest; the architect's solution was split levels on a pinwheel plan around a central stair. Major living areas such as the living room and master bedroom are grouped under a large skylight covered with operable shutters that control light and heat gain, as well as provide insulation.

PROJECT: Vuolo house, Lloyd Harbor, NY
ARCHITECT: Alfredo De Vido Associates, Architects; New York, NY
AREAS: 1,900 square feet, plus 750 square feet unfinished, plus 475-square-foot garage
DATE COMPLETED: 1980
COST: $125,000

SITE WORK
Septic, well, and electrical (underground) connections were made. A gravel driveway was built to the existing road.

GRIDS AND MODULES
The house was built in accordance with the architect's modular system.

MATERIALS
Materials consist of shiplap cedar boards 8 inches wide and ¾ inch thick on 15-pound building paper on ½-inch plywood on 2-x-6 studs filled with R-19 insulation. Interiors are ½-inch sheetrock throughout on walls and ceilings; floors are carpet or tile on plywood. Double-glazed skylights are stock sizes from sliding doors. Beams were spaced to fit the glass sizes.

CONSTRUCTION TECHNIQUES
Builder's standards were followed throughout, with the exception of the skylights over the living room/master bedroom and the kitchen-breakfast area. These required unusual techniques: beams needed flashing with metal at the tops to prevent leaks and condensation runoff, and the glass had to be securely anchored. The movable insulating shades had to be installed carefully as well; the added expense was justified by desirable sun control and the insulating value of the shades.

Above: Insulating shades roll down to protect the glass from the sun and to provide night and winter insulation.

Right: A second-floor bedroom cantilevered over the main entrance shelters the stair to the foyer.

Right: The planes of this cubistic combination, although freely placed, line up with those on other floors, greatly facilitating construction.

Below: The continuous skylight over the living room and master bedroom is interrupted at midpoint by a small flat roof. This serves as a collection point for the three flues.

Opposite page left: The economical square plan is extended in all directions at various levels to form larger rooms where required.

Opposite page right: The side elevation clearly shows the architect's vertical module. Note the alignment of window and door heads and the bottom of the soffit over the entrance.

Section A

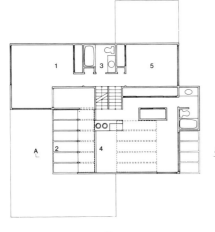

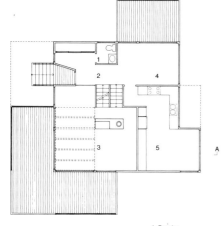

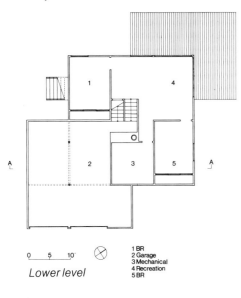

INTERIORS

The design concept of the interiors depends on the relationships of the various spaces within the split-level plan. The organization and interrelation of spaces are important factors in small houses because they can make the spaces seem larger. Rooms can overlook each other, yet still be private if shutters, fixed glass, or interior windows are used.

THERMAL COMFORT AND PLUMBING

Movable shutters over the large skylights control sunlight and insulate as well. They are electrically operated and can be thermostatically controlled. Two heat-producing fireplaces are centrally located on the middle and upper levels. The house is otherwise centrally heated, and an oil-fired hot-air furnace is planned for future air conditioning.

LIGHTING

Natural light, modulated by the movable shades, is generous. The shades have an intermediate position that permits light to diffuse through them. Artificial light is provided by recessed fixtures and task lighting in the kitchen and bathrooms.

MANAGEMENT AND DOCUMENTS

Plans consisted of four 24-x-36-inch sheets, with ¼-inch-scale plans and sections, and interior elevations. Structural and lighting notations were placed directly on the plans, as were the specifications. Exterior elevations are at ⅛-inch scale. The job was conventionally bid and awarded to the low bidder. The lower level was left unfinished as an economy measure.

SPECIAL DESIGN TREATMENTS

Spaces were arranged on two levels around the core stair, adjacent to which are the fireplaces and the flues; all is contained within a cube. Spaces and decks project from this cube, and recesses are made to accommodate the slopes of the skylight. These connections of space result in unexpected views and an apparent increase in the sizes of rooms. Glass areas and voids are grouped and contrasted with solid walls to direct views and provide solid surfaces against which light can reflect.

Openings to other spaces make individual rooms appear larger. Skylights were made of stock pieces of insulating glass from sliding doors. Beams were spaced to fit these sizes.

BOOTH / HANSEN & ASSOCIATES
CHICAGO, IL

Economy is no hindrance to quality of design

This firm views economic constraint as a spur to design quality, not as a restriction. Based on their belief that architecture should be available to a wide segment of the public, the architects avoid luxury finishes and work instead on the relationships and proportions of the spaces within their houses as the key to economical construction. They order structures and spaces within the discipline of modules, poetically equating their system with the repetition of simple details in nature. Important considerations in the firm's designs are ease of construction, flexibility of space usage, and economical maintenance.

Although each building program, site, and client are different, the examples share a basic approach. The architects select and size a structural system that fits the program, local construction practice, and economical use of materials and labor (see Chapter 2). This underlying repetitive structural system gives the spaces their proportions. All finishes, such as kitchen cabinets, bathrooms, and wall materials, may then be selected from a wide variety of possibilities, either costly or not. The architects believe that simple shapes and lines result in economy and lasting beauty.

HOUSE 17
BOOTH/HANSEN & ASSOCIATES

Artist built his own house

The client, an artist of talent, wanted as much space as possible for his studio and house. Because of the size of his sculptures, the area of the studio had to be as large as that of the living quarters. He intended to, and did, build the entire structure himself, so it was important that it be as simple as possible to construct. The artist wanted to be in touch with nature, so the architects designed large glass areas with vistas of rolling farmland and woods.

PROJECT: Barr house, Northville, MI
ARCHITECTS: Booth/Hansen & Associates; Chicago, IL
Project Associates: Laurence Booth and Steve Rugo
AREAS: 3,888 square feet on 28 acres
DATE COMPLETED: 1979
COST: $50,000, plus owner's labor

SITE WORK

The site, 30 miles west of Detroit, is a rolling farm with few trees and surrounded by woodland. Additional trees were planted informally. The house is reached by an improved construction road.

GRIDS AND MODULES

The structure was devised to maximize the efficiency of 2-x-10-inch joists 16 inches on center, which resulted in structural bays of 12 x 18 feet organized into an overall plan of 36 x 54 feet. That happens to be a square and a half in plan, a double square in one elevation, and a triple square in the other elevation.

MATERIALS

The frame, windows, and doors are wood; the roofs are made of built-up tar and gravel and corrugated metal roofing. Wood siding is 1 x 6 inches. The lower floor is a concrete slab on grade, with hardwood flooring on 1-x-2-inch wood sleepers 2 feet on center as a finish. The architects specified 6-inch-diameter pipe supports for the porticoes overhanging the house on each side. The interiors are ⅝-inch sheetrock ½-inch sheetrock is more usual in house construction, but the greater thickness was necessary because 2-x-6-inch studs were employed on 2-foot centers.

CONSTRUCTION TECHNIQUES

Conventional building techniques were used. It was particularly important to keep details simple because the owner, rather than a professional builder, was doing the work.

INTERIORS

All interiors are wallboard, painted in various values of white. The hardwood flooring was left natural and polyurethaned for easy maintenance.

THERMAL COMFORT AND PLUMBING

Electric baseboard units and a wood stove provide heat; there is no air conditioning.

LIGHTING

Recessed lights and light tracks were used.

MANAGEMENT AND DOCUMENTS

Plans, sections, and elevations were ¼-inch scale; the roof plan, plumbing diagrams, schedules, and pipe diagram were ⅛-inch scale. All were on four sheets, 24 x 36 inches. The architects supervised the owner only in the sense of guiding him with regard to details. In lieu of fees, the architectural services were bartered for the owner's artwork.

SPECIAL DESIGN TREATMENTS

The architects designed a house that they felt incorporated the artistic ideas of the artist, whose art reflects structuralism and constructivism. To them, the design is evocative of both the twentieth-century artistic tradition and the rural tradition of the villas of Andrea Palladio.

Left: The site plan shows the relationship of the approach drive to the skew roof above the rectangular house.

Opposite page above: Elevations reveal the careful composition of stock windows on the facades, which provide a lively pattern.

Right: The surprising effect of the skewed pitched roof is heightened by its support on a free-standing group of columns at the gable end.

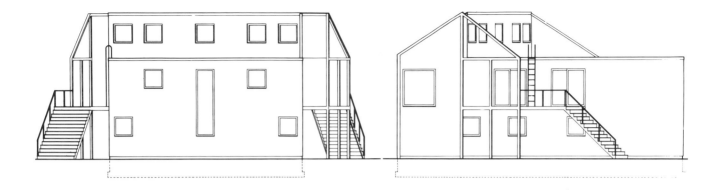

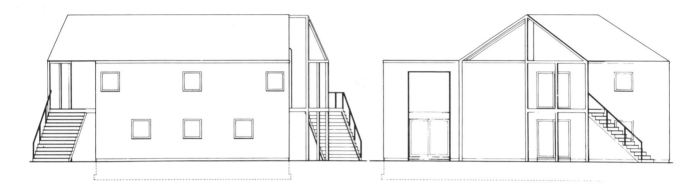

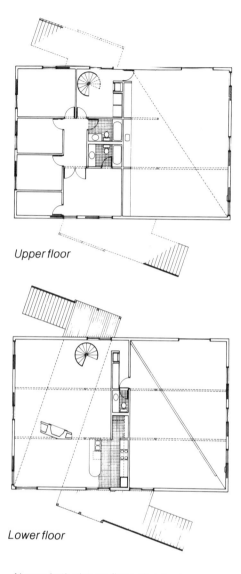

Upper floor

Lower floor

Above: In the lower-floor plan, bedrooms are grouped under part of the upper floor; a circular stair provides access. The studio has a two-story portion, cut on a diagonal. The upper-floor plan illustrates the main entrance to the large living/dining/kitchen space. A door communicates to a balcony over the studio below.

Right: The fireplace serves as a free-standing space divider, but is tied into the structure by its relation to a free-standing beam resting on top of it.

HOUSE 18
BOOTH/HANSEN & ASSOCIATES

House incorporating a simple structural system is raised on stilts to avoid site work

The site, on an island in Washington, is very steep, so the architects selected a simple structural system that would require the least amount of site work and the removal of only one tree. The choice was made in deference to Nature as well as to economy.

The lower level has two sleeping rooms for the children; the middle level contains a large living room, dining area, kitchen, and powder room. The top floor, for the adults, provides the best views of surrounding mountains and forests.

The architects emphasized the assemblage of simple spaces within the chosen module and exposure of the structural elements to create interesting surfaces.

PROJECT: Magnuson guest house, Vashon Island, WA
ARCHITECTS: Booth/Hansen & Associates; Chicago, IL
Project Associates: Laurence Booth and Steve Weiss
AREAS: 2,000 square feet on 5 acres
DATE COMPLETED: 1975
COST: $60,000

SITE WORK

Vehicular access to the house is provided by an existing service road to a house beyond. The house was set on pier footings in the natural landscape, which was left untouched.

GRIDS AND MODULES

Modules were 12 x 12 feet in plan and 9 feet high floor to floor.

MATERIALS

Tongue-and-groove 1-x-4-inch cedar siding, applied diagonally to strengthen the structure, was left natural to blend with the surrounding forest. Builtup roofing was applied over a ¾-inch plywood deck. Floors were laid diagonally on 2-x-2-inch sleepers, 24 inches o.c. each way, with sand between sleepers as sound baffling between floors over a ¾-inch subfloor and extra insulation where upper floors project. Interiors are ½-inch sheetrock throughout.

CONSTRUCTION TECHNIQUES

The exposed frame of 3-x-8-inch main structural members is bolted to 8-inch-square glu-lam piers, 12 feet o.c., on 4-x-4-x-1-foot spread footings. Laid over this were conventional 2-x-12-inch floor joists, 16 inches o.c., and 2-x-8-inch roof joists, also 16 inches o.c. This structural system is not always acceptable in areas where local building codes require continuous foundations, but where permitted it is a good way to preserve the landscape and save money. It is essential to bolt the framework to the pier and provide lateral bracing to prevent lateral deflection.

INTERIORS

The inside of the house is composed of simple cubical spaces, the details of which were designed to complement the volumes rather than call attention to themselves. A contrasting approach was used in Houses 39 through 41, where details are emphasized. Builtins, mainly baths and cabinets, were detailed carefully.

THERMAL COMFORT AND PLUMBING

A heat-producing fireplace is provided in the living room. Baths and kitchen are lined up over the lowest floor, since part of the house is supported on piers.

Above: The structural system is clearly expressed outside.

Right: Diagonal siding, recalling the diagonal decks in the plan, provides a decorative accent on the simple side elevation.

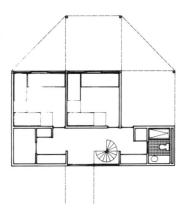

LIGHTING

Ceiling-mounted track was used extensively, with recessed lights provided in such areas as baths and kitchens.

MANAGEMENT AND DOCUMENTS

Plans consisted of six sheets, 24 x 36 inches, comprising ¼-inch-scale plans, sections, and elevations; 1½-inch typical wall sections; twenty-seven partial details at a scale of 3 inches = 1 foot; and ½-inch interior elevations, mainly of kitchen and baths.

Although there are few sheets and details, specific conditions were carefully spelled out, for example, in the twenty-seven details at the large 3-x-1-foot scale; this practice is in keeping with the simple volumes and precise details.

Supervision was minimal, because of the distance between the architects' home base and the site, but the simplicity of the concept resulted in a quality finished product.

SPECIAL DESIGN TREATMENTS

The basic modular concept allowed inexpensive and durable materials to be assembled in an economical way. The proportions, junctures of materials, and positioning of windows and doors were the important considerations.

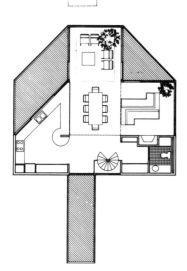

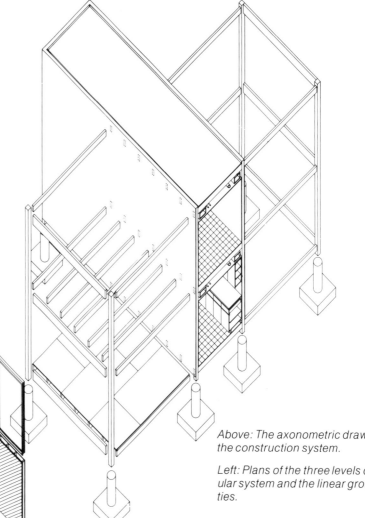

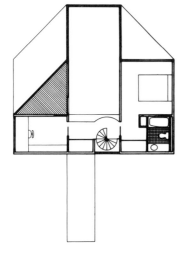

Above: The axonometric drawing illustrates the construction system.

Left: Plans of the three levels clarify the modular system and the linear grouping of utilities.

Above: Panel infill between columns and beams is varied in locations such as this balcony and parapet.

Left: The concept of the structure as a kit of parts is accented by the use of a different material as infill between the structural elements.

WILLIAM P. BRUDER, ARCHITECT
NEW RIVER, AZ

Combining complex geometries with industrial materials

In all his projects, the architect begins with a detailed discussion of the program to establish the clients' basic space needs and understand their architectural awareness. He also discusses the advantages of owner participation during construction, which is often critical for unusual, labor-intensive design solutions. If the clients are inclined toward "hammer and nails" involvement in building, Bruder determines tasks that they might reasonably undertake. In projects with a more conventional approach to construction, he defines the level of craftsmanship and relates it to budget restrictions; different budgets generate different levels of detail, structural and geometric complexity, and material finishes.

After establishing a relationship with the clients, Bruder evaluates the building site, which often has been acquired prior to his involvement with the project. He believes that it is important to discover why the owner chose the property and what the owner saw as its attributes; location, size, views, topography, vegetation, and cost are only some of the important factors. Careful integration of the house into a site does not always represent initial dollar savings (bulldozers can move mountains), but the long-term paybacks of minimum landscaping and the intangible value of using natural features are important. Topographic maps and surveys are invaluable to a cost-conscious solution; money spent on them is generally repaid by good integration of building and site.

HOUSE 19
WILLIAM P. BRUDER, ARCHITECT

Owner's contracting skills are employed to best advantage

The site, near a park in central Phoenix, has fine views of the city and surrounding mountains. The clients are a couple with four children; the owner, a sheet-metal contractor, did most of the construction himself.

The plan concentrates group activities in a funnel-shaped, two-story, masonry-walled structure, containing the entry, living room, dining room, and kitchen on the lower level and a library loft above. Changes in floor and ceiling levels and cylindrical metal and wood walls define the spaces. Along the wide south elevation of the funnel is a deep covered veranda overlooking the pool and downtown skyline.

Two cylindrical service towers housing bath, laundry, and mechanical functions are engaged into the sides of the funnel. Adjacent to these are the bedrooms, a series of cylinders.

PROJECT: Karber house, Phoenix, AZ
ARCHITECT: William P. Bruder, Architect; New River, AZ
AREAS: Main residence, 3,200 square feet; garage, 550 square feet; covered terrace, 600 square feet; lot, 11,850 square feet
DATE COMPLETED: 1980
COST: $125,000, including pool, fences, and landscaping

SITE WORK

Instead of doing costly excavation, the architect worked with the slight slope of the lot (approximately 3 to 4 feet north to south) by stepping the main living level of the house down 2 feet 8 inches; this also reduced the visible profile of the structure. Natural desert landscaping on the site blends with the desert of the nearby mountains and keeps maintenance costs to a minimum. The driveway is desert granite, and walks are washed aggregate circular pavers.

GRIDS AND MODULES

Two primary modules are combined: (1) The large brick funnel contains the main open living areas. The roof and floor framing of conventional wood and the brick paving are laid out either parallel or perpendicular to the centerline of the funnel. (2) A series of cylindrical forms in various sizes and finishes contains private and service areas. The radial grid of their pinwheel (2-x-4-inch) compression trusses and simple curved plywood wall plates made them quick and easy to frame.

MATERIALS

The owner's sheet-metal business and his brother's brick masonry business were the keys to the design concept. The architect made extensive use of two standard galvanized industrial metal sliding patterns on the circular forms and combined them with simple jumbo brick (8 x 4 x 16 inches). These materials are economical, not only in initial cost but also in maintenance costs. Incorporated into the walls of the stair and dining room are fir "sill blocks," which were found as salvage.

All cylindrical units are roofed by pinwheel trusses, the hubs of which serve as skylights. Radial segmented metal ceiling panels clip to the 2-x4-inch cords of the pinwheel trusses. Floors and walls of the main spaces are brick masonry. Carpeted walls that match the floors in sleeping modules provide acoustical privacy. An interlocking rib pan of copper was used as cladding for the interior of the dining room and stair. Main ceilings are 4-x-8-foot rough-sawn plywood sheets.

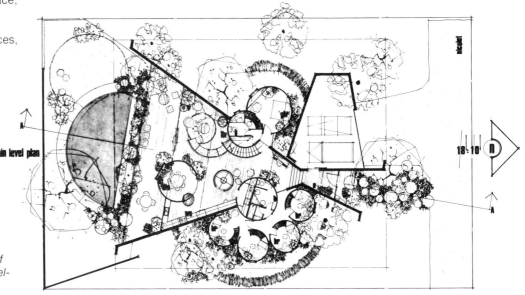

main level plan

The main level plan shows the grouping of small circular bedrooms around the funnel-shaped main living space.

Right: The upper-level plan continues the circular elements of the main level and creates voids over the entry and living room. The relation of the flat roof to the long brick walls that define the central space is evident in section.

Below: Brick exterior walls are a strong visual anchor for the fanciful circular sheet-metal elements.

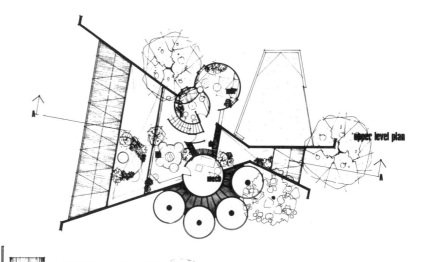

upper level plan

section A-A

CONSTRUCTION TECHNIQUES

The geometric forms are related in plan by angle references and dimensioned center points. Masonry walls are kept as planes without penetrations, headers, or numerous height changes. Angled brick corners are interlocked to avoid sawn brick angles, a technique that is ornamental and economical at the same time.

Pinwheel trusses have common compression and tension-ring details and a radial repeat grid, which allowed precutting and preassembly. Circular windows are fixed glass set in stainless-steel hoops with silicon structural sealant. Bedroom vent panels are vertical metal-clad plywood doors with piano hinges, crank operators, weatherstripping, and fixed screens; these are cheaper than operable circular windows.

INTERIORS

The materials of the interior—brick, metal (galvanized copper and stainless steel), and wood—continue on the outside. Built-in cabinets, beds, and desks in the circular areas save space. The distinctive exposed pinwheel truss in the dining room acts as a decorative element while showing how the house was built. All color is derived from the natural building materials and fabrics. Clear penetrating sealers and oils reduce painting costs.

THERMAL COMFORT AND PLUMBING

A solar water-assisted heat pump system conditions air. The pool and domestic hot water are also solar-heated. The solar panel array serves as a balcony rail for the roof garden deck. Pool aeration acts as a heat exchanger to aid the air-conditioning system. A mechanical room is centrally located in the second level of the east tower for economical duct distribution.

The house works passively: in winter the south-facing funnel traps the sun for the main living area. The plan channels prevailing north-south breezes through screened doors on the entry and patio elevations. Plumbing is stacked in the two main service cylinders. Insulation in the curved walls is high-efficiency salvaged fiberglass duct board, which was available as waste from the owner's company.

LIGHTING

Insulated skylights and extensive clerestories provide natural lighting. Inexpensive porcelain sockets with clear special G bulbs and recessed cans are built into the interiors for nighttime use.

MANAGEMENT AND DOCUMENTS

Working drawings (eleven sheets) and an outline spec served as construction documents. Supervision involved weekly site visits to help the owner coordinate his owner / builder / contractor activities. Many field sketches were required to clarify construction details. The owner's skills and available materials were used as much as possible.

SPECIAL DESIGN TREATMENTS

Angels and circles create privacy and views in private spaces while maintaining openness in the public spaces; the concept is an attempt to integrate a large program on a small site.

Sheet metal is employed on the porch roof adjacent to the pool. Note the decorative brick corners; this detail avoids having to cut bricks on an angle.

Exterior materials are repeated on the interior. Note the relation of the plywood roof sheathing to the recessed lights.

Wall shapes are reflected in the paving patterns. The circular windows are fixed. Ventilation is provided through crank-operated metal panels.

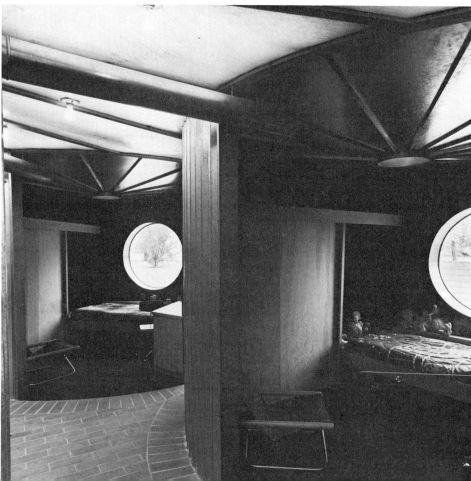

Opposite page: From the road, the front curve of the house leads visitors gently to the entrance.

HOUSE 20
WILLIAM P. BRUDER, ARCHITECT

Solar adobe features walled garden courtyard

The ancient building material of adobe is combined here with modern building systems to create a house that harmonizes with the desert and the needs of a contemporary energy-conscious family. The site is a double lot on the north side of a small cul-de-sac in the western area of Phoenix. The curvilinear plan of the house relates to the cul-de-sac. Another important design idea was the use of thick adobe walls to serve as a thermal sink in order to maintain a stable and comfortable temperature range throughout the year. A south-facing solar greenhouse with water heat-storage tubes and wood-burning stoves supplies heat during colder weather; an evaporative cooling system is used in hot months.

The combined living/dining/kitchen/greenhouse connects with the sunken and walled east patio. The other main space to the north of the primary living area is a long narrow master bedroom and bath complex with a den and crafts area in a loft. A circular guest bedroom with a skin of metal contrasts with the natural adobe walls. Above the guest room is a deck with a vista of the mountains to the west.

PROJECT: Matthews house, Maricopa County, AZ
ARCHITECT: William P. Bruder, Architect; New River, AZ
AREAS: 2,345 square feet plus two-auto carport on approximately ⅓ acre
DATE COMPLETED: 1981
COST: $105,000, including compound walls and landscaping

SITE WORK
Two small flat lots were excavated to provide earth to make 30,000 adobe blocks for the project. Because of a change in the construction process, however, only 4,000 adobe blocks were owner-made; the rest were purchased. The remaining dirt was trucked away. The setting of the house 2 feet 8 inches below grade creates an unobtrusive profile on the street.

GRIDS AND MODULES
The center point of the cul-de-sac is the prime layout focus of the house. Radial lines from it define all the exposed rafter centers. The owner established the framing grid in the concrete floor with redwood strips. As construction continued, this floor pattern was used to project the radial grid to the ceiling plane. In addition, four other center points control the plan's geometry. A separate plan drawing showing only center points and radials simplified the layout.

MATERIALS
Stabilized mud adobe, conventional exposed 2-x-12-inch framing with industrial-grade plywood exposed at ceilings, corrugated galvanized metal siding, "Roughtex" fir plywood sheets, and exposed concrete floors make up the materials list. A sprayed 4- to 8-inch-thick foam insulation system and liquid rubber "flashingless" roofing system economically solve the problem of weatherproofing the unusual roof.

CONSTRUCTION TECHNIQUES
This house took almost two years to build, and the owner's participation was important. Both husband and wife worked, with some help from the architect, on such tasks as pouring footings, making adobe, carpentry, wiring, and sealing wood and adobe.

Among the more interesting features is a curved (in plan) plywood box beam in the living room/carport, which was less expensive than a curved glulam beam would have been.

INTERIORS
Exposed concrete floors with radial wood inserts combine with adobe walls, exposed plywood, rafters, and corrugated metal inside and out. The elegant craftsmanship of curved red oak cabinets and simple glass detailing contrasts with the rough materials.

THERMAL COMFORT AND PLUMBING
A solar greenhouse and wood-burning stoves provide heating. In summer, thermal mass works with air-conditioning units in three zones, distributed through exposed galvanized ducts.

LIGHTING
Porcelain fixtures with clear spherical G bulbs and spots are used. Skylights and clerestories allow daylight to penetrate to interiors.

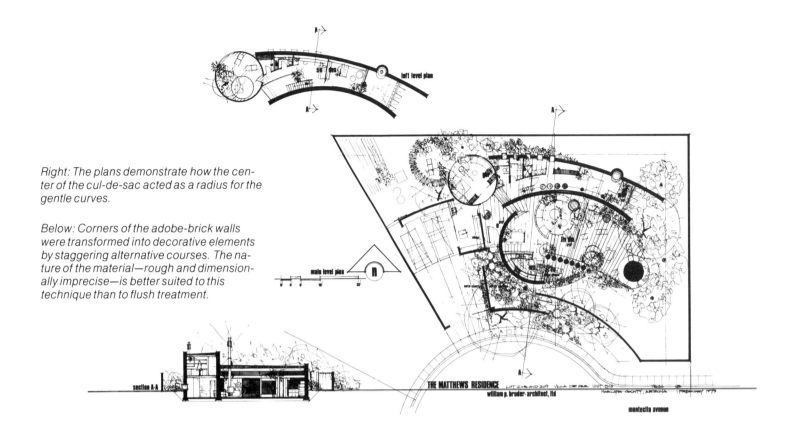

Right: The plans demonstrate how the center of the cul-de-sac acted as a radius for the gentle curves.

Below: Corners of the adobe-brick walls were transformed into decorative elements by staggering alternative courses. The nature of the material—rough and dimensionally imprecise—is better suited to this technique than to flush treatment.

THE MATTHEWS RESIDENCE
william p. bruder·architect, ltd

The gradual curve of the walls provides inviting passageways along which to walk.

The radial pattern of the roof beams and the corresponding floor dividers can be seen clearly in this interior view.

MANAGEMENT AND DOCUMENTS

Fourteen sheets of working drawings were produced. The architect furnished numerous ''yellow pad'' detail sketches to refine conditions unique to the adobe and complicated geometric intersections. The project was owner-built and owner-contracted, but the architect was responsible for total supervision.

SPECIAL DESIGN TREATMENTS

The clients' fondness for and prior experience with adobe construction while they lived in New Mexico became a major design input. It is utilized in this project as a plastic material forming soft curving walls. Gate and scupper details, high ceilings, and exposed wood framing give the house a southwestern flavor.

CANATSEY/WEINSTEIN ARCHITECTS
SEATTLE, WA

Partners work together in unusual way to meet project goals

These architects have established a working method that allows both partners to collaborate on every project without being co-designers. They describe their relationship as that of "author and critic"; both interview the clients, refine the program, analyze the site, and establish a mutually agreeable point of departure for the project. At that point one of them becomes the primary designer, and the other assumes the role of the critic. This second opinion helps control the construction budget and ensures that clients get what they want.

A communication tool they often use to help each other is an annotated series of drawings that state their understanding of a problem and their ideas for its resolution. For example, a diagram may show the master bedroom on the second floor, overlooking the living room, in response to a client's wish for a high living room. An objective observer might ask whether it would be better to have a different room adjacent to the living area. These drawings focus on key issues and serve as a reminder of the architects' intentions.

HOUSE 21
CANATSEY/WEINSTEIN ARCHITECTS

Clients required traditional look in weekend/vacation house

This house is a weekend and vacation home for a working couple who are approaching retirement age. Their program dictated a low-maintenance and efficient residence for their present use. In the near future, it will become their permanent home, with office space for their scaled-down business. Their requirements included a living/dining/kitchen/entertainment zone, master bedroom and bathroom, office space/guest bedroom, bathrooms, utility and storage areas, and basement workroom.

More important than the listing of program elements were the clients' wishes that the house look like a traditional beach house, combining architectural elements from their childhood experiences of such houses.

PROJECT: Pedersen house, Belfair, WA
ARCHITECTS: Canatsey/Weinstein Architects; Seattle, WA
AREAS: 2,692 square feet on 30,000 square feet
DATE COMPLETED: 1980
COST: $133,000

SITE WORK

The long, narrow, heavily wooded waterfront lot is oriented toward the northwest. Spectacular views across Hood Canal to the Olympic Mountains are exposed at the crest of a severe slope that falls to the beach. The owners had previously installed a drain field in the only flat area at the top of the slope, leaving a very narrow envelope 32 feet wide in which to locate the house while still providing panoramic views. Electricity, water, and telephone connections were required to the road. A septic field was necessary for sewage disposal.

GRIDS AND MODULES

The house is divided into two parts: a living zone and a service zone. Both zones are 24 feet square in plan; they are linked internally by corridors and externally by a continuous breezeway. The living zone contains the living and dining area, the kitchen, and the master bedroom, which is located at the crest of the hill for optimal views. The service zone, which contains the utility room, bathrooms, carports, and office, is located at the rear.

MATERIALS

All windows are stock white enameled aluminum. Exterior walls are ½-x-6-inch cedar beveled siding on ½-inch plywood sheathing on 2-x-4-inch wood stud walls, fully insulated. Interior wall finishes are ½-inch sheetrock throughout, with wood in the living, kitchen, and dining rooms. The floor is quarry tile in the entry, kitchen, and light well; carpet in the living, dining, and bedrooms; vinyl in the master bath and other upstairs bath.

CONSTRUCTION TECHNIQUES

Floor beams and roof rafters, 16 inches o.c., all run in the same direction bearing on glulam beams where spans are long, as in the living room and carport, or bearing walls, which run across the long axis of the house and define smaller rooms such as bedrooms. The framing in this house is simple, with its regularly spaced bearing points and one-directional beams and rafters. Since much of the cost of a wood house is framing labor, this simple framing method resulted in economical and quick erection of the structure.

Washington is a seismic zone, and some additional reinforcement and strength were required in the poured-concrete footings and walls. The wood frame needed additional work in the form of plywood diaphragms to resist lateral seismic pressure.

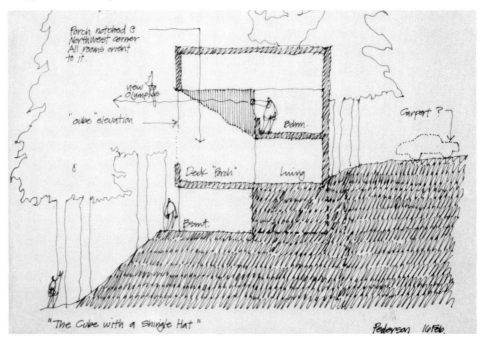

This is a sample of the type of developmental sketch architects use within the office as a communication device.

Left: The bowed front of the breezeway adds great variety to this house. Although important visually, the balcony was not expensive; it consists only of a railing and a deck floor.

Southwest elevation

Section

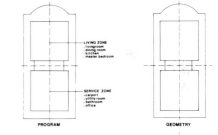

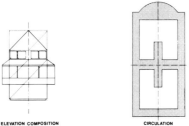

Diagrams

INTERIORS

The walls of the living / dining / kitchen half of the house are accented with wood. The quarry-tile floors of the recessed center foyer extend into the adjacent pantry / utility room and downstairs bath. A light well to the second story in the entry foyer at the middle of the house dramatically emphasizes this important space.

THERMAL COMFORT AND PLUMBING

A heat pump provides summer cooling and winter heating. Plumbing is concentrated in the front half of the house and stacked.

LIGHTING

Recessed lights are regularly spaced as required for task lighting over kitchen counters, bath vanities, and fronts of closets in bedrooms. Other lighting consists of fixed units over the high space in the living room and the light well in the central foyer. The bedroom / office over the carport is lit more generously with a series of recessed lights above desk areas.

MANAGEMENT AND DOCUMENTS

The drawings for this house were well detailed. There were twenty-two sheets in all, 24 x 18 inches, including floor plans, elevations, and sections at ¼-inch scale, a framing plan at ⅛-inch scale, interior elevations at ⅜-inch scale, wall sections at ¾-inch scale, and selected details at 3-inch scale. This quantity of drawings is costly to produce, but it can be justified if the architect gets an adequate fee.

SPECIAL DESIGN TREATMENTS

The architects acknowledged their clients' remembrances of East Coast beach houses with the steep roof pitch, breezeways, and latticework. The square grids in plan and elevation helped everyone understand the design solution. This aid to understanding usually elicits a more sympathetic price from the builder.

Above left: The number and types of windows and doors were kept to a minimum. Supports for the breezeway roof are lined up with the window or door.

Top: The basic shapes of the house and the cantilevered breezeways are shown in the section drawing.

Above: Diagrams illustrate the architectural principles governing the design.

Above: The most difficult part of the handrail construction was cutting the bottom plate and top handrail. This was accomplished with a template and short sections of stock lumber.

Right: The visual clarity of the exterior is reflected inside. Note the alignment of trim pieces at the bottom of the clerestory windows with the balcony rail.

Living and service zones are clearly separated on each floor and stacked above the corresponding zone on the floor below.

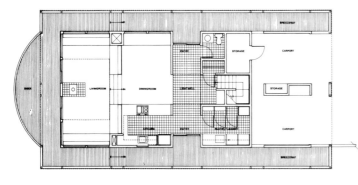

Main floor

Upper floor

DONALD SINGER, ARCHITECT
FORT LAUDERDALE, FL

Unifying concept is most important factor in developing design

All three projects shown on the following pages exemplify this emphasis on an overall unifying concept, to which he assigns primary importance in the design process; other factors play a secondary role. Developed in a broad initial phase, the concept is based on the client's program; site factors such as topography, sun, access, vegetation, privacy, prevailing breezes, and noise; and budget. In the case of House 23, for instance, the site and program suggested a distinctive L shape facing an outdoor "room." House 24 emphasizes prefab techniques and a "tropical" method of spatial organization.

After he determines the concept, the architect considers the following specific guidelines:

MATERIALS
1. Use materials common in local practice.
2. Use materials requiring little or no finish.
3. Use materials requiring little or no maintenance.

GRIDS AND MODULES
1. Establish organizational principles around the sizes of standard components: masonry, windows, and doors.
2. Use a modular (spatial) grid to aid in dimensional consistency, a good proportional device.

CONSTRUCTION TECHNIQUES
1. Work out well-integrated spatial and structural systems selected for their economy and adherence to the concept.
2. Follow common practice when possible.
3. Develop a system of products and details that work together in repetitive patterns. (Detail repetition results in consistency and simplicity.)
4. Use a minimum of details to ease the contractor's comprehension. This results in less confusion and better work.

INTERIORS
1. Carry through in interiors the same concept developed as a solution for programmatic and site problems.
2. Use the three "systems" (spatial, structural, and mechanical) as a basis for interior design (in many cases nothing more is required).
3. Develop ideas for furniture that fit the budget and the space.

HVAC AND PLUMBING
1. Convince clients that these parts of their houses are the most costly; extravagance here can wreck the budget and leave little money for other important factors such as space and details.
2. Develop minimum criteria that meet the client's physical needs.
3. Minimize duct and piping runs.
4. Avoid costly interference with structural components.

LIGHTING
1. Avoid elaborate lighting systems; they are very expensive.
2. Evaluate initial installation and fixture costs versus operating and maintenance costs.
3. Keep lighting minimal and simple—use task lighting and lamps for specific areas and fluorescent light where its quality is acceptable.
4. Situate outdoor floodlights strategically to create lighted landscapes and extend the limits of interior space during nighttime hours.

MANAGEMENT AND DOCUMENTS
1. "Avoid overly detailed design and documentation, which consume more time than can be justified to a client. Cut the time spent on routine tasks, such as repetitive details, and use the saved time for larger concerns, such as the organization of space and structure.
2. Synthesize and refine materials specifications so that three or four details at most can be used in any circumstance. This saves architect's drawing time as well as contractor's effort.
3. Rely on contractors who are sympathetic to and experienced in your way of doing things. Clients may question this type of cronyism, but inform them that time and effort saved during construction can be used more productively in the design phase.

HOUSE 22
DONALD SINGER, ARCHITECT

Builder's house encouraged experimentation

Designed for a builder trained as an architect, this house was built around a concept that evolved from an earlier, more complex one that would have cost twice as much. The key to an economical organization that was not too fussy was a concept of three interlocking spaces, two horizontal and one vertical, linked by walkways and decks.

The client was willing to experiment, so the architect tried out an open children's room and a foundation system that avoids the roots of adjacent banyan trees. The concept of clearly defined spaces reveals basic materials and simple details.

PROJECT: Weinberger house, Miami, FL
ARCHITECT: Donald Singer, Architect, Fort Lauderdale, FL
AREAS: 1,920 square feet on 16,113 square feet
DATE COMPLETED: 1968
COST: $22,400

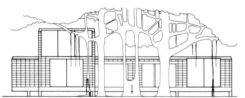

Elevation

Plan

The elevation indicates the placement of the main floor above the ground level to avoid conflict with the spreading banyan-tree roots.

SITE WORK

The lot was a nursery before the client purchased it. The client characterized his site work as "creative removal"; no elaborate landscaping was done.

GRIDS AND MODULES

Three units establish an economical modular pattern:
- The size of standard concrete blocks.
- The maximum span dimension of the wood decking, which established the width of major spaces. All units were equal to minimize cutting and waste.
- The widths of openings were made alike so that all sliding glass units could be the same standard, off-the-shelf dimension.

MATERIALS

The locally made concrete block was chosen as the basic unit because it was cheap and it worked with the architect's idea of exposing the structure (the client liked the idea too). In detailing, every effort was made to plan so that the blocks did not have to be cut and to leave openings for standard-size windows. The blocks also act as the inside wall surface; there are very few sheetrock partitions and no plaster work, which would have messed up the blocks. Room sizes were planned for off-the-shelf decking lengths.

All floors are 2-x-2-foot unfinished concrete tile, spanning between precast concrete joists. The roof decking, all 16-foot lengths, is left exposed.

CONSTRUCTION TECHNIQUES

The foundation accommodates two giant banyan trees on the site. The roots of these trees grow at the surface of the ground and can destroy any structure placed over them or under which they can spread. Holes were dug to determine root depth, and concrete footings were placed well below that level. Short columns were poured up to the grade beam elevation. The roots surround these columns but never go deep enough to disturb the footings.

The foundation supports a grade beam, and 16-foot-long precast joists were set into the grade beam forms at 2-foot intervals. These in turn support the concrete floor tile. The open space below allows air to circulate, which helps cool the house in summer.

The block is stabilized for 150 mph hurricane winds with in-cell reinforcing steel vertically and truss wall reinforcement horizontally. The two-piece design of the roof flashing enables it to be used in both typical situations—over walls and over windows.

The sliding glass window was selected for its simplicity of installation.

INTERIORS

The only finish materials necessary were the few sheetrock partitions, the wood ceiling in the dining room (to carry air-conditioning ducts), and wall tile in the bathrooms.

THERMAL COMFORT AND PLUMBING

The house is heated and cooled with a split (outside condenser) heat pump. The air space below and the tree cover above all but eliminated the need for cooling. The system is centralized to minimize duct runs, as is the plumbing.

LIGHTING

Little daytime lighting is necessary because of the openness of the house. Only a few fixtures were installed: in the dining room, kitchen, and one in each bedroom and bath.

MANAGEMENT AND DOCUMENTS

Two 24-x-36-inch sheets of drawings were used; one detail was added during construction. Further documentation was unnecessary because the owner acted as his own contractor.

SPECIAL DESIGN TREATMENTS

The trim concrete forms contrast with the lush site. The circulation routes between the three discrete spaces are expressed in the design.

Above: Some openings, such as the patio doors here, extend to the underside of the roof planks, thereby eliminating the need for a lintel.

Left: The walls supporting the two-story portion of the living room align with the exterior opening to the adjacent one-story space. This arrangement is visually attractive, and it simplified structural connections.

Openings in the masonry construction are expressive. The windows and sliding doors in this house are grouped. Note the step-down pads that provide access to the porch; they are separate from the structure, which is a simpler way to build them.

The use of lintels of the same depth as adjacent block coursing avoids costly on-site cutting of masony units.

HOUSE 23
DONALD SINGER, ARCHITECT

Good relations with a quality contractor freed time for design refinement

The owner, who was sensitive to craftsmanship and to the building process, preselected the contractor for this house. The architect notes, "It was a privilege to work with this man . . . not cheap, but a bargain at any price. The owners were able to get beyond the low-bid syndrome and have been rewarded. . . ." Dealing with an excellent contractor freed time usually spent on documentation, so the architect was able to spend more effort on the design of the house.

The house was placed tight against the building setback line on the north side of the property. The closed wall screens the use areas from the northern neighbor, also close to the line. The house is open to the yard and the screened patio at the east end along its entire southern elevation.

The patio, a public space accessible from the living area, was a bonus created by roofing the open area between the carport and the enclosed house. The siting was used to greatest possible advantage; it becomes almost an adjunct living room.

PROJECT: Ritchie house, Fort Lauderdale, FL
ARCHITECT: Donald Singer, Architect; Fort Lauderdale, FL
AREAS: Air-conditioned space, 1,294 square feet; carport and storage, 320 square feet; total, 2,254 square feet; lot, 8,050 square feet.
DATE COMPLETED: 1970
COST: $31,461

SITE WORK
Existing trees were left in place. With the exception of a 20-foot-wide gravel drive 35 feet long and the septic system, there was no site work.

GRIDS AND MODULES
The 8-x-8-x-16-inch concrete blocks served as the primary module within which the window system was inserted. The window unit became a module of its own—an off-the-shelf awning vent with a fixed glass middle. The entire length of the corridor acts as a modular curtain wall of standard economy components.

MATERIALS
The block, which requires neither finish nor maintenance, was set early. It was more economical to place electrical and mechanical systems in nonblock walls.

Wet trades above the walls can ruin exposed block finishes, so the architect selected a wood roof system (beams and decking) and plywood-covered partitions, a choice influenced by the contractor's skill with millwork and carpentry. All living areas are carpeted, with the exception of the kitchen (vinyl asbestos tile) and the baths (ceramic tile).

CONSTRUCTION TECHNIQUES
Using builder's standards in a booming area can result in poor workmanship, particularly when a house is to be undecorated with wall coverings and paint. The architect therefore sought economy in structure rather than in workmanship.

The floor is a concrete slab on the cleared and leveled earth; the foundation is incorporated into the slab as a thickened edge. The block rests on the slab with a neoprene waterstop set into a continuous sawcut, made the day after the slab was poured.

Instead of beams running laterally across the space, a single member was run lengthwise, which reduced the framing considerably and allowed minimal-dimension wood decking to span in the lateral direction. A smaller member runs lengthwise over the windows, spanning the short distances between the posts.

INTERIORS
The exposed structure and block required no finish. A skylight enhances the shower in the parents' bedroom.

THERMAL COMFORT AND PLUMBING
The centralized location of the electric heat pump's fan coil unit reduced the need for ductwork. Cooling is essential in the middle summer months.

Plumbing was simplified by placing baths and kitchen in line and adjacent to each other.

LIGHTING
This is held to a sensible level with inexpensive fixtures and floodlights in the planting under the eaves to expand the space at night.

MANAGEMENT AND DOCUMENTS
All drawings were done on 8½-x-11-inch paper. The plan was the only one done with a straightedge; the others were freehand. The architect used this technique one other time with the same contractor, and it worked well. He does not recommend it for every situation, but the freehand detailing is a time saver if the detail system is simple and repetitive. The contractor's interest and involvement with the project from its inception were a help.

SPECIAL DESIGN TREATMENTS:
The house is conceived as a grouped series of enclosed spaces organized around an open outdoor "room." The concept and quality of the materials require no treatment.

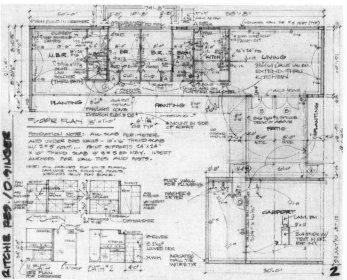

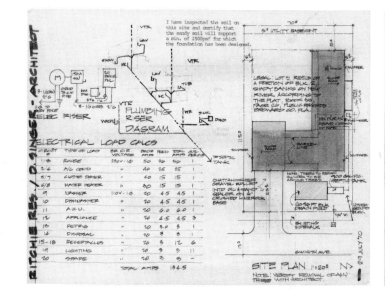

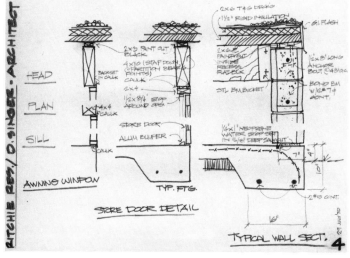

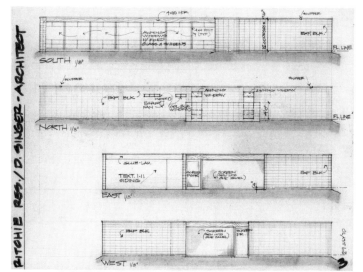

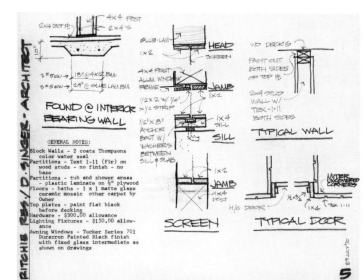

Opposite page: The condensation of all essential information for this house into six 8½-x-11-inch sheets is part of the design process. The brevity of the documents complements and reinforces the simplicity of the design.

Left: The orientation of the house toward the outdoor room is an integral feature of the design. The lush tropical vegetation softens the linear quality of the house.

Below: On the front elevation, the entrance patio is centered between the carport and the house.

Architect explores industrialized systems in own house

For his own house, the architect tried to design in a "tropical" mode using contemporary materials with an industrialized system of prefabricated changeable panels. He listed his requirements under two broad headings: the practical considerations of space allocation, maintenance, and a factory-built wall component; and the aesthetic considerations of the tropical vernacular, separation of structure and enclosure, and a visual expanse of apparent space. The result is a house developed as a pavilion, with wide eaves on freestanding columns, constructed of materials suited to the hostile hot-wet, hot-dry climate.

The first basic system was the structure, which was all concrete. The second system was in-fill (an aluminum sandwich panel, glazed where necessary) spanning between floor and and roof planes.

PROJECT: Singer house, Fort Lauderdale, FL
ARCHITECT: Donald Singer, Architect; Fort Lauderdale, FL
AREAS: Air-conditioned space, 2,400 square feet; covered porch, 420 square feet; carport, 384 square feet; total, 3,204 square feet; lot, 21,968 square feet
DATE COMPLETED: 1976
COST: $67,000

SITE WORK

The site was overgrown with live oak, sable palms, and ferns. Codes called for a floor level fully 2 feet above grade and a similarly high septic system. To avoid extensive regrading, the house was set on a 2-foot base and the septic system placed within the confines of the "front porch." This also eliminated the need for costly fill.

GRIDS AND MODULES

Columns were arranged on a 16-x-16-foot grid, which was modified to 16 x 12 feet along the northern edge to accommodate trees that would otherwise have had to be removed.

The 6½-inch-thick roof slab was laid out on a 4-x-8-foot grid that corresponded to the column grid and also allowed complete reuse of the plywood concrete forms. (A prearranged sale of 125 sheets of the ¾-inch plastic-coated plywood was a major cost offset.)

The wall system was planned around a 4-foot-wide panel. Singer notes that there were variations, and he learned a lesson: he vows to use only one size on his next panel project.

MATERIALS

Concrete, aluminum, and glass were the three basic materials. The insides of the aluminum panels were painted to match interior partitions.

The wall panel is the most important item. A stock panel was chosen to serve as a curtain wall inset. The panel, 2¼ inches thick, is built around a rigid urethane insulation core with ⅛-inch cement asbestos laminated to each face to protect the aluminum overlay from dents; an aluminum skin is laminated over that.

The panels are costly, but they need no other support in the wall. They self-span the 9½-foot distance between the floor and roof slabs. They also have superior insulating qualities. The architect learned about the detailing on the job by installing the panels himself with the help of friends.

CONSTRUCTION TECHNIQUES

Columns were poured in place using cardboard forms. They were all one size (12 feet) and proved to be a quick and easy system. Scaffolding was rented to form the roof slab.

A cardboard tube similar to the column forms was coated with resin and laid in the ground to carry conditioned air to the west side of the pavilion after the architect discovered that standard underground duct systems would have cost 10 times as much. The solution was acceptable to local code interpretation.

The panels were installed in a U channel top and bottom (slip up, in, and down), and the joints were closed with a sealant.

The 4-foot-wide panel system, shown here with window inserts, spans the 9½ feet between floor and roof slabs.

The joints between the plywood panels that form the roof are expressed, as are the form markings of the cardboard tubes that formed the columns.

INTERIORS

Very little finishing was done. Partitions were placed to reinforce the open-pavilion concept. Doors were installed only where required for privacy.

THERMAL COMFORT AND PLUMBING

The architect took advantage of an insulation manufacturer's computer program to relate insulation cost and thickness, per-ton HVAC equipment cost, per-kilowatt-hour electrical cost, and local use characteristics for heating and cooling to select an optimum combination of insulation and HVAC and equipment size.

He then cut the heating capacity of the system in half, recognizing that manufacturer's criteria are designed for the most extreme conditions. The result is yearly power bills that are much lower per square foot than those with comparable systems. Such a decision, perhaps possible only when designing for yourself, involved accepting potential discomfort in extreme conditions in the interest of large overall savings.

LIGHTING

Abundant natural light makes artificial lighting necessary only at night. Outside spaces are lit with lamp holders that also expand the interior space at night. Often only the outside lighting is on, which throws a backwash of soft light through the glass to the interior space.

MANAGEMENT AND DOCUMENTS

Functioning as owner, architect, and contractor made coordination easy on this project. The danger in such a relationship, however, is a tendency to lose the discipline usually applied to more standard arrangements.

Drawings were done in terms of the systems of construction—foundation, columns and roof slab, panels, partitions, plumbing, electricity—to facilitate off-site manufacturing as well as subcontracting.

SPECIAL DESIGN TREATMENTS

The architect chose to express the structure separately from the prefabricated panel system.

The separation of the round structural columns and the infilled nonstructural walls is evident in plan.

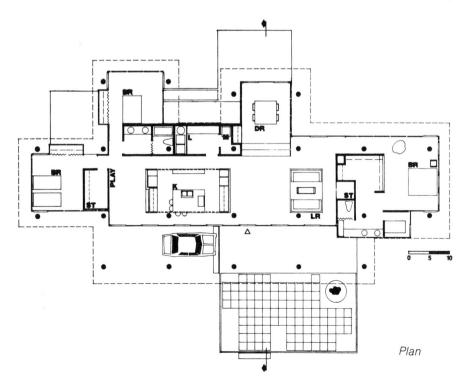

Plan

The depth of the overhang is flexible, as is
the type of infill between roof and floor slabs.
Seen here are panels with partial windows,
full-length sliding glass panels, jalousies,
and solid panels.

MASSDESIGN
CAMBRIDGE, MA

Firm emphasizes cost effective energy design

Massdesign is interested equally in low first costs and low operating costs; this interest is reflected in their low-energy, low-maintenance designs. They note: "If we are successful in completing houses to a high standard within tight budgets, it is attributable to the fact that we study each house very thoroughly prior to commencement of the working drawings. Typically, we will build at least two models both for our benefit and to assist the client and builder in visualizing accurately the spaces and the junctions to be built. The first model, generally to ⅛-inch scale, is an aid to establishing exterior form. The second, generally at ¼-inch scale, allows us to explore and explain room relationships, plus structural and spatial expression. We have found these larger models are appreciated by the builder preparing the final estimate.

"Probably our most important cost-saving approach is our effort to stress building costs in our earliest discussions with the client. Typically, we develop an overall project budget at the first meeting. We demand realism, challenging and testing the client's needs. Often we are able to revise the client's initial program by introducing a more flexible approach to room uses and sizes. This is probably the best way to reduce overall building costs."

HOUSE 25
MASSDESIGN

Solar house combines good design with low operating costs

The clients, an active couple in their fifties, requested a simple house that would both support and express their appreciation of the surrounding natural environment. Although the overall house area was to be modest in size, they desired the greatest possible sense of spaciousness. They also needed some extra space to accommodate offspring who visit occasionally.

The site was an abandoned apple orchard in a Massachusetts farming community first settled in the eighteenth century. The entrance door opens into a compact vestibule, which can be separated in winter from the adjoining solarium/breakfast area and kitchen. The five principal ground-floor spaces of the house (living/dining, kitchen, solarium/breakfast, study, and master bedroom) are connected in a line, creating surprisingly long views and assuring each space a "front-row seat" facing the sun. Only the two-compartment bathroom/laundry faces north. The second floor contains a large guest bedroom with raised study alcove, plus a smaller room with a balcony overlooking the living area. A small basement houses the solar tank, domestic hot-water heater, and rock store.

PROJECT: Thompson house, eastern Massachusetts
ARCHITECTS: massdesign; Cambridge, MA
AREAS: 1,750 square feet on 4 acres
DATE COMPLETED: 1978
COST: $88,000

SITE WORK

A short gravel driveway and path connect house and garage. Additional site work involved constructing the septic system, well, and electrical connections. Grading was kept to a minimum.

GRIDS AND MODULES

Studs and beams are spaced 2 feet o.c. throughout the house.

MATERIALS

The ground-floor slab is 4-inch reinforced concrete poured over rigid insulation and a continuous vapor barrier. Exterior 2-x-6-inch stud walls sheathed with ⅝-inch exterior plywood contain 5½-inch foamed-in-place insulation. A 4-mil polyethylene vapor barrier forms a continuous lining to studs and rafters.

Exterior wall finish is 1-x-6, and 8-inch shiplap pine boards treated with a light buff preservative stain. Fascias and all exterior trim are stained dark brown. The roof is finished with buff-colored asphalt shingles over plywood sheathing on 2-x-10-inch wood rafters 24 inches o.c.

Stock wood windows and doors are all casements or fixed, with the exception of thermal-break aluminum sliding doors. Wooden skylights in the roof are operable. All window trim is redwood, 6 x 1¼ inches. For interior walls that are exposed to the sun, two layers of ⅝-inch gypsum board provide added thermal mass.

CONSTRUCTION TECHNIQUES

Standard wood framing is used, except for 6-x-14-inch cross rafters 12 to 18 feet on center, placed periodically across the length of the house, each with a ¾-inch steel tie rod. These brace the walls of this long space, which otherwise would tend to spread.

INTERIORS

Gypsum walls are painted with a variety of pale earth tones. The wood beams, wood decking over study and kitchen, and door and window trim are all lightly stained and clear-finished.

Interior walls that face the sun are lined with two layers of ⅝-inch sheetrock for additional thermal mass. The north-facing hopper windows located above second-floor rooms provide induced summer venitlation.

Axonometric

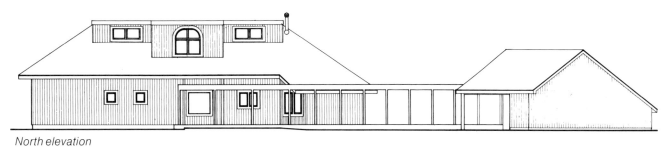

North elevation

South elevation

Comparative elevations show contrast between open south elevation and closed north elevation.

THERMAL COMFORT AND PLUMBING

All south-facing rooms contain energy-storing ceramic-tile floors over a concrete slab in areas that receive extended hours of sunshine. A 2-foot roof overhang and fairly deep spaces provide each southern room and its occupants and furnishings with necessary shelter from excessive direct sunlight and glare.

A row of north-facing, hopper-type clerestory windows runs continuously through the two second-floor rooms, allowing efficient summertime extraction of heated air induced by the prevailing southwest wind. In winter the two upper rooms are isolated from the remainder of the house when not in use, serving as an additional insulated attic.

A half-horsepower fan, activated by a conventional thermostat, circulates air between the house and a rockbed energy store beneath the kitchen. One high- and three low-level extract points are provided to prevent stratification of the air in the heated spaces.

Five water-cooled flat-plate collectors on the roof, a 500-gallon basement water tank at atmospheric pressure, and a pump and a differential controller constitute the active solar heating system. Its primary function is the preheating of domestic hot water; in spring and autumn, surplus tank heat is available from a fan-coil unit that heats house air circulating through the storage area. The house contains no furnace; all auxiliary heat requirements are met by the efficient wood stove. (The owners burn 1 ½ cords of hardwood per year.)

LIGHTING

The principal spaces receive ample daylight from south windows and skylights. Recessed ceiling fixtures provide light in kitchen and bathroom / laundry work spaces.

MANAGEMENT AND DOCUMENTS

Drawings, 18 x 30 inches, include three mechanical and one electrical sheet. Plans, sections, and elevations are ¼-inch scale; framing plans are at ⅛-inch scale. Half-inch full wall sections are combined with 3-inch partial details.

The job was estimated by several contractors, and a contract was then negotiated with the selected builder.

SPECIAL DESIGN TREATMENTS

The visible solar energy features of this house (collectors, greenhouse, and south sliding doors) are unobtrusively incorporated within the clearly expressed image of a simple house under a broad, sheltering roof. The two-car garage is linked to the house by means of a covered walkway.

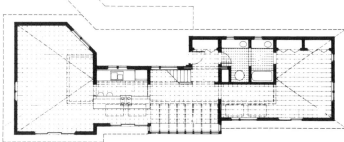

Ground floor

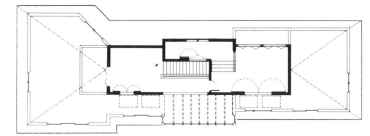

Second floor

Above: All major rooms line up to face the sun—an important consideration in passive solar design.

Top: Windows and doors are visually accented with a surround of wide boards. The five solar collectors above the large solarium skylight are used primarily for domestic hot-water heating.

Left: The solarium, besides providing solar gain, is a pleasant place in which to eat.

Below: The tile floor is set on a concrete slab to provide thermal mass. The wood-burning stove is the only backup source of heat.

ACORN STRUCTURES, INC.
CONCORD, MA

Prefab manufacturer maintains high design quality

This housing manufacturer, established thirty-five years ago, achieved early success with factory-built components and preassembled modular units, and it evolved a precut, factory-assembled panel system. Acorn Structures is continuing its series of energy-efficient, solar-oriented houses with the Independence series, begun in 1974.

The materials called for on working drawings are linked with an inventory of windows, stairs, and other parts through computers. The designs are based on a 4-foot planning grid, four roof pitches, and limitations of geometry and details. Within these restrictions, design flexibility is maintained to achieve a wide variety of models.

In order to sell its products successfully to the varied U.S. housing market, the company stresses the advantages of the prefab approach.

- Costs are predictable, and quality is high. Although factory assembly of building components permits quality control and speed in erecting the building shell, it does not guarantee lower costs. Acorn, however, controls costs in three areas: design, purchase of materials, and, importantly, a nationwide network of franchised builders with a reputation for reliability.
- Guidance in obtaining permits, financing, and builder selection is provided for the purchasers of Acorn units.
- Design quality has always been important. The company hires talented architects to design the houses, and its literature is graphically attractive. A monitoring system has been set up to check feedback from customers who occupy their units.
- Recognizing the fact that fewer than 20 percent of sales are built as shown in the catalog, the houses were designed to anticipate   and invite individual adaptations to fit different programs and sites. The company maintains a permanent staff of architects, designers, and sales representatives to work on those changes. The company indicates that roughly 40 percent of the models are routinely modified (plans reversed, a garage added, windows and non-load-bearing walls changed, and other such modifications), and another 40 percent are radically redesigned or designed from scratch. When clients ask Acorn for a custom design, the company's architects work with outside architects to devise a package based on their system of roof pitches, stock details, and components. This leaves considerable latitude for individual finishes, special details, and site design.

Site plans are not offered because manufactured housing must be designed to fit a variety of sites and climates. For instance, stock plans allow for entry from two or three sides, a garage in several directions, or expansion of a family room, kitchen, or sunspace. In the case of the solar-oriented Independence series, such items as the quantity of solar mass, the mix of direct and isolated solar gain, and the number of layers of glazing can be modified.

INDEPENDENCE SERIES
GENERAL SPECIFICATIONS

ERECTED SHELL

Foundation: Poured concrete or concrete block foundation (10" or per plan) asphalt coated, and nominal 4" slab floor with vapor barrier; or concrete or block piers. Foundation and pier footings below frost line. Ducted and insulated thermal mass in Independence III and IV.

Floor Construction: Girder—Fir 4 x 10 (or larger per plan). Joists 2 x 10 16" o.c. Floor 5/8" T & G plywood, glued and nailed to joists. Porch posts, joists, decking, open stairs and rail per plan.

Exterior Walls: Panels assembled as indicated. Framing 2 x 4 16" o.c. #3 T & G cedar boards, field applied on ½" CD sheathing. Optional sidings available. Windows - Pella wood casements or awnings with screens and storm sash installed in panel. Picture windows with insulating glass. Triple glazing for all windows not covered with thermal drapes. Trim #2 Idaho pine.

Interior Partitions: 2 x 4 framing 16" o.c.

Exterior Doors: Insulating core prehung. 1¾" steel flush door or steel door with safety insulating glass per plan, compression weatherstripped with trim, lock and hardware. Wood sliding patio door with screen and safety insulating glass per plan.

Roof Construction: Trusses 24" o.c. or rafters 16" o.c. per plan. Sheathing ½" plywood. Roofing 290 lb. (25 year warranty) asphalt seal tab shingles, with 15 lb. roof felt, metal drip edge and flashings. Soffit 3/8" exterior plywood with vent strip.

Stairs: Open or closed stairs with oak treads, risers, and railings per plan. Supplied with Acorn materials package for installation during Rough Finish and Finished House stage.

Hardware: Nails, screws, plates, bolts.

Cabinets: Prefinished oak cabinets for kitchen and vanities for bath per plan. Supplied with Acorn materials package for installation during Rough Finish and Finished House stage.

Interior Trim and Doors: Trim for doors, base and windows: pine. Interior doors flush 1 3/8" hollow core ash, hinged or slider, prehung with hardware. Closets, shelving and rods. Supplied with Acorn materials package for installation during Rough Finish or Finished House stage.

ROUGH FINISH

Plumbing and Bathroom: Lavatory, water closet, tub or metal stall shower, medicine cabinet and wall accessories per plan. 80 gallon electric water heater. Fittings and tubing to complete plumbing to kitchen, bathrooms, and to outside wall. Single bowl 24" stainless steel kitchen sink, deluxe fittings.
Tub Enclosure: Ceramic tile, marlite or fiberglass.

Electrical Service: 100 amp service (or larger with electric heat), wire, circuit breakers, 40-160 outlets depending on size. Light fixtures extra.

Heating: Oil fired warm air. Isolated gain space heat transfer and ventilation system in Independence IV. Variable speed fan, proportional controller and automatic damper for winter/summer operation with smoke detector cutoff.

Insulation: Cantilevered floors fiberglass with vapor barrier R32. Ceilings fiberglass with vapor barrier R32. Walls fiberglass with ¾" foil faced rigid insulation R19.

Interior Walls & Ceilings: ½" sheetrock on walls and ceilings. Optional: 1 x 6 T & G #3 cedar panelling.

FINISHED HOUSE

Interior Trim and Doors: Install interior doors and trim, closet shelving and rods.

Kitchen: Size per plan. Install cabinets. Supply and install formica countertop, 30" slide-in electric range with timer. Dishwasher per plan.

Fireplace: Masonry fireplace and chimney or freestanding stove as shown on plan.
Optional: Heatilator Energy Pack Fireplace.

Painting: One coat stain on all exterior surfaces. Two coats stain/sealer or paint on interior doors, trim and sheetrock.

Finished Floors: Floor tile for baths, kitchen entries, and utility rooms. Pile carpet for living, dining, bedroom areas. Bluestone (or equivalent) in solarium in Independence III. Optional: wood flooring.

Energy Features: Sunwave® 70-300 Domestic Hot Water System in finished house stage. Optional: 210 Space and Domestic Hot Water System. Thermal drapes in Independence I, II and III.

Acorn Structures provides all materials printed in black. Other materials, foundation, plumbing, electrical, etc. shown in red print are provided by Acorn Builders. Please ask your local builder or the factory for detail specifications which separately describe materials provided by Acorn and materials provided at the site. Site clearing, excavation, water sewerage, driveway and electric fixtures will be priced separately by local builders.

Transportation is priced according to distance from Concord, Massachusetts.

Solar house maintains traditional look

In this series of designs the manufacturer continued the evolution of its solar designs. Although they were having good success with the solar series (see page 135), Acorn Structures wanted to broaden the market by combining solar features with a more traditional look. The house illustrated here is an adaptation of one of the models in this series, called the Cottage series. The plan places the family room adjacent to the kitchen, with the dining room beyond, as a part of the living room. Four bedrooms are located on the second floor, but there is a study/bedroom on the first floor. This example includes the optional garage, with an ample mud room entry so often required in the New England area.

PROJECT: Furtney house, Acorn Cottage series, Hollis, NH
ARCHITECTS: Acorn Structures, Inc.; Concord, MA
Architectural Design: Betsy Lee
Energy Systems Design: Mark Kelley III
Sunwave Solar Systems Design: John Bemis, Jr.
AREAS: 2,835 square feet
DATE COMPLETED: 1982
COST: Specific costs for the Furtney house are not available. The manufacturer's estimated finished house price range for the standard Cottage 2500 house with attached garage and Sunwave® solar system is $165,000 to $175,000. This price range includes design fees, foundation, carpentry, insulation, plumbing, heating, electrical work, painting, fireplace, and kitchen, but does not include transportation, sales tax, site work, septic or water systems.

SITE WORK
Site work is not a part of the package; owners must rely on a local builder to perform these services.

GRIDS AND MODULES
The Acorn component building system is based on a 4'0" horizontal planning module. The 4'0" modular grid runs to the outside stud line. Vertically, the gable section develops in 4'0" increments horizontally, starting with the sidewall height and increasing in height according to the roof pitch. Roof pitches available are 4/12, 6/12, 8/12, and 12/12.

MATERIALS
See page 131 for options.

CONSTRUCTION TECHNIQUES
The exterior shell of the house consists of preassembled wall panels 2 or 4 feet in width and of varying heights. These panels are of 2-X-4 frame construction and ½-inch plywood sheathing, with the windows and doors factory installed. The floor system includes factory precut 2-X-10 floor joists at 16 inches on center with ⅝-inch plywood sheathing assembled in the field. Similarly the roof system consists of factory precut 2-X-10 rafters at 16 inches on center with ½-inch plywood sheathing.

Interior structure consists of a factory precut post and beam system with nonbearing partitions assembled in the field by the builder. A majority of the homes are built with field-applied siding of either 1-X-4 vertical cedar boards or 1-X-6 cedar clapboards.

The manufacturer cautions builders on the importance of starting out with sills and floor deck that are level, square, and on dimension. The company recommends that the foundation be held undersize ½ inch all around to ensure that the exterior shell dimensions do not grow, causing problems all the way up. Acorn Structures provides the builder with an extensive detail book since many of the construction details are not builder's standard because they are engineered as part of a total component system.

The exterior suggests some of the more enduring traditions of American house design: steeply pitched roofs, a generous porch, and decorative accents at the tops of gables.

INTERIORS

Acorn supplies all interior doors, trim, stairs and railings, and kitchen and bath cabinets as part of the house package. Because local building inspectors and fire underwriters generally need to inspect plumbing, wiring, heating, and insulation before the walls are closed in, the wall panels are shipped open and installed in the field by the builder.

Most interior finishes are selected by the owner, so interiors vary in houses of the same series. However, the manufacturer supplies recommended details for interior finish to be consistent with the clean-looking square-edge trim provided with the package.

THERMAL COMFORT AND PLUMBING

Space heating is provided by a combination active and passive solar system with a conventional backup heating system. In addition to space heating, the active solar system supplies heating for the domestic hot-water system. The Sunwave® active system manufactured by Acorn comes as part of the house package. The direct gain passive system employs masonry thermal storage and between-room air transfer grills to assist the distribution of solar gain. The backup heating equipment (gas, oil, or electric) is provided by the builder.

Plumbing fixtures are provided by the local builder based on specifications and allowances prepared by the manufacturer and approved by the owner.

LIGHTING

All lighting and wiring are provided by the local builder, based on specifications and allowances prepared by Acorn Structures and approved by the owner.

MANAGEMENT AND DOCUMENTS

Floor plans are drawn with a reference grid representing 4 feet on a ¼-inch scale. Many elements on the plans are keyed to this grid and often may not be otherwise dimensioned. When grid-line relationships are not clear, locations are specified by dimensions.

Outside dimensions are given to the module line, which in plan is the exterior stud line. Interior dimensions are given to the centerline of interior partitions.

The dimensions are expressed in a three-part number system, representing feet, inches, and sixteenths. The dimension 10-8-12, for instance, means 10 feet 8 inches 12 sixteenths, or 10 feet 8¾ inches. This system enables the manufacturer to check dimensions more easily than with the normal fractional system.

Drawings for this house are shown on eighteen 24-X-18-inch sheets, with plans, elevations, and framing plans at ¼-inch scale, sections at ⅜-inch scale, and selected details at larger scales. Documents are furnished with a bound book on 8½-X-11-inch paper showing details at larger scale.

The company forecasts an estimate for the assembled house, including a fixed price on the package and estimates for subcontractor work. The local builder is the contracting party with the owner. The company will also sell the package of manufactured items separately, leaving it to the owners to select and deal with a builder of their own choice.

SPECIAL DESIGN TREATMENTS

The Cottage series of houses is an attempt to broaden the appeal of a solar-oriented house with the simple shapes and details of early colonial houses. Prominent gables, long saltbox shapes, and generous porches formed by steep wrapping roofs are the prominent features.

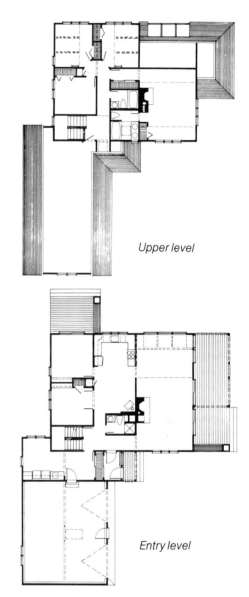

Upper level

Entry level

Four bedrooms are grouped on the second floor, entirely filling it with the exception of a high ceiling above the dining room/solarium. On the entry level, a small family room is adjacent to a large country kitchen. Opposite is a large dining/living room.

Above: Rendering in sales brochure shows this house in a flopped position.

Right: The country kitchen is the heart of the house. From there can be seen the screen porch beyond the spacious dining / living area. The solarium is to the left.

HOUSE 27
ACORN STRUCTURES, INC.

High-performance passive solar house series developed with consulting architect

These houses were designed with Massdesign (see page 125) to fill a need in Acorn's product line for a more traditional look in passive solar homes. The four original designs in the Independence series include passive strategies that vary in complexity, cost, and performance. The model illustrated here is a three-bedroom house with a two-story isolated gain solarium, the primary solar buffer and collector, which also visually expands the compact spaces adjacent to it. Direct access into the solarium promotes its use as a sunny garden in which to eat or just sit.

PROJECT: Potter house, Acorn Independence series, Butler, MD.
ARCHITECTS: Acorn Structures, Inc.; Concord, MA
Architectural Design: Douglas Govan
Acorn Staff: Bruce Hampton
Energy Systems Design: Mark Kelley III
Massdesign, Architects and Planners
Principal: Gordon Tully
Principal: Tudor Ingersoll
Design Associate: Stu Roberts
AREA: 2,000 square feet
DATE COMPLETED: 1982
COST: Specific costs for the Potter house are not available. The manufacturer's estimated finished house price range for the standard Independence IV (1,896 square feet) is $120,000 to $130,000, including the Acorn Sunwave® Domestic Hot Water system, isolated gain space heat transfer and ventilation system, and ducted remote thermal storage slab. See House 26 for more details on pricing.

SITE WORK:
Similar to House 26.

GRIDS AND MODULES
Similar to House 26.

MATERIALS
See page 131 for options.

CONSTRUCTION TECHNIQUES
Similar to House 26.

INTERIORS
The owner has finished the isolated gain space with a quarry-tile floor and cedar siding.

THERMAL COMFORT AND PLUMBING
The energy-conserving design of this house follows a set of simple procedures to achieve the goal of minimal auxiliary fuel use. Since this house was manufactured as a panelized system, several constraints were placed on the design. The difficulty of shipping the heavy materials required for thermal mass was economically resolved by adding a network of ducting within concrete floor slabs on grade, utilizing "already purchased" construction, and requiring no added space.

The construction techniques and details involved in the thermal collection and storage system were kept simple to allow on-site construction by the average home builder. The design includes the following energy conserving features:

Foil-faced taped isocyanurate insulation boards were installed on the inside of fiberglass-packed stud walls to yield R-19 walls without thermal, short circuits.

A polyethylene vapor barrier was placed between the fiberglass and the foam board for additional infiltration protection.

Foam caulking was sprayed around cracks and electrical boxes.

Triple glazing was used on all but buffer spaces.

A large solar collection area is provided by an isolated sunspace, which allows additional living space and controls overheating and glare.

To control solar gain, doors and windows at the back of the sunspace can be opened to augment the natural flow of heat throughout the house.

The sunspace is coupled to the concrete floor storage mass with a thermostatically controlled ducted fan system.

The storage mass discharges its heat passively by natural radiation and convection.

A battery of underground heat-exchange tubes provides fresh air and summer cooling.

LIGHTING
Recessed and surface-mounted track lighting was mounted on top of beams in the solarium.

MANAGEMENT AND DOCUMENTS
Similar to House 26.

SPECIAL DESIGN TREATMENTS
The traditional forms of this house include saltbox shapes with a stepped-out second floor on the south and a steeply pitched north roof. Windows are located in the center of the walls above the greenhouse to the right of the sunspace, another traditional location.

The sunspace is the most prominent feature of the south facade. A smaller greenhouse to the right is accessible from the basement. The upper level is stepped out over the entry level, providing summer shade for the windows on that level.

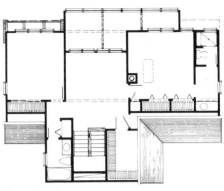

Upper level

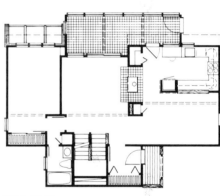

Entry level

Above: A large dining area facing the kitchen is the principal feature of the entry level. This room can also serve as a family gathering place on cold winter evenings. The sunspace, on the other side of the kitchen, is usable particularly in warm weather, as well as on sunny winter days. On the second floor are the master bedroom and another bedroom around a sitting area overlooking the sunspace.

Left: Because sunspaces can overheat or cool down excessively, all rooms opening to it can be closed off with operable windows and doors. The room is paneled with wood boards and tiled over the concrete slab, making the space an intermediate zone between inside and out.

LOUIS SAUER/ARCHIRIS
PITTSBURGH, PA

Architect achieves design variety using standardized townhouse construction

One of the building types that this firm specializes in is townhouses. Sauer has worked out a construction system to effect savings that stresses the efficiency of standardized and repetitive building methods. He finds that whenever builders have to change the way they build or use unfamiliar products or materials, construction costs rise. Before he starts designing, therefore, Sauer spends time investigating local traditions of materials use and assembly; these off-the-shelf systems become his design palette.

Sauer suggests limiting the number of special design conditions when laying out drawings, such as foundation dimensions; locations of walls, doors, windows, and equipment such as kitchens and baths; and finishes, trim, and details. He also advocates reducing the number of construction materials and subcontractors, because costs rise as these increase. For instance, it is generally more expensive to construct both flat and sloped roofs for the same project.

The problem with standardized townhouse design, however, is monotony, which creates a marketing problem. When purchasing a house, people seek a neighborhood, a floor plan, and a street facade that relate to their life-style. Sauer's firm determines a group of standardized design elements that permit plan and elevation variations within a type and a mix of sales costs.

HOUSE 28
LOUIS SAUER/ARCHIRIS

Townhouses in urban-renewal area echo surrounding restored historic buildings

The site, located within Baltimore's Inner West Harbor renewal area, was adjacent to a cluster of already occupied historic townhouses that had been recently restored. The architect and the developer did not want the new construction to contrast too starkly with the old, which would destroy the character of the neighborhood. They therefore used the same building type—townhouses—and similar fenestration and details such as front doors and door lights, brick, band coursing, and window trim.

After a survey of urban townhouse types, the architect did site and floor-plan studies to determine the widths of the two- and three-bedroom units, as well as the organization of vertical sections. He developed facade and stoop-stair alternatives, as well as combinations and variations of the two basic plan types.

PROJECT: Harbor Walk, Baltimore, MD
ARCHITECT: Louis Sauer; Pittsburgh, PA
AREAS: 100 units varying from 1,080 to 3,370 square feet on a 3.4-acre site
DATE COMPLETED: 1982
COST: $97,500 to $187,500 per unit (sales prices), depending on model and options

SITE WORK

Site costs for townhouses are relatively low because of their high density: utility runs are short and the paved areas around them are small. Landscaping is also minimal. In this project, parking ratios of 1:1 for two-bedroom townhouses and 2:1 for three-bedroom townhouses were achieved within a net density of twenty-nine units per acre. In-house garages for the three-bedroom units and surface parking for the two-bedroom units are located off small informal alleys between private yards.

After study and consultation with marketing specialists and city and community organizations, the architect selected an 18-x-70-foot property size for three-bedroom units with an additional 2 feet for corner properties and a 14-x-59-foot property size for two-bedroom units.

GRIDS AND MODULES

The property sizes of 14 and 18 feet were the basic controlling modules.

MATERIALS

Exterior front and side walls are 4-inch face brick on 4-inch concrete block, with 2-x-4-inch studs inside; rear walls are 4-inch steel studs with gypsum-board sheathing and stucco walls filled with full thick fiberglass insulation and covered with ½-inch sheetrock. Wood casement windows and aluminum sliding doors were used throughout with ⅝-inch insulating glass. Party walls are 8-inch concrete block furred out on each side with stripping and finished with sheetrock. Roofs are asphalt shingles on ½-inch plywood.

CONSTRUCTION TECHNIQUES

For all floors, 2-x-4-inch wood trusses were used, spanning 14 and 18 feet. These truss sizes are economical for multi-unit construction because the amount of material is minimal. They are less economical for single-family detached houses, for which there is no advantage of mass production (most of these trusses are not off-the-shelf items). Roof construction consists of 2-x-4-inch trusses 2 feet on center spanning from front to back.

Set-back units with stoops can be combined with units that are flush with the building line. Such options provide visual variety within the overall unity created by the use of similar windows and brick.

Above: The steel-stud, stucco-clad rear walls join brick-faced side walls at the corners. This change of materials was made in the interest of economy, but as handled it provides needed visual relief from the brick.

Below: Careful site planning was essential so that the buildings could receive unobstructed light and air. Amenities such as paving patterns and trees cost comparatively little but add much to the neighborhood.

INTERIORS

Builder's standards were adhered to throughout. Sauer used "clamshell" profile moldings, sheet vinyl floors in kitchens, ceramic tile in baths, and carpet over plywood subflooring elsewhere. Oak stairs were left uncarpeted. Closets have bifold doors.

THERMAL COMFORT AND PLUMBING

Heat pumps are used for both air conditioning and heating, boosted electrically at lower temperatures. Heat pumps have an operating cost advantage over conventional methods of heating and cooling because they extract heat from the air in the heating cycle and eject warm air in the cooling cycle.

LIGHTING

Recessed can-type fixtures provide general illumination, except in dining areas, where buyers were given options. Kitchen lighting was provided with undercabinet fluorescents.

MANAGEMENT AND DOCUMENTS

The architects had two separate contracts, one with the city for utility and surface landscaping and the other with the developer for buildings and private yards. Full services were provided in collaboration with a local architect for on-site construction observation. Fifty drawings were produced. The owner/developer served as general contractor.

SPECIAL DESIGN TREATMENTS

The architect noted that facade organization in townhouses is similar throughout the country, except for details and artifacts on the facade, their color, and their size. For the Harbor Walk project he decided to vary the entrances and their stoops, stairs, planting beds, and special details such as stripes of precast concrete. Within, he provided some spatial options: for example, a single-story living room with a large master bedroom/dressing/sitting room over it or a two-story living room with a small study balcony above.

To provide greater visual diversity within the two townhouse types (two and three bedrooms) and their facades and stoop-stair alternatives, Sauer provided two additional variations: a corner variant with two entrances and a carriage-house unit that could be located in the rear yard of corner properties. In the three-bedroom units, different materials were used for the street-front facade, which is brick, and the rear-alley facade, which is stucco.

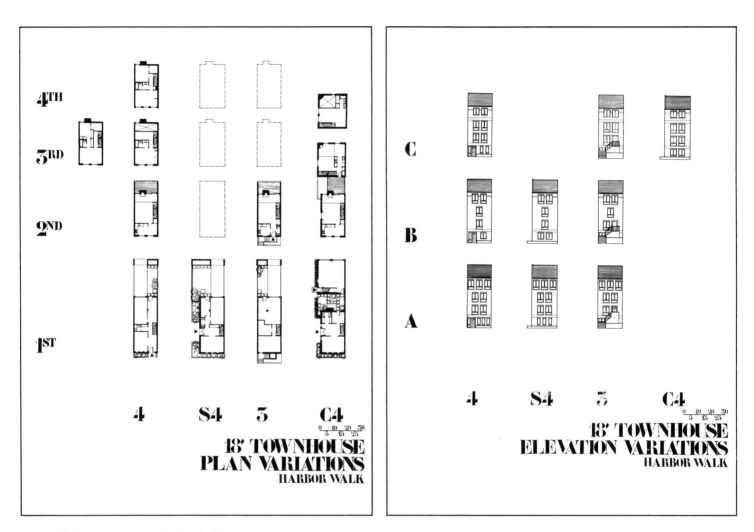

4TH

3RD

2ND

1ST

4   **S4**   **3**   **C4**

18' TOWNHOUSE PLAN VARIATIONS
HARBOR WALK

C

B

A

4   **S4**   **3**   **C4**

18' TOWNHOUSE ELEVATION VARIATIONS
HARBOR WALK

Above: Stairs are generally located in the same position; entries vary, depending on whether the building is entered from the side or from the front.

Above right: The number and size of windows and the width of the horizontal bands are the chief variables of the elevation.

MLTW / TURNBULL ASSOCIATES
SAN FRANCISCO, CA

Architects apply same philosophy over wide geographic area

William Turnbull says his firm has the same problems as any other. ''The clients want more than what they can afford, and our job is to pull the rabbit out of the hat and provide dreams as well. Essentially we are purveyors of dreams—three-D makers of all those special things that keep people going through the chaos of existence. We do it by dealing in images and metaphors, using simple materials and not too expensive detailing. Our vocabulary is space and light and color, and we see buildings not as discrete objects but as part of their physical and psychological settings. To this end we get mixed up with plant materials and grandmothers' heirlooms. We make a fabric for people to inhabit either formally or casually; and if we have done our job well, they enjoy the process of living their lives with heightened enthusiasm.''

HOUSE 29
MLTW/TURNBULL ASSOCIATES

House in Hawaii deals with problems of the tropics

The site for this house is 200 feet from the beach on the northern shore of the Hawaiian island of Kauai. The climate—tropical and extremely wet—and the owners' style of living—outdoor-oriented and casual—seemed to indicate an open, informal, "porchlike" house. Because this region of Kauai is susceptible to *tsunami,* or tidal waves, structures must be elevated; thus the house is essentially an airy pavilion supported by wooden poles, floating amid tropical foliage, open to cooling sea breezes and views of ocean and mountain.

Within this light-filled and airy enclosure, the living spaces of the "inner" house are arranged symmetrically about the north-south axis of the central veranda, which is the core of the house (see plan). Access from ground level is from both sides, responding to the fact that the property itself is bounded to the north and south by two roads, one leading to the town of Hanalei and the other providing access to the ocean. A freestanding stair/planter is stationed at each end of the central veranda; each has a swing-down wooden drawbridge that can be pulled up when the owners are away. Within the central veranda, a stairway topped with a planter leads up on each side to a sleeping/play loft, which forms the roof deck of the two halves of the inner house below.

PROJECT: Davidow house, Kauai, HI
ARCHITECTS: MLTW/Turnbull Associates; San Francisco, CA
AREAS: 1,172 square feet on ⅓ acre
DATE COMPLETED: 1982
COST: Not revealed

SITE WORK
The house sits above the natural landscape, which surrounds it. Landscaping was done by the owners under separate contract.

GRIDS AND MODULES
The spacing of the poles supporting the house sets up a structural module 10 feet on center under the main house; shorter spacings on the perimeter support the encircling porch.

MATERIALS
The poles supporting the house are treated with creosote. Otherwise the structure is Douglas fir. Exterior board siding is ¾-x-4-inch square-edge western red cedar, tongue-and-groove, with resawn face, clear, kiln-dried.

Interior wood finishes and trim are clear western red cedar. Cabinets are hardwood closed-grain face veneer for paint finish with laminated plastic tops.

Exterior decks are covered with a composite Neoprene Hypalon membrane over plywood. Roofing is lapped-seam formed metal panels, 25-gauge corrugated, over bedrooms, living areas, and kitchen. The veranda is roofed with translucent corrugated fiberglass panels. Windows are louvered glass; wooden sliding doors provide access to the veranda and surrounding porch.

CONSTRUCTION TECHNIQUES
To withstand tidal-wave action, floor beams are bolted to 10-inch round poles. Four 12-inch poles reach the roof at the corners of the veranda to support trusses.

INTERIORS
A line of "tilt-up" doors around the inner house shields the living spaces from inclement weather or encloses them for privacy as occupants see fit. When the doors are up, they form a ceiling for the porch, encircling the house. The four quadrants of the inner house then extend all the way out to the lattice porch enclosure, greatly enhancing the sense of spaciousness and openness.

THERMAL COMFORT AND PLUMBING
Heating and air conditioning are generally not required in Hawaii, but backup electrical heating was provided in this house for unusual weather. All ventilation is natural.

LIGHTING
The house is naturally lit through the translucent roof panels during the day. Movable and recessed fixtures supply nighttime lighting.

The perspective view shows the house form in its entirety. The actual house is much more enclosed by the lush Hawaiian vegetation.

Section looking west

South elevation

Above left: The piers that support the first level line up with partitions and structural members above.

Above: Such decorative features as the semicircular plate at the juncture of truss members add appealing touches of whimsy to an otherwise straightforward elevation.

Above: The piles supporting the first floor are relatively inconspicuous because of the vegetation at the base of the house. The central veranda permits sunlight to enter, providing an accent of light.

Right: All rooms in the symmetrical plan adjoin the central veranda, where much of the life within the house takes place. Bedrooms are buffered from the space for privacy.

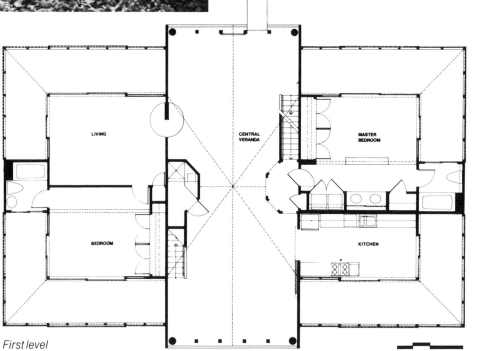

LIVING

CENTRAL VERANDA

MASTER BEDROOM

BEDROOM

KITCHEN

First level

0   5   10

MANAGEMENT AND DOCUMENTS

The architects set up six bid alternates: changing the fiberglass roofing over the veranda to corrugated metal roofing to match the rest of the house, changing the lumber to two different grades, changing the type of tilt-up door, adding a security system, and deleting the prefabricated fireplace. These alternates were intended to give the owners flexibility in selecting options.

The architects included a project closeout section in the specifications. This required the contractor to submit certification that work had been completed in accordance with contract documents and to submit as-built drawings showing the location of all utilities and services, warranties, and evidence of compliance with all inspection requirements of governing authorities.

Numerous job difficulties were related to two main factors: distance from materials sources and communication. Most of the materials had to be shipped in from several thousand miles, and some piece was always wrong or missing.

Communication was also a problem. Even with the telephone it was hard to direct the job. Normally the firm would use a field architect for on-site inspection and answering questions, but could not find one for this project. The result was frustration on the contractor's part and unhappiness on the architects'. Trips were made as required, sometimes at the owner's expense, sometimes at the firm's, depending on the problem being addressed.

The architects urge using a field architect to work out daily problems on a project, to foresee problems and to solve them in advance, to maintain goodwill on the job, and to alleviate frustration.

SPECIAL DESIGN TREATMENTS

The overall form of the house reflects indigenous Hawaiian dwellings.

Above left: Barn doors close off adjacent spaces from the central veranda.

Above: The simple detailing was easily built. Note the pulley for raising the drawbridge.

HOUSE 30
MLTW/TURNBULL ASSOCIATES

House plan suggests Cape Cod vernacular

The site for this house is a protected sand-pine forest overlooking the marshes and estuary of Chappaquiddick Island on Martha's Vineyard. The problem was to create a spacious summer dwelling for a college president, his wife, and their three children. The house will eventually become a full-time retirement residence; the architects therefore had to think in the long term while stretching the short-run budget.

The economical 2,000-square-foot plan encompasses three bedrooms, study, kitchen, and living/dining room. An unusual feature is the first-floor breezeway separating the living/dining/kitchen area from the two first-floor bedrooms, which thus have more privacy. (In summer resorts it is advantageous to provide separate areas for guests and rental use.) Although protected at each end by sliding doors, this 8-foot-wide corridor is otherwise open. The second-floor master bedroom and study are reached by a stairway within the breezeway. This type of plan, common in the South and highly appropriate for New England summers, is excellent for catching breezes through the center of the house.

PROJECT: Edwards house, Chappaquiddick, MA
ARCHTECTS: MLTW/Turnbull Associates; San Francisco, CA
Design: William Turnbull
Job Captain: Heather Trossman
AREAS: 1,600 square feet on 100 acres
DATE COMPLETED: 1982
COST: Not revealed

SITE WORK
A septic system and well were provided. An underground electrical connection was made to a remote electric meter in concealed wood housing.

GRIDS AND MODULES
Trusses are spaced regularly over the living room, 8 feet on center, with supporting 6-x-6-inch posts.

MATERIALS
The materials list includes white cedar shingles over 1-x-4-inch strips on the roof, over rigid insulation, 15-pound felt, and 1-x-6-inch diagonal sheathing on the sides. Windows are wood casements or double-hung; sliding patio doors are aluminum. The barn doors screening the patio are diagonal 1-x-6-inch tongue-and-groove boards on a 2-x-6-inch frame hung on a heavy-duty track protected by a metal cap. The diagonal sheathing boards are left exposed in the interior, seen through the 2-x-4-inch studs.

CONSTRUCTION TECHNIQUES
The lower level is supported on continuous foundation walls supporting 2-x-8-inch floor joists 16 inches on center. A continuous girder up the middle supports these beams and is supported on pier footings 7 to 8 feet on center. Exterior walls are exposed studs 16 inches on center supporting 2-x-8-inch joists 16 inches on center at the second floor. The roof is composed of 2-x-8-inch rafters on 2-x-4-inch exposed stud walls.

Wood trusses are provided 7 to 8 feet on center to support the ridge beam. These scissors-type trusses keep the side walls from spreading as they support the ridge beam. Second-floor bay windows extend 1 foot 2 inches from the main frame and are bracketed above the floor line with diagonal braces 16 inches on center.

This axonometric drawing shows the decorative effect achieved with additional horizontal bracing on the side wall.

INTERIORS

The interiors depend on the exposed structure for their decoration and richness. This type of construction is effective and economical because it makes interior finishes unnecessary. Care must be taken to use good pieces of framing material, not warped or overly split and knotty ones. Carpenters must be advised of this technique early in the project so that they will fasten members together with care.

THERMAL COMFORT AND PLUMBING

No heating was provided other than a wood stove in the center of the living space. Ventilation is natural, facilitated by the long, thin plan with generous window openings on both sides. The two bathrooms are stacked. There is a screened sleeping porch off the second-floor master bedroom.

LIGHTING

Kitchen lighting is a combination of fluorescents and incandescents mounted between the exposed rafters supporting the second floor. Electrical outlets are placed horizontally, centered between studs in a continuous 1-x-8-inch baseboard. This solves one of the difficulties of exposed-structure house construction: electrical wiring, normally run through studs and rafters by the shortest possible route, would be unsightly if left exposed; a builtin raceway is therefore a good idea.

MANAGEMENT AND DOCUMENTS

Five 24-x-30-inch sheets included three architectural, one electrical and plumbing, and one structural drawing. Architectural drawings contained ¼-inch plans and elevations and a ½-inch scale section through the entire house, which served as the main detail drawing. This minimal set of drawings is adequate for a simple house like this one that has no eating or elaborate finish details.

There were no owner problems; however, the contractor's problems included finishing the job after having underestimated how expensive it is to do simple things. The architect's problem was quality control on an island where substitutions are the name of the game and subcontractors can be tyrannical.

SPECIAL DESIGN TREATMENTS

The house expresses New England vernacular through the use of horizontal bevel siding, corner board, and the simple overall shape of the building.

Top: Shingles, corner boards, and exterior rolling shutters are regional traditions incorporated into the design. Besides being still appropriate, the use of these traditional elements is economical, because local builders are familiar with the techniques necessary to construct them.

Above: The open balcony above the kitchen can serve as a study or an extra bedroom for guests.

Above left: Decorative exposed studs and bracing within the house provide nooks for the placement of objects. They also create an appropriate summery ambience.

HOUSE 31
MLTW/TURNBULL ASSOCIATES

Court of house in hot, arid climate provides shelter from the sun

The program for this design was a comfortable residence for a family with three children, two of whom were away at school. One edge of the property, which is an old hayfield in California's hot central valley, is a recent subdivision and vineyard; the other is a public road and tree-lined bank above the floodplain of the Stanislaus River. Summertime temperatures there often rise into the hundreds, and there were no trees on the building site. The solution was an encompassing barnlike gable roof that extends beyond the sides of the building as a lipped porch around a large protected courtyard.

PROJECT: Allewelt house, Modesto, CA
ARCHITECTS: MLTW/Turnbull Associates; San Francisco, CA
AREAS: 3,000 square feet on 18 acres
DATE COMPLETED: 1978
COST: Not revealed

SITE WORK
The architects planned the landscape work, but it was not included in the general contract; the owner later contracted for it separately. The architects' work included layout of extensive tree groves, gravel walks, driveways, and horse stalls and rings.

GRIDS AND MODULES
The spacing of framing is builder's standard 16 inches on center.

MATERIALS
Materials are ½-inch rough-sawn redwood plywood with 1-x-4-inch battens over 15-pound building paper on 2-x-4-inch studs. Interiors are ½-inch sheetrock. The court area is finished with ¾-inch-x-6-inch square-edge tongue-and-groove redwood siding, with resawn face, clear, all heart, kiln-dried.

Interior materials besides sheetrock include clear Ponderosa pine jambs, bases, and casings; Douglas fir windowsills and miscellaneous trim; and red oak stair treads and flooring.

Roofing is wood cedar shingles 16 inches long, 6 inches exposed, over 30-pound felt and ½-inch plywood on 2-x-10-inch joists. Walls and rafters are fully insulated with fiberglass batts. Casements and double-hung windows are aluminum or wood.

CONSTRUCTION TECHNIQUES
The architects used standard building techniques for this area of California, where deep footings are unnecessary because there are no deep and penetrating frosts. The house is built mostly on a 4-inch concrete slab with woven wire mesh reinforcement and thickened edge footings. The dryness of the region and the lack of extended cold eliminated the necessity for roof ventilation, which is required in many other parts of the country.

Redwood plywood siding with battens is common in this part of California because of the proximity of the redwood forests. The atrium is paved with bricks set in sand.

Opposite page: An important component of this design is its relationship to the benign California climate: the house permits easy access to the outdoors at all times of the year.

Above: The architects planned tree groves, walks, and driveways as means of softening the otherwise open site.

Left: The central roofed court is an important element of summer cooling. It provides shade, which draws warm air from the adjacent rooms and sends it out through the open roof.

MBR

ST

ATTIC

ATTIC

BR

The chimneys for the first-floor fireplaces provide lively accents on the roofscape in combination with the freely arranged roof louvers.

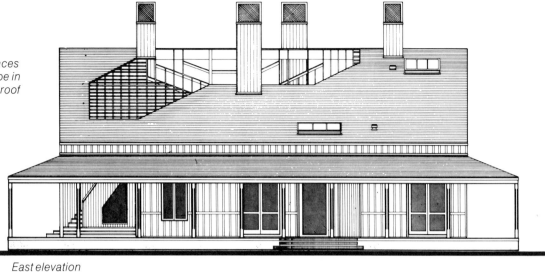

East elevation

The surrounding portico echoes the slope of the main roof. It is differentiated by the break at the juncture with the vertical walls of the house.

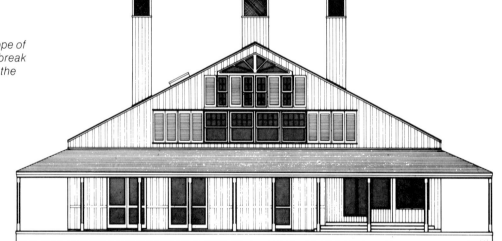

South elevation

Within the central court the windows are freely arranged. The supports for the open lattice above are oversized for a sculptural effect.

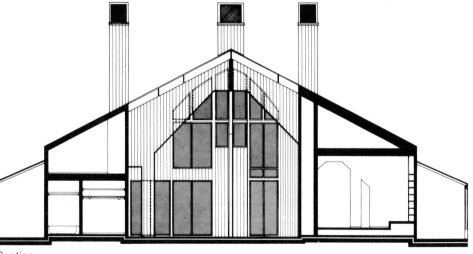

Section

0 1   5   10

INTERIORS

The most important interior space is the roofed court, which is open to the sky but screened from the sun with a decorative pattern of rafters and 1-x-4-inch stripping. Fireplaces are accented with tile surrounds. Interior spaces focus on large assemblages of ordinary double-hung windows. The repetition of such a simple and inexpensive element looks quite dramatic from the interior. On the south elevation, wood shutters on the outside of these grouped windows provide diffused light patterns inside.

THERMAL COMFORT AND PLUMBING

The house is heated by electric air-cooled heat pumps with resistance booster heaters. Two heating/cooling zones are designed for a 45-degree temperature differential for heating and a 30-degree differential for cooling. Ductwork is embedded in concrete below the floors. The use of electic heat pumps is feasible in this warm climate. It can be expensive in other areas, where temperature differentials are 70 degrees or more, because it is necessary to supplement the pump by conventional means at the low end of the heating cycle.

LIGHTING

The decorative sunscreen over the interior garden court provides changing light patterns to all the rooms around it. Sliding wood shutters control strong sunlight on the south elevation. Wood verandas surround the house on all sides and shield sunlight on the lower level. Artificial lighting is wall-mounted or recessed.

MANAGEMENT AND DOCUMENTS

The 24-x-36-inch drawings included thirteen architectural, one swimming pool, and three structural drawings. Specifications on 8½-x-11-inch sheets totaled sixty-six pages arranged in the Construction Specifications Institute (CSI) format, plus fourteen pages of structural calculations required in California for seismic reasons. Supplementary drawings issued during construction consisted of nine other 8½-x-11-inch sheets, covering such items as fireplace details, tile layouts, and cabinet modifications.

The architects worked the job in stages; contractors checked with them on design. Field trips were made every week to ten days, and there were lots of telephone calls. No special difficulties occurred. The contractor was outstanding; his only problem was that his bid was too low. The architects worked closely with him, and he stuck with the job without lowering his standards, even though he lost money. Both the contractor and the principal in charge wanted the job to be right.

SPECIAL DESIGN TREATMENTS

The architects separated the structure into two distinct dwellings unified by one roof. To the north is the grownups' area, including the kitchen, dining room, and living space. To the south are the children's bedrooms and playroom. The center of the house is open at the southeast and northwest to catch and funnel summer breezes; the court thus becomes a cool exterior summer living room while it separates the parts of the house.

The surrounding veranda shades the house from the hot summer sun and gives way to lawn, garden, and pool areas. The house is a layered island of shade and shadow in the hot California sunshine.

Shadow patterns from the freely arranged latticework of the roof create interesting and changing contrasts throughout the day.

MITCHELL / GIURGOLA ARCHITECTS
PHILADELPHIA, PA

Firm utilizes design-team approach

This Philadelphia- and New York-based firm is committed to the belief that architecture is capable of enriching the daily lives of the people who experience it. In their buildings they seek to create a distinctive sense of place that stems from the program. At the inception of a project, staffers are assigned to a design team under the direction of a project architect, who in turn works directly with one of the two principals. This team designs, details, and monitors the construction of a building. It is the firm's belief that this approach assures that the original design intentions will be realized.

HOUSE 32
MITCHELL/GIURGOLA, ARCHITECTS

New kitchen/breakfast area transforms townhouse facade

The owners of a magnificent 1810 vintage townhouse in Society Hill, Philadelphia, wished to replace the 1950-ish kitchen that had been installed in the grandly scaled original front (west) dining room with a new kitchen/breakfast area in the rear yard whose east wall would border the parking lot of other townhouses built in 1967. In the floor plan the architects developed a curved glass wall for the breakfast area, which faces the main part of the house. Privacy is provided by a new brick wall along the parking lot.

PROJECT: Bershad addition, Philadelphia, PA
ARCHITECTS: Mitchell/Giurgola, Architects, Philadelphia, PA
Project Architect: John Lawson
AREAS: 350 square feet attached to existing townhouse
DATE COMPLETED: 1978
COST: $29,500

SITE WORK
The existing kitchen was demolished and the site prepared for the new addition.

GRIDS AND MODULES
None.

MATERIALS
Exterior materials are brick, glass, and lead-coated copper sheathing on the half dome. Interior materials are quarry tile on the floors and sheetrock walls and ceilings, except for the interior of the half dome, which is plaster.

CONSTRUCTION TECHNIQUES
The half dome is the most interesting part of the construction and the most difficult to build. The half circle in plan was divided into twelve equal segments. Laminated plywood ribs were constructed on an 8-foot radius of three ¾-inch-thick exterior-grade Douglas fir plywood ribs. All joints were staggered, and sections were glued with waterproof glue and serrated shank nails.

So that too many ribs did not come together at the peak of the half dome, two 2-x-8-inch headers were installed at 30-degree intervals 2 feet 8 inches from the center of the dome. Shorter ribs were fastened to these at 15-degree intervals. Two layers of ¼-inch plywood were installed on top of these ribs with staggered joints to form the dome's surface. Sixteen-ounce lead-coated copper flat-seam roofing was arranged in a circular pattern.

INTERIORS
Interiors are simply defined with custom woodwork at windows and J beads at the termination of plaster and sheetrock.

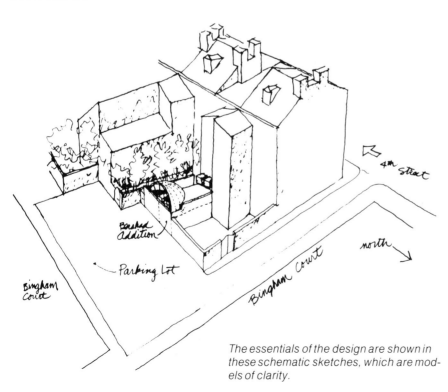

The essentials of the design are shown in these schematic sketches, which are models of clarity.

Looking East

THERMAL COMFORT AND PLUMBING

Connections were made to the main house systems; additional air-conditioning work was needed.

LIGHTING

An indirect light fixture just below the semicircular window lights the half-dome ceiling. Kitchen lighting is recessed in the ceiling; there are fluorescents under the cabinets.

MANAGEMENT AND DOCUMENTS

The plans include three 24-x-36-inch sheets, mostly devoted to construction of the semicircular dome.

SPECIAL DESIGN TREATMENTS

The architects committed themselves to solving the problem of a new addition to a historic house located next to several contemporary houses. Their solution was related to the existing building by the use of brick; the glass fanlight, although not of this scale, was a common component of nineteenth-century house design. The size of the fanlight is a result of the half dome, which is in scale with the existing high ceiling spaces.

Note the amount of information contained in these sections and elevations.

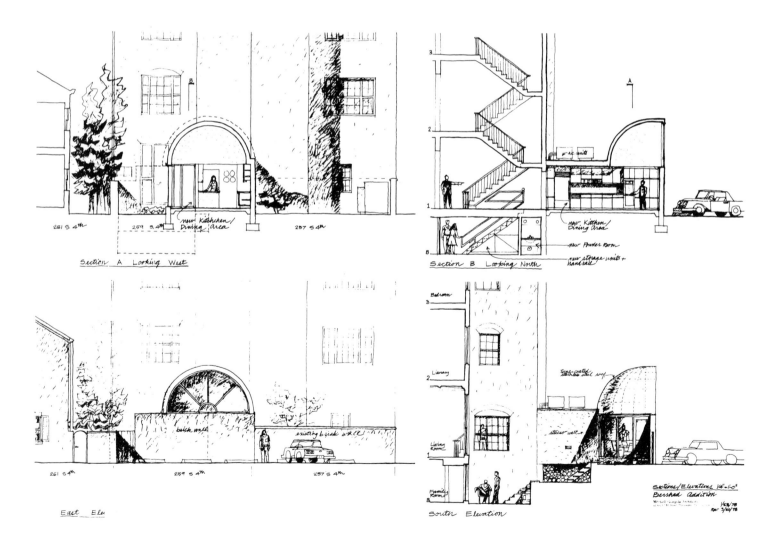

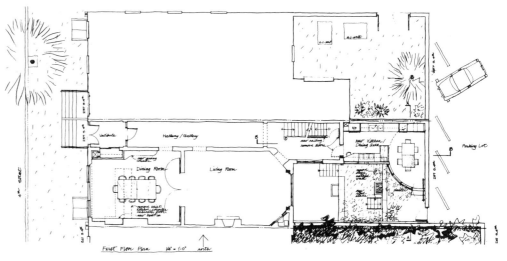

Above: The back of the half-dome over the dining room forms part of the view from the family room. Note the interesting contrast with the towers in the background designed by I. M. Pei.

Above right: The conventional townhouse plan has been transformed by the kitchen / dining room addition, which creates an important view from both the living and family rooms.

Right: The fan window brings plenty of light into the dining room without sacrificing privacy. From the parking lot, it is a striking landscape feature.

HOUSE 33
MITCHELL/GIURGOLA, ARCHITECTS

Budget limitations prompt phased construction

The clients for this house, a family of four—a college professor, a stockbroker, and their two boys, aged nine and ten—have informal living habits and requested an open living, dining, and kitchen area. Budget limitations suggested a program of phased design and construction: the master bedroom temporarily occupies the boys' playroom and will be constructed in phase 2.

The cleared open site is ringed with scrub trees. Development of the site anticipated the establishment of gardens, orchards, and a swimming pool and the construction of a garage, barn, and guest house. Two levels have direct access to grade because the house is built into the gently sloping site. Views of the hills and farmlands from southeast to southwest are the major attributes of this location.

The plan is direct: living spaces on the lower level, sleeping areas above. The attached screened porch provides shade for the terrace on a site that has no natural shade. The windows are placed to take advantage of the spectacular views, admit morning sun, and limit the entry of the afternoon sun.

PROJECT: Kasperson house, Conestoga Township, PA
ARCHITECTS: Mitchell/Giurgola, Architects, Philadelphia, PA
Project Architect: Harold Guida
AREAS: 2,600 square feet on 20 acres
DATE COMPLETED: 1980
COST: $70,000

SITE WORK

The only site work was that needed to gain access to the building site. The owners bought the land in January, hired the architects in the spring, broke ground in August, and moved in on Labor Day. Because construction was so hurried, there were no utility connections when the owners moved in; they used a camp stove for cooking and brought in bottled water.

GRIDS AND MODULES

None, other than conventional builder's spacings of materials.

MATERIALS

The house was built by Amish builders with local materials: red painted wood clapboard siding over a wood frame, standard operable wood windows and doors, and gray asphalt shingle roofing. The screened porch, master bedroom, and fireplaces are plastered with natural-finish stucco. Floors are wood on the lower level and carpeted on the upper level. Interior walls and ceilings are plastered. The fireplace is brick.

CONSTRUCTION TECHNIQUES

Builder's standards were followed in construction, except for walls that don't meet at right angles and the roof, which slopes in two different directions.

INTERIORS

The open floor plan and high ceilings help to expand the modest floor space.

THERMAL COMFORT AND PLUMBING

The central, interior location of the fireplace provides the most efficient heating. Most of the glass is on the south facade; there are no north-facing windows. Backup heat is oil-fired warm air.

LIGHTING

Convenience outlets are provided for floor and table lamps. Builtin wall fixtures are provided in halls.

MANAGEMENT AND DOCUMENTS

The owners did much of the work themselves. They comment: "Architects are not for everybody. The owner, the architect, and the builder have to work together as a team, or you end up living a nightmare until the house is built, and maybe after you move in. You don't start thinking about an architect until you get beyond the $50,000 or $60,000 price range. But you don't have to get much beyond that price before having an architect begins to make sense."

Originally the Kaspersons decided on a budget of $48,000. "The first thing to go was the budget," they said. "We just wanted to do too much, so the cost went up pretty quickly. But we still didn't spend an outrageous amount of money on the house, and the replacement cost and the market value have also gone up."

Using local builders and standard materials held down costs. In addition, the architects provided only design services, not supervision and materials specifications, so their fee was minimized. The clients believe their investment in an architect was worth more money than they paid. "Very often architects' fees will account for 10 percent or more of the construction cost. We didn't pay that much because we did the supervision ourselves, and our contractors did some of the design work. The heating system, for example, was designed by our heating contractor. I did the wiring. And the Amish builder took pains to see that the house was built the way the architect designed it and the way we wanted it."

SPECIAL DESIGN TREATEMENTS

The house is a traditional "bank-barn" type with masonry lower story set into the hill. The large windows make this small house appear big.

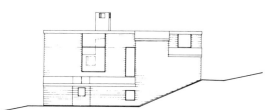

Northeast elevation

Southeast elevation

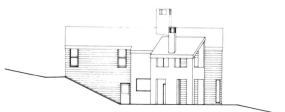

Southwest elevation

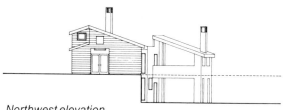

Northwest elevation

Above left: On the entrance facade, which faces north, most of the glass is grouped over the entry.

Above: Elevations show how few openings there are in the exterior walls. These openings relate closely to the building setbacks.

Left: The different orientations of skew elements are further reinforced by changes of material, from horizontal wood planks to stucco.

157

Left: The skewed elements result in a narrowing stair to the second floor that looks much longer and grander than it actually is. Such manipulations of scale in a small house can add complexity to an otherwise simple design.

Above: Brick accents the fireplace / chimney mass. Sculptural niches provide display space for plants and decorative objects.

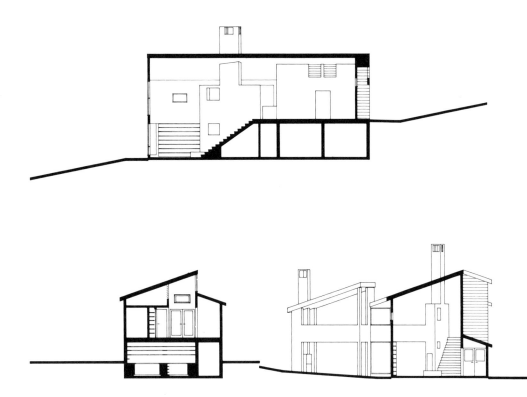

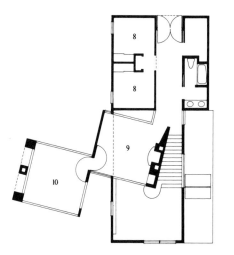

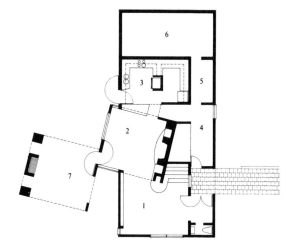

The skewed dining room and master bedroom and their adjacent open pavilion spaces are the predominant features in this simple design.

RICHARD C. TREMAGLIO
CAMBRIDGE, MA

Architect's interest in building explores crafted details and client/tradesman participation

Working with both the client and the tradesman on the job is of great importance to this architect. He says, "My role as architect/teacher/builder has been to prepare a basic design with the clients which during construction may be altered, interpreted, and added to. It is a process of education and building in which client, architect/builder, and craftspeople work together to evolve the final building. My intention is to make inhabitants conscious of their own activities, then to help them interpret the place in which they live, and to encourage craftspeople to share in design and building decisions. The buildings are in some cases highly crafted and in some crudely so. In all cases there is the imprint of those who have participated."

The architect always forces the issue of client participation, in both the design and construction stages. He discusses at length the siting, the relation of the house to the rest of the neighborhood, and the client's program.

Tremaglio outlines desired end results for people such as plumbers and electricians. They generally have specifications carefully spelled out and are not used to interpreting for themselves ways to accomplish the desired installation or finish, but Tremaglio looks to them to take responsibility for some of the design decisions, such as the routing of pipes and conduit and the juncture of floor patterns. This approach has been successful because of the architect's constant presence at the job site and because his subcontractors have been able to judge intelligently which decisions to make themselves and which to refer to the architect.

Tremaglio likes to assemble elements—beams, windows, doors, and the smaller things that surround or subdivide them—thematically within a "field." For example, the idea of a predominantly skew assemblage as expressed in House 35 is carried through in all the parts, including site work. A more rectilinear plan, such as that of House 34, has right angles without diagonals of any sort. The architect believes that the building parts are his vocabulary; the way he uses them, the basis of architectural grammar. Applying this theory results in a do-it-yourself look—basically skew or rectilinear arrangements filled in with crafted wood details and open space planning. The architect has frequently worked on his jobs as a carpenter, designing details as work progresses.

The two houses that follow must be examined in terms of their function in particular lives. The architect's "process" approach—his solicitation of and insistence on the collaboration of client and workers—is successful because it enlists the skills and interest of all parties, which in turn generate quality and efficiency.

HOUSE 34
RICHARD C. TREMAGLIO

Close liaison with contractor is key to complex yet economical house

Unlike the owners of the other houses in this architect's portfolio, the clients for this one wanted to set an initial fixed price and did not wish to participate extensively during the construction process. They furnished Tremaglio with a detailed program, listing room relationships and family activities; then they discussed with him the philosophy of the design. The clients liked another of the architect's houses (House 35), particularly the use of wood, the natural lighting, and the windows, angles, and corners. They also wanted a design with a solid look that would harmonize with the rocky natural landscape of the site. The architect's complex massing in earlier work appealed to them, and they felt it would harmonize with the roofscapes of other houses in Marblehead.

In his previous work, the architect had promoted the participation of his clients and tradesmen as well as the making of design decisions on the spot. When he got this commission, however, he realized that he had to work faster and more efficiently because the clients wished to have the work finished when they moved in. Looking to the future, he also realized that he could not continue to spend as much time on houses as he had previously (three to six years), so he decided to do a more complete set of drawings that would determine the basic plan, structure, and shape of the house. He also predetermined finishes, but detailing was done on the job.

PROJECT: Arena house, Marblehead, MA
ARCHITECT: Richard C. Tremaglio; Cambridge, MA
AREAS: 3,700 square feet on 2 acres
DATE COMPLETED: 1976
COST: $138,750

SITE WORK

The site was left natural, in keeping with the client's request that the house look as if it were part of the site. Water and sewer pipe connections to local utilities were required, and gravel drive was provided.

GRIDS AND MODULES

A grid of 9 feet 8 inches with a 45-degree diagonal was set up. The architect, who also worked as a carpenter on the job, thought that the diagonal of a 9-foot-8-inch square was about the size of beam that one or two workers could handle. The grid also allowed for window and door sizes and placement of a window next to a door.

MATERIALS

Cedar bevel siding, applied over ½-inch plywood and 2-x-4-inch walls, was used on the entire exterior with the exception of terraced areas, which are brick. Interior wall surfaces are ½-inch sheetrock with 1-x-6-inch source-edge base. Roofs are cedar shingles on ½-inch plywood on 2-x-8-inch rafters. Interior sloped ceilings are 1-x-6-inch #2 pine. Good-quality stock wood windows were used.

CONSTRUCTION TECHNIQUES

Standard wood-frame construction was used throughout. The foundation required some stepping to accommodate the rocks on the site.

INTERIORS

Trimmed with wide fir boards, the interiors convey a predominantly natural appearance. Floors are wood or tile. Doors are paneled rather than flush. All details contribute to the richness of the interior.

THERMAL COMFORT AND PLUMBING

Heating is by oil-fired warm air; there is no air conditioning. Plumbing was installed back to back on the second floor, with stock fixtures.

LIGHTING

Generous natural lighting is supplemented by plug strips on wood brackets and track lights. The plug strips are inexpensive and permit ordinary light bulbs to be plugged in wherever desired. When mounted on a piece of trim, they can be decorative as well as functional.

MANAGEMENT AND DOCUMENTS

The drawings were more detailed than those the architect prepared for houses in which he had a more active building role. In this case, ¼-inch plans, elevations, and sections were supplemented with ⅛-inch framing plans and typical wall sections at a scale of 2 inches = 1 foot. To explain the concept to the client, he prepared a scale model and a colored set of drawings.

SPECIAL DESIGN TREATMENTS

An important part of the design is the wealth of detail. The architect notes that there are three orders of details in the house: small, specific details, like window trim; larger details affecting the house forms, like the bay window in the family room and window seat above in a bedroom; and details that builders themselves add, such as baseboard. The bay window/seat occurs where two major walls meet at a corner; although it looks like an addition, it is the result of a geometric crossing at that point.

The building method helps determine many details—for example, placement of a post next to a fireplace, the size and location of trim pieces, and even placement of doors and windows. The cost-saving implications of this approach are hard to quantify because the architect and client must commit themselves to spending a lot of time actually working on the job. Design time may be cut before construction, but it certainly increases on site after construction starts.

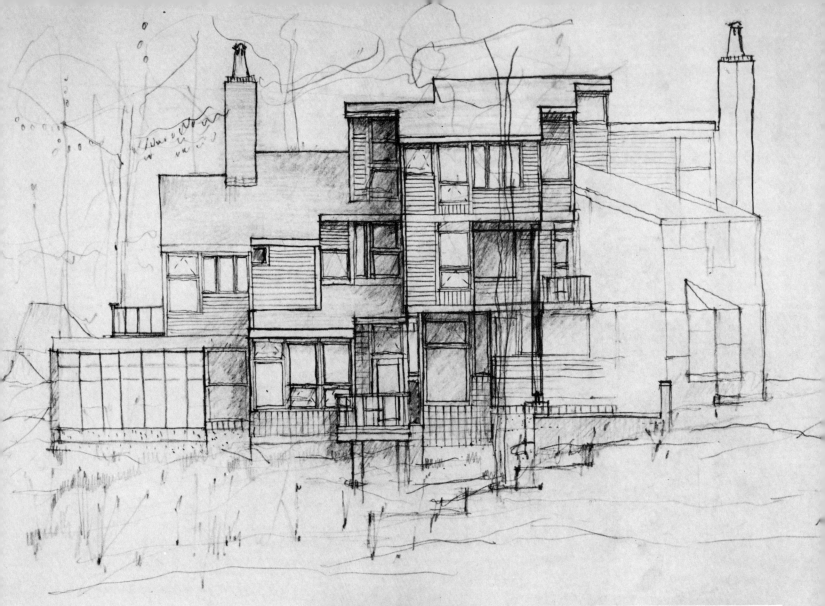

Above: The architect uses sketches like this one to study elevations as well as to present essentials of his design to clients.

Right: Construction of the profusion of gables, overhangs, and window sizes required frequent site visits by the architect to ensure that his design intent was carried out.

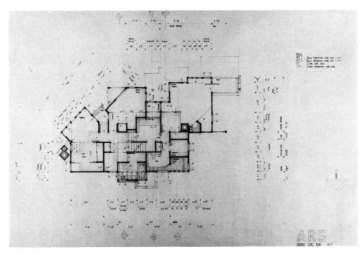

Second level

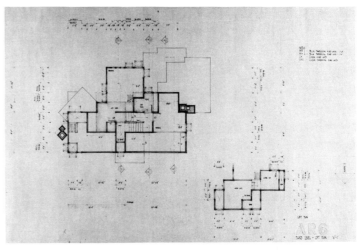

Third level and loft

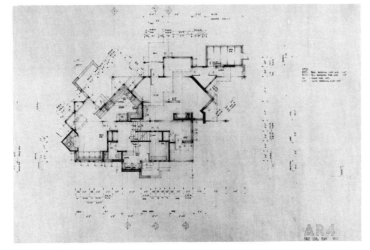

First level

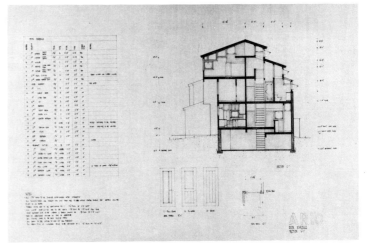

Section

An unusual feature of these rendered plans
is the delineation of awning windows in plan.

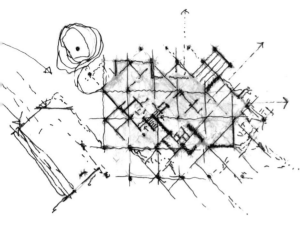

Above: These are office studies for the design.

Right: The row of tiles between wood walls and concrete foundations is an unusual and inexpensive design feature.

Details are important in this design. The wood post shown here, for example, is turned at an angle to the beam it supports, and the wood flooring is wrapped around the post's base.

Bolted connections are exposed in the beam connection to the post. The beams supporting the upper roofs are held up by the wall, but the support function is expressed by short brackets below.

HOUSE 35
RICHARD C. TREMAGLIO

Barn renovation is an assemblage of original, recycled and new materials

For over a hundred years the clients' family had owned this barn. Having long admired it, they finally decided to live there and asked the architect to renovate it. While doing so, they wanted him to keep it as "barnlike" as possible. The client's intention was to preserve the spaciousness of the building (the original structure was 40 x 80 feet) while creating smaller private spaces. They also wanted to preserve the hand-hewn beams and posts and the original·siding, as well as the simple elegance of the space.

The owners described the work process as follows: "Within the framework of the overall plan provided, we all worked out the details of design together, often by standing in the barn and actually marking off spaces with boards on the floor. We made windows wherever we wanted air, a view, or more light. The original barn construction provided the original framework for added structural beams placed on the diagonals moving between bays. New levels were added. The central fireplace complex took shape as a source for the geometry of the new construction. Many details were sketched out on the scraps and ends of the boards as we wandered around the building talking and planning.

"The location of major living spaces was determined by the sun and the predominant southwest breeze.

"Working on the diagonals of the building offers continuity and movement from one area to the next. Spaces are not clearly defined as to use but lend themselves to different functions. Cooking, eating, visiting, reading or special projects, and children's playing all occur in the same general area without segregation. The only totally private rooms are bedrooms, bathrooms, the laundry, and the dining room."

PROJECT: Burnes house, New England
ARCHITECT: Richard C. Tremaglio; Cambridge, MA
AREAS: 3,200 square feet on 5 acres
DATE COMPLETED: 1974
COST: $50,000, plus owners' labor

SITE WORK
Since this was an existing building, only access roads, paths. and connections for utilities were required.

GRIDS AND MODULES
New work was organized on a 45-degree diagonal within the basic 13-foot-6-inch column grid of the existing structure.

MATERIALS
In addition to the existing palette of materials in the barn, recycled old materials, such as windows and lumber, and new materials, such as windows and fixed glass, were used.

CONSTRUCTION TECHNIQUES
The post-and-beam construction of the original barn was preserved, and additions were made in a similar way. Heavy plank floors and tile were used in the interior, and the exterior was sheathed with beveled siding. Stud-wall construction was used for secondary infill.

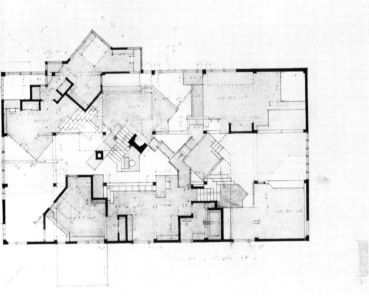

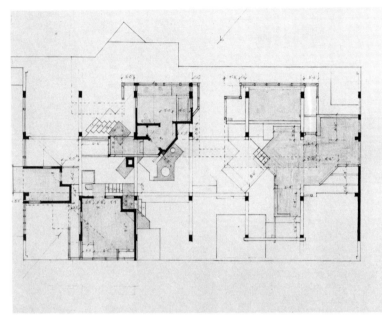

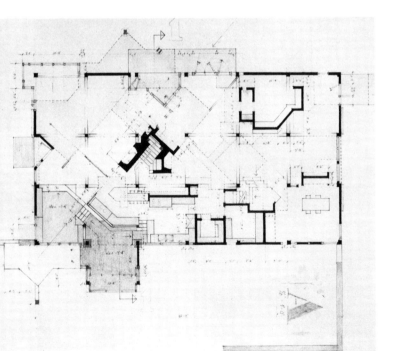

Above and left: These drawings are prints of the original plans, which were colored with pencils. They also served as presentation plans to clarify the various levels for the client as well as working documents while the house was under construction.

Opposite page: Posts and bracing members are expressed on the exterior. Stock windows are set in groupings of fixed glass.

It is virtually impossible to detail such a pro-
lific assemblage of elements completely. Instead, the architect must, and in this case
did, spend a lot of time on the site.

Minimal drawing such as this provides the
basis for field decisions.

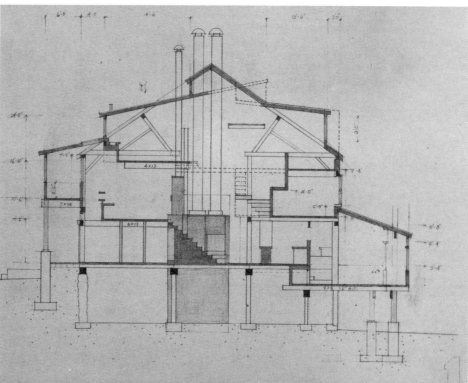

The interior is an ornate assemblage of posts, beams, stairs, connections, and household objects.

Following page: Informal groupings of furniture, personal mementoes, and everyday objects fit easily into this environment.

INTERIORS

Rough natural fixtures predominate. Heirloom furniture and country objects are placed casually, reflecting the busy texture of exposed beams, both old and new. The overall appearance is a rich assemblage of handsome, well-aged natural materials.

THERMAL COMFORT AND PLUMBING

Heat is supplied by oil-fired warm air; there is no air conditioning. The routing of plumbing required careful planning within the exposed structure of the interior.

LIGHTING

The multiple windows provide natural light, supplemented by floor and area lamps.

MANAGEMENT AND DOCUMENTS

The four drawings reproduced on pages 167 and bottom 168 are the only ones the architect produced for the renovation. They indicate simply the scope of the project and major structural decisions; everything else was decided on site by the architect, working in residence, and the owners. The clients did a lot of the work themselves, ranging from hammering subfloors through sanding, staining, and grouting tile.

SPECIAL DESIGN TREATMENTS

Exterior additions are picked out with red shingle roofs to distinguish them from the existing structure, shingled in black. Recycled materials, from the owners' collection, range from structural timbers to turned columns, barn siding to polished oak balustrades, lacy Victorian grates to marble sinks. The exposed construction gives a strong impression of roughness and durability.

HARTMAN-COX, ARCHITECTS
WASHINGTON, DC

Architects work with site and adjacent buildings to achieve compatibility

The work of Hartman-Cox, centered mainly in the builtup Washington, DC, area, is not primarily residential. Most of the firm's commissions have been for buildings in restricted metropolitan or suburban areas. Many of the sites have been problematic, including the one for the project shown here.

The Washington area, unlike many other U.S. cities, has a strong neo-classical architectural tradition. Hartman-Cox is frequently called upon to produce designs that blend with this tradition to satisfy clients and design review boards. Since they have chosen to follow their own personal design direction, they continue the scale and quality of the neighboring buildings in unique ways.

HOUSE 36
HARTMAN-COX ARCHITECTS

Privacy concerns in carefully zoned suburban house

This small corner lot, thought to be un-buildable, has an entry point off an attractive alley cul-de-sac at its inside corner. There are major highways on two outer sides of the lot. The house is in a high-density sub-division of good neocolonial houses.

The first problem was providing the privacy that the lot lacked. The second was planning three separate areas that could be reached without passing through the others: a suite for mother and grandmother, a bedroom and bath for a college-age son, and living and dining areas and kitchen. The yard was fenced to provide for privacy and pets.

The architects designed three courts, entered off the cul-de-sac, with maximum closure to the outside and linked, open spaces inside. There are two wings, pitched at right angles to each other. The south wing contains the suite for mother and grandmother on the ground floor; the son's bedroom is over that. The east wing houses the living room, dining room, and kitchen, over which are the son's bath and a storeroom. All areas can be entered directly from the stair hall. A small courtyard is off the dining room and kitchen and another is off a bedroom.

PROJECT: Phillips-Brewer house, Chevy Chase, MD
ARCHITECTS: Hartman-Cox, Architects; Washington, DC
AREAS: 2,500 square feet on 9,000 square feet
DATE COMPLETED: 1968
COST: $61,000

Right: The design concept can be understood in this photograph: shed roofs stepping down toward the rear and intersecting on the diagonal, starting at the entrance and terminating at the rear garden.

Opposite page left top: The setback line cuts across the enclosed garden; this was permissible within zoning regulations. The architects were thus able to close the composition at this point, while providing areas required by their program.

Left middle and bottom: A series of open spaces is arranged on the diagonal, proceeding from the entry, to the hall, to the court, and finally to the rear garden.

SITE WORK

On-site gravel parking and a brick entrance patio were provided. Site grading was restricted to the entrance area. Utility connections were made underground to gas, sewer, water, and electrical lines.

GRIDS AND MODULES

None.

MATERIALS

The materials consist of 1 ⅛-inch-square battens 6 inches on center over ⅝-inch exterior-grade plywood over ⅝-inch sheathing. Providing battens closely spaced over plywood eliminated an aesthetic concern about having plywood on the exterior; the battens cover the joints and break up the scale of the wider sheets of plywood. Plywood can also look wavy when subjected to oblique sunlight; the battens eliminate this visual effect. The exterior materials of board and batten were selected because brick was too expensive.

Major interior materials are ½-inch sheetrock and ⅝-inch plywood; carpeting was supplied by the owner. Roofing is wood shingles over ½-inch plywood.

CONSTRUCTION TECHNIQUES

The framework is wood, 2 x 4 inches, on a concrete masonry unity foundation over a crawl space. Holes were drilled through the roof rafters to provide ventilation above the insulation. Exterior wooden doors and fixed glass are set in wood frames. Shields and perservatives applied to wood members in contact with concrete and within 1 foot 6 inches of grade provide protection from termites.

INTERIORS

Kitchen cabinets are epoxy-coated Douglas fir. The entrance hall, paved in brick, features a white-painted circular stair leading to a small landing hall at the top, which is painted flamingo red. The library is paneled in red oak and is reached by two steps down from the hall. The dining room has a double-height ceiling and glass wall opening to a brick-paved dining courtyard.

Right: A large skylight sheds light on the vertical mass of the fireplace.

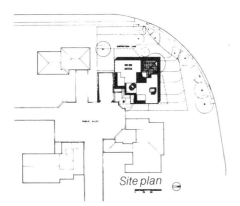

Site plan

Second floor

First floor

THERMAL COMFORT AND PLUMBING

Heating is by gas-fired warm air; air conditioning is central.

LIGHTING

Exterior fixtures in the courts are standard molded aluminum lamp holders dressed up with a wooden enclosure. Interior lights are wall-mounted metal cylinders and recessed fixtures.

MANAGEMENT AND DOCUMENTS

Documents consisted of nine 24-x-36-inch sheets with ¼-inch-scale plans, elevations, and sections. Selected details at 1½-inch scale were shown.

Allowances were called out in the drawings for the vacuum-cleaning system ($400), circular stair ($700), mailbox and house number ($50), finish hardware ($700), tree removal ($100), and prefab fireplace ($400). These allowances, although totaling only a small percentage of the budget, are important, because they can be indeterminate at the time of bidding (such as required tree removal) or difficult to decide upon quickly (such as hardware or the circular stair).

Other items such as the builtin vacuum-cleaning system are price-competitive, and the contractor would not have the time to shop for the best price when bidding; the owner can usually buy these items more cheaply.

SPECIAL DESIGN TREATMENTS

The house takes its color, scale, pitched roof, and broken massing from its neighbors, and its diagonal plan from the corner site. The courtyards provide privacy on the tight lot. The intent was to design a house that was specific to its site and compatible with its neighbors.

The gently sloping roofs are carried up to the giant tree in the garden court. The location of this tree was an important design consideration.

The detailing of the small garden court recalls the batten detail of the building skin.

BOHLIN POWELL LARKIN CYWINSKI
WILKES-BARRE, PITTSBURGH, AND PHILADELPHIA, PA

Varied means are used to accommodate special circumstances

After becoming as familiar as possible with their clients' needs and desires and with the nature of a particular site, these architects search for simple means and details to achieve rich emotional effects. They often accomplish this by developing a modest concept for the building that relates to the particular qualities of the site and then deliberately warping elements within the design to fit particular circumstances and requirements. In combination with relatively economical materials and construction techniques, this no-holds-barred approach results in an eclectic mix of elements ranging from slick pipe rails to classical columns and industrial windows.

Set in a forest, House 39 (Bohlin residence) is the oldest of the three houses shown here. It is a simple green-stained shed modified with unexpected industrial elements, color, and a carefully controlled sequence of spaces. Recently the architects have become more eclectic and nostalgic in their references to childlike gabled house forms and rural imagery. Traditional elements of house architects such as windows, stairs, columns, and fireplaces are used to intensify the emotional qualities of Houses 37 (caretaker's house) and 38 (Gaffney residence). The resulting buildings are skewed, slightly unfocused, and soft-edged, as are childhood memories. Using such deceptively simple means, these houses gain strength both from thoughtful relationships to their sites and from rich spatial qualities and a sensitive handling of sunlight.

In a time of shrinking budgets, these architects have generally used the same relatively straightforward detailing for each house. They have explored the decorative possibilities of simple millwork details, varying their width, shape, and color. One of the most important means the architects have used to enrich their houses is one of the most modest: color. Color can emphasize potent elements, heighten their symbolic or allusive qualities, and strengthen elements that mark territory or movement. Color also emphasizes or changes the apparent scale of elements, masses, and spaces.

HOUSE 37
BOHLIN POWELL LARKIN CYWINSKI

Small house is part of larger complex, saving on construction coordination

This small residence was designed to accommodate the staff caretaker/naturalist at the Shelly Ridge Girl Scout Center, an 84-acre nature preserve just north of Philadelphia city limits. It was to be grouped with a maintenance facility, a garage, and an existing barn.

The program called for the equivalent of a two-bedroom apartment, an office for the caretaker's administrative work, and a bathroom to serve office visitors and those using the adjacent maintenance building. The first floor accommodates the office and public bathroom and the living/dining/kitchen area of the residence. Tucked inside the gable are two bedrooms and a bath.

The first floor is organized around a wood stove whose hearth is surrounded by four columns arranged in the manner of a baldachino. The ceiling between the columns is open to the second floor, so the stove's heat rises through the central well of the house. The bedrooms have shuttered interior windows to this well, and the bathroom draws light from it through interior windows.

An entrance vestibule provides direct access to the office and a water closet. The undercut entrance, with its bench for waiting visitors, is linked to the adjacent maintenance facility by a wall that continues into the latter's entrance while serving as a fence to set off the caretaker's private outdoor area.

PROJECT: Caretaker's house and office, Springfield Township, PA
ARCHITECTS: Bohlin Powell Larkin Cywinski; Wilkes-Barre, Pittsburgh, and Philadelphia, PA
AREAS: 1,068 square feet on 84 acres with other buildings
DATE COMPLETED: 1981
COST: $87,000

SITE WORK
Part of a larger complex of buildings, the house is worked into a grassy clearing. Other than restoring the damage caused by construction, landscaping is limited to encouraging the growth of indigenous vegetation to provide privacy for the yard and the seasonal planting of simple gardens.

GRIDS AND MODULES
None were used, other than spacing of beams and framing members.

MATERIALS
The exterior is a mixture of stained wood clapboards, vertical siding, and shingles, the same materials used in all the site's buildings.

CONSTRUCTION TECHNIQUES
Techniques were builder's standard, with the exception of trim and detail features such as the chair rail that drops down in a geometric pattern to pass under and integrate with wide window trim, salvaged wood columns, and custom windows. Walls are framed in 2 x 6s for additional insulation thickness, and rigid insulation is applied on the inside.

INTERIORS
Cabinetwork and details were finished with carefully selected subtle colors, particularly where they emphasize important features such as the baldachino hearth and the sun dormer. The baldachino columns and trim are painted several dark green tones. The area surrounding the sun dormer is a peach color; pale gray wood trim surrounds the window.

An unusual decorative detail is the exposed beams supporting the second floor under the open walkway above. When those same beams pass the enclosed rooms, they are covered with sheetrock to provide acoustical insulation and to hide plumbing and wiring. These details are effective, yet they are economical because they rely on standard materials put together in a simple way and enlivened by color.

A garden plot and some ornamental shrubs align with the two square windows above.

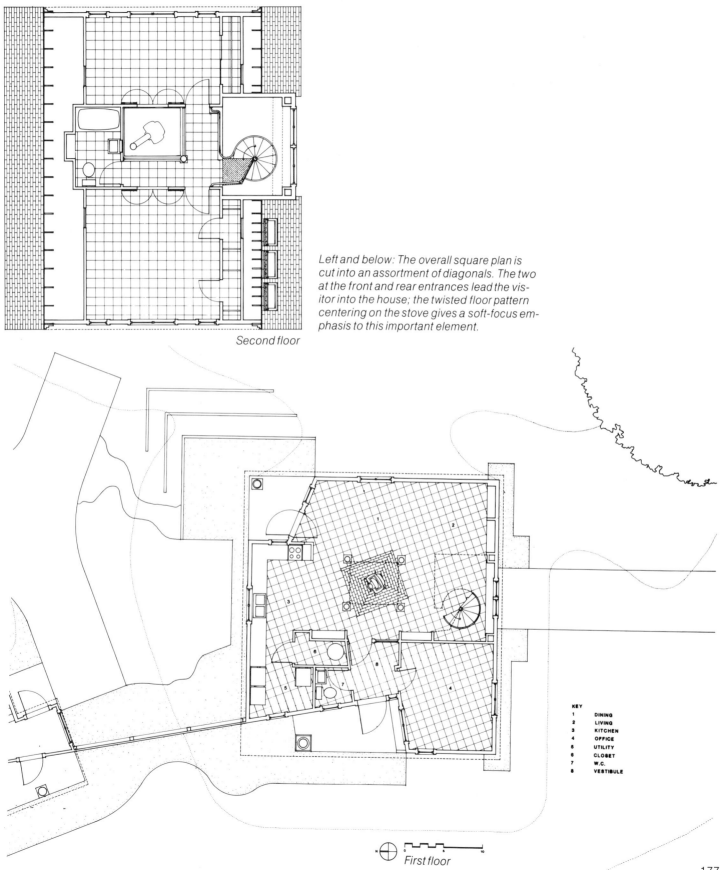

Left and below: The overall square plan is cut into an assortment of diagonals. The two at the front and rear entrances lead the visitor into the house; the twisted floor pattern centering on the stove gives a soft-focus emphasis to this important element.

Second floor

KEY

1	DINING
2	LIVING
3	KITCHEN
4	OFFICE
5	UTILITY
6	CLOSET
7	W.C.
8	VESTIBULE

First floor

An example of the straightforward detailing of the buildings can be seen in this rear view of the maintenance shed.

THERMAL COMFORT AND PLUMBING

The central well of the house promotes air circulation and extends to form a large south-facing gable with overscaled windows. These windows are covered at night with insulating shades and in daytime admit sunlight to provide about 15 percent of the house's heat. They are set in a thickened wall that accommodates the shades and conducts warm air from a fan at the top of the dormer back down to the living area. The house is heated by the wood stove with backup electric heat. The upstairs bath is situated above the kitchen, simplifying plumbing runs.

LIGHTING

Wall-mounted adjustable fixtures are provided for illumination of specific features such as the well and dormer windows. Lighting elsewhere depends on convenience outlets or recessed fixtures.

MANAGEMENT AND DOCUMENTS

Because the house was part of a larger project, drawings were incorporated into the set that included the other buildings. Plans were drawn at a scale of ⅜ inch = 1 foot. A typical detail drawing included sections of other buildings. All aspects of the house were managed as part of the larger scheme, thereby cutting the amount of time the architects had to spend on this portion of the job.

SPECIAL DESIGN TREATMENTS

Although the residence is not tailored to a particular individual's needs, it is adapted to the organization's goals and to the site. The Girl Scout Council wished its buildings to be special, yet simple and modest. One overriding concern was the expression of a positive attitude toward nature, energy, and the sun, motivated as much by educational and philosophical reasons as by economics.

Cutaway axonometric drawing shows the complexities of the interior balcony, column, and railing relationships.

Right: An axonometric drawing shows the relation of all buildings in the composition.

Below: The relationship of the house to the adjacent service buildings is visible in the elevation.

Bottom: The long wall screening the entrance to the maintenance building leads visitors to the office in the house.

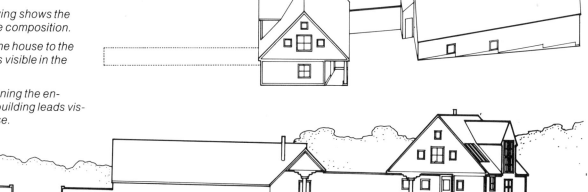

0   20   40

West elevation

Above: The second floor reveals a bracketing of the sheetrock at the sides of the windows to add thickness to the wall, which is needed for the exhaust fan.

Right: Four columns surround the woodburning stove and its skewed floor pattern. The sheetrock covering the underside of the floor above is partially cut away in a decorative curve, which is echoed by a similar curve in the handrail above.

HOUSE 38
BOHLIN POWELL LARKIN CYWINSKI

House is built within stone barn foundation

This house is located on an old farm in Chester County near Philadelphia. The client, a bachelor, grew up on a farm in Wisconsin and spent several years with the Peace Corps in Peru and the Philippines. His program called for spaces defined not so much by function and area as by mood, feeling, and atmosphere. He wrote of childhood memories of the farm, of predilections for courtyard gardens such as he had seen while abroad, and of a feeling for "openness with privacy." His ideas provided the key to the architects' approach; the site determined the plan.

The stone foundation of a burned barn, set on a knoll overlooking a meadow to the southeast, was located near the southwest corner of the 9-acre rural site. Like most other barns in the region, it faced south into a courtyard enclosed by lower stone walls. After carefully studying the possibility of building on the foundation, the architects decided that they could best fulfill the client's requirements by building within it, using the walls both as part of the house and as part of the courtyard.

The house is scaled in miniature, but the profile and construction of the house are derived from the local farmhouse vernacular. The plan and section are arranged so that spaces are open to the exterior yet visually private within. The three-story building is 13 feet wide at its upper story and is placed 4 feet away from the existing stone walls on its west and north faces. A glazed slot skylight intensifies the relationship between the house and the previous barn's stone walls by clearly separating them.

PROJECT: Gaffney house, Coatesville, PA
ARCHITECTS: Bohlin Powell Larkin Cywinski; Wilkes-Barre, Pittsburgh, and Philadelphia, PA
AREAS: 1,430 square feet on 9 acres
DATE COMPLETED: 1977
COST: $68,000

SITE WORK
Other than required utility connections and the garden, no site work was undertaken. The house is approached from an existing farm lane that terminates in a small grass parking area. A path leads to the front entrance between existing stone walls at the building's west face. Care was taken to relate the house to the local landscape; for example, the small raised garden at the end of the entrance walk is seen at eye level just outside the kitchen window and is a reference to the surrounding farm landscape.

GRIDS AND MODULES
None, other than standard spacing for framing members.

MATERIALS
The exterior is gray-stained vertical wood siding over 2-x-4-inch wood studs 16 inches on center. Interior walls are mostly covered with drywall. Steel and concrete columns, pipe rails, and wide wood trim are mixed with the wood frame. Windows are wood residential units; where greater openness was desired in the living room, steel industrial sash were installed. The roof is covered with red asphalt shingles.

CONSTRUCTION TECHNIQUES
The builder's standard wood frame was built within the barn foundation. Special areas such as the kitchen and entry have a glass roof that rests on the existing wall.

INTERIORS
Soft colors are used on such elements as the steel columns, the pipe rails, the steel corner window, the entry door, and the exposed framing under the balcony and cabinetry. The balance of the drywall and simple wood-trimmed interior is painted in shades of gray.

THERMAL COMFORT AND PLUMBING
A cylindrical wood stove on the first floor is backed by a decorative striped brick-and-block wall, which also forms a recess for the metal chimney that extends upward to the third floor, visually strengthening the stove and masonry mass. The masonry not only protects the wood framing from the stove and flue; it also acts as thermal storage. Because of the wood stove, the house's sheltered position within the barn walls, and its predominantly south-facing glazing, the building requires a small amount of fuel.

LIGHTING
Adjustable wall and ceiling lighting is provided where overall illumination was desired. Task lighting was installed where needed, recessed over kitchen counters or with desk and floor lamps.

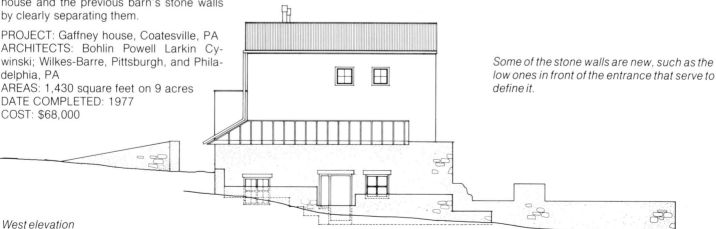

Some of the stone walls are new, such as the low ones in front of the entrance that serve to define it.

West elevation

Right: Some spaces borrow light from other skylit interior space, while others look across a void to see through a remote window.

Below: Some of the openings in the barn were reused, such as the main entrance and the other two windows visible in this view. Also shown is the glass roof bridging the gap to the walls on the north and west, which makes the house appear to be free-standing.

Section

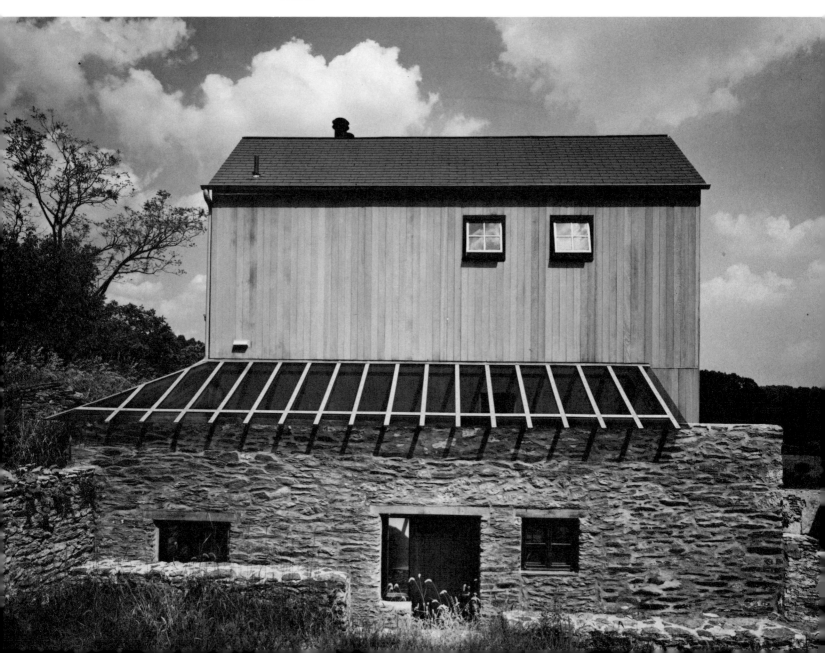

MANAGEMENT AND DOCUMENTS

Documents for this project were completed in a straightforward manner. The project was bid and the low bidder, a local contractor, was selected. The owner did a substantial amount of work himself, which reduced the overall cost.

SPECIAL DESIGN TREATMENTS

The building has been "adjusted" in various ways. For example, the kitchen and stair were set at an angle to turn the stair toward the view and to enlarge the kitchen space. Steel pipe columns, gloss-painted light green and rose, support the "box" at the kitchen and cutout wall across from the entrance door.

An angled oak "barn beam" supports the second floor between the dining and living spaces, permitting a round concrete column to extend freely for two stories. This column is placed at the pivot point of a glazed corner of gray-blue painted steel sash facing across the court to the southeast view of meadow and forest.

A slick gray-painted steel pipe rail surrounds the second-floor balcony overlooking the living area, which is furnished with a variety of wicker chairs. The trim band at the second-floor line and balcony edge is painted a pale gray rose. The stair rising through an L-shaped slot in the third-level den floor reinforces its "attic" quality.

The den has a slightly askew false end wall incorporating a desk, a small bookcase, and storage. The proportions of the multihued wall are slightly distorted, as are other elements in the house. The desk overlooks a tall, narrow space extending up from the bedroom below, and its shuttered window lines up with a square exterior window overlooking the entrance lane.

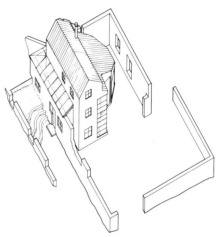

Axonometric

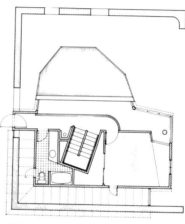

Third floor

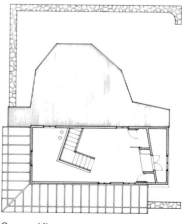

Second floor

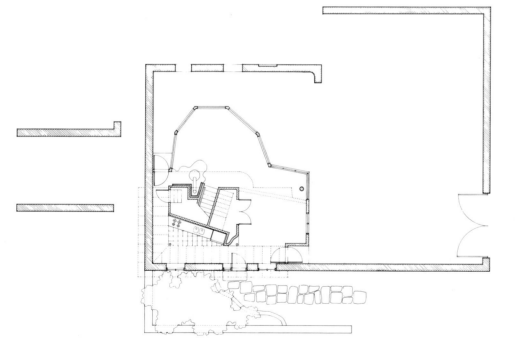

Above and right: The house sits mostly within the walls of the old barn foundation, but it rests on them on the north and west. There is a glass skylight over the kitchen.

Top: The house can be seen from the approach road through a gap in the stone walls. The road was left in its rustic state, appropriate to this design in its recall of farm tradition.

Above: From the entrance door, seen at the left penetrating the stone wall, a continuous passage leads to the kitchen at the back or to the main living spaces, which are in the foreground.

Right: Some of the architects' design quirks can be seen in this view: the concrete column left with exposed formwork, or the rough beam supporting a portion of the second floor. The steel tube railing and industrial sash add further variety.

HOUSE 39
BOHLIN POWELL LARKIN CYWINSKI

Summer house for architect's parents called for simplicity

This residence was planned for summer and weekend use by a retired couple. The requirements were a living/dining space, kitchen, master bedroom with bath on the living level, and a guest bedroom with bath. They wanted a den that could be used as an overflow space for guests, particularly children. No garage or car shelter was needed.

PROJECT: Bohlin house, West Cornwall, CT
ARCHITECTS: Bohlin Powell Larkin Cywinski; Wilkes-Barre, Pittsburgh, and Philadelphia, PA
AREAS: 1,800 square feet on 18 acres
DATE COMPLETED: 1974
COST: $81,000

The long entrance walk leads to the house over the forest floor. An industrial lighting fixture marks the beginning of the walk.

SITE WORK

The 18-acre site is located on a forested hillside facing northeast and extending along a paved rural road. The upper portion of the site is covered with mature evergreens; the lower extends into woodland. A gravel access road, septic well, and electrical hookup were required.

GRIDS AND MODULES

None, other than standard spacing for framing members.

MATERIALS

The exterior is sheathed in tongue-and-groove cedar siding stained green to match the surrounding forest. Three concrete columns that extend up through the building are painted dark red; the remainder have been left natural. The steel industrial sash at the living-area window wall and stair have been painted dark red; all other metal window frames have a black factory finish. The roof is corrugated aluminum.

The interior drywall and wood trim are painted in light gray tones, and the oak flooring is stained gray. Exterior wood decks are treated with a gray bleaching stain that matches the color of the forest's weathered gray granite boulders.

CONSTRUCTION TECHNIQUES

Construction of the residence consisted of conventional wood framing supported by Sonotube-formed concrete piers. Some materials, such as the corrugated aluminum roofings, are uncommon in houses, but installation is within the ability of the average house builder.

INTERIORS

The 16-foot-wide building is organized on two levels, with a shed roof pitched up to the southeast sun and all spaces oriented in that direction. The living room extends to the roof and is glazed with steel industrial sash painted dark red; the den overlooks this space. The dining area also faces a deck and a forest clearing. The kitchen extends beyond the face of the building toward the sun under a glazed roof. The stair connecting both levels is fully glazed from landing to roof with steel sash painted dark red.

THERMAL COMFORT AND PLUMBING

Because it is a summer home, primary emphasis was placed on summertime comfort. The large expanses of southeast-facing glass are shaded by trees, and there is much cross ventilation. The two bathrooms are stacked to simplify plumbing.

LIGHTING

Adjustable fixtures are provided for illumination of specific features. Lighting elsewhere depends on recessed fixtures or convenience outlets.

MANAGEMENT AND DOCUMENTS

The documents for this project were completed in a simple, direct fashion. The contract, with a local contractor, was negotiated on a cost-plus basis.

SPECIAL DESIGN TREATMENTS

This house gains much of its strength from a sensitive relationship to the natural landscape. It is a simple, modestly sealed building that has been modified by various devices to make it seem richer and more comfortable. These devices include the use of such out-of-the-ordinary elements as the steel industrial sash and such small details as the shedlike glass skylight for the kitchen and the careful "wrapping" of the deck around existing trees. The most important of these devices is the use of color.

The dark red used for various items such as the RLM lighting fixture at the entrance bridge, the three columns, the entrance door, and the steel sash marks potent elements in the progression from the dark evergreen forest through the house to the sunlit deciduous forest at its far end. Conversely, the green-stained exterior has a chameleonlike quality, making the house seem to disappear in the forest when viewed from a distance. Similarly, the soft neutral gray of the interior takes on the changing qualities of the reflected light from the surrounding forest.

Right: Color is used dramatically on the exterior. The house itself is stained dark green; the round column in the corner is painted red.

Opposite page top left: The simple long, rectangular plans are modulated by diagonals in the floor plan of the living room, a kitchen projection, and a slice into the plan for the entrance walk.

Top right: The penetration of winter sun and the blocking of summer sun are illustrated in the section drawing. Warm air is vented within the enclosure via the high windows.

Below: The simply furnished den overlooking the living room can be converted into an additional bedroom. Built-ins are located along the low end of the shed roof in a space that is otherwise not sufficiently high for standing.

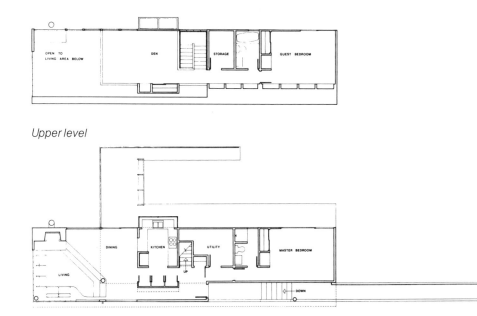

Upper level

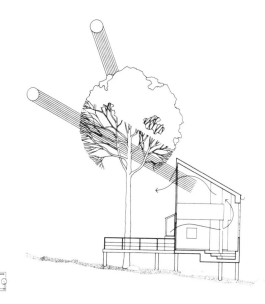

Lower level

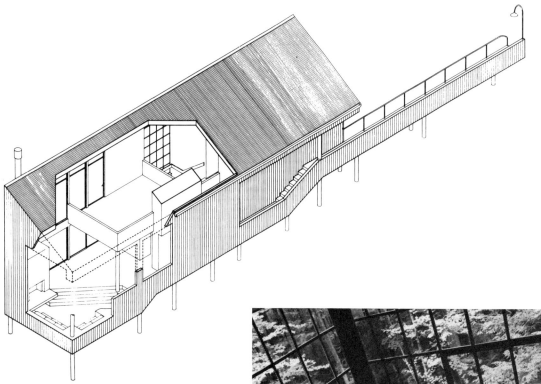

Cutaway axonometric drawing reveals relationship levels with bottoms of exterior walls.

Right: The high living room is opened to the forest with a tall grouping of industrial sash. Built-ins are used to make the most of the small space. The broad diagonal steps are useful for additional informal seating.

MORPHOSIS
LOS ANGELES, CA

Architects' system of aesthetics stresses complexity

This team of architects, Thom Mayne and Michael Rotondi, makes a point of using simple, inexpensive materials such as asphalt shingle siding in a richly decorative way. The materials are inexpensive to the point of cheapness, but the architects assemble them uniquely, lifting them above their mundane connotations. They also focus on the assemblage of parts by using working drawings that detail them (below); windows, stairs, and levels are expressed on the exteriors. Careful detailing makes their buildings out of the ordinary.

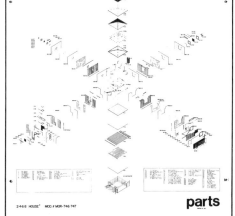

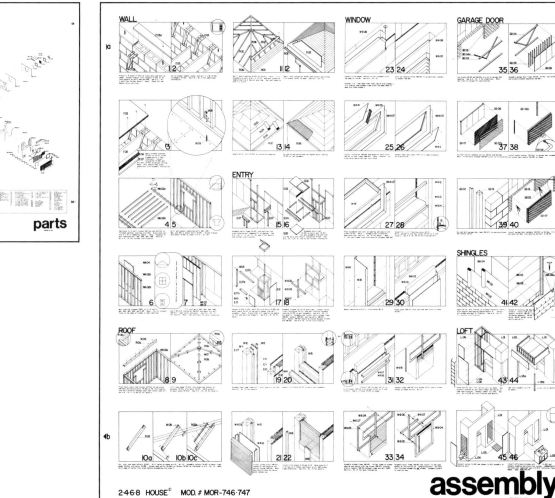

HOUSE 40
MORPHOSIS

Studio addition incorporates kit of parts

This project is a studio space added to an existing 1920s beach bungalow. The client desired privacy, a room removed from the main house that could be used for a broad range of activities.

The architects produced drawings that document the project in a format that the client could easily understand. The two posters shown on page 189 catalog the building materials and describe the step-by-step assembly. These were the major means of communication between client and architect.

In order to respond to the client's request for a retreat, the architects conceived the studio as a detached house behind the existing residence. The building is one space, with a modest provision for kitchen and bath, over a two-car garage.

PROJECT: 2-4-6-8 house, Venice, CA
ARCHITECTS: MORPHOSIS; Los Angeles, CA
AREAS: 324 square feet on top of a garage on a 30-x-80-foot site
DATE COMPLETED: 1981
COST: $26,000

Despite the use of ordinary materials, the house achieves a striking presence in the neighborhood.

SITE WORK

The building is on the site of the owner's house. All utilities were connected to the house system.

GRIDS AND MODULES

The house was designed as a kit of parts, documenting and explaining the project in a straightforward, easily understood way.

MATERIALS

The base is a concrete slab; concrete-block walls are laid in alternating bands of pink and gray. The upper floor is a wood frame covered with asphalt shingles. The structure of the roof is steel and wood, topped with metal-standing seam roofing. The exterior has wood windows with a wood handrail; a wood slat fence provides privacy for the yard.

CONSTRUCTION TECHNIQUES

The wood frame of the upper story rests on the concrete-block base. It is built of 2-x-8 studs rather than the normally used 2-x-4 studs because the architects wanted deep reveals around the windows. Although the reveals were not necessary from a structural standpoint, the additional cost was minimal and was worth the price in its effect on the design of this simple house.

Roof rafters are graduated in size and connected to the steel ridge members with metal plates.

INTERIORS

The main room upstairs has 12-foot-high walls and a pyramidal peak rising to 18 feet. The materials are handsomely crafted. The variation in window size is an important design feature (the name of the house, 2-4-6-8, derives from the sizes of the square windows). The views in four directions through these windows result in a striking effect with little impact on the budget.

THERMAL COMFORT AND PLUMBING

The building is neither heated nor cooled mechanically, but rather depends upon the windows for heat, cooling, and ventilating. The sun is controlled through external motor-operated blinds. The space is naturally ventilated by manually operated lintel/vents on three sides and a hatch over the entry. Water is heated by the solar collector panels.

LIGHTING

Lighting is natural or supplied by floor lamps.

MANAGEMENT AND DOCUMENTS

The owner and architects served as general contractors during the two years of construction. Two posters (shown on page 189) were drawn to document the assembly of the kit.

SPECIAL DESIGN TREATMENTS

Scale is manipulated by the progression of window sizes. Within, all walls are the same size, but the window sizes vary. Outside, the sills are all at the same height, but headers drop and widths decrease, causing rooms to look as if they might be much higher within. Frames and mullions are proportioned to the window size.

On the exterior a yellow cross is superimposed on the window frames. Above the cross is a blue lintel, which tilts for ventilation, and a red scupper extending only slightly beyond the lintel. These strong colors contrast with the variegated grayness of the asphalt shingles. On the west wall, the largest window (8 x 8 feet) incorporates a balcony entrance and a stair leading to it.

Right: The isometric rotates the house and shows the relationship of adjacent walls on all four quadrants.

Below: This drawing shows the plan and exploded elevations, as well as an ant's-eye view of the roof construction.

Following page, above: The windows are graded up from the smallest (shown left) to the largest (right). All are located in the same-size wall, displaying an interesting scale variation.

Below: The sills of the windows are at the same height on all four walls.

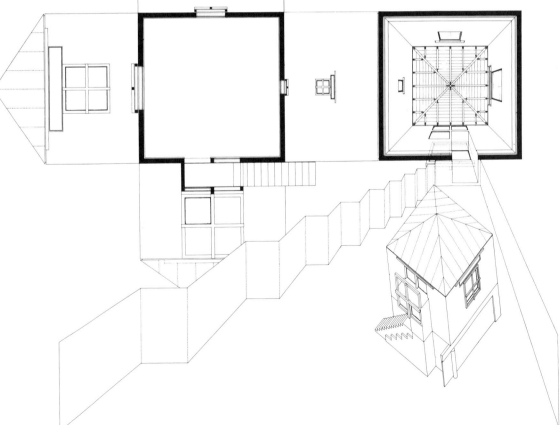

HOUSE 41
MORPHOSIS

Detached library/studio seems larger through manipulation of scale

The Sedlak library/studio/retreat acts as a visual end to the backyard of a typical suburban house. As in House 40, the living spaces are placed above the garage facing an alley, but this house differs in its inward focus and the wall that will eventually become a garden green wall. The green wall will be complete when the vines planted at the base of the scored west wall cover it completely, leaving bare only the metal-clad top part of the building.

The facade is divided horizontally into a plaster base scored diagonally, a middle band of horizontal siding, and a metal cap with vertical ribs. These material separations overlap irregularly on all elevations except the west so that there are no conventional endings of different materials; thus the expanse of each seems greater.

PROJECT: Sedlak addition, Venice, CA
ARCHITECTS: MORPHOSIS; Los Angeles, CA
AREAS: 700 square feet, plus 600-square-foot garage
DATE COMPLETED: 1981
COST: $70,000, including all built-ins

Below: The elevations show the patterns and material changes that manipulate the scale to make the house appear larger than it is.

Far right: This cutaway elevation study of the interior reveals the continuity of the roof rafters with the wall structure.

SITE WORK
All utilities were connected to those of the main house.

GRIDS AND MODULES
None.

MATERIALS
The materials list includes stucco, horizontal redwood siding, and standing seam metal roofing on a wood frame. Interiors are sheetrock with custom cabinetwork.

CONSTRUCTION TECHNIQUES
The wood frame of the upper story rests on the stuccoed concrete-block base of the garage, overlapping it on wood piers that are also covered with stucco. Walls are conventionally framed. The interior of the metal-clad portion on top of the house is covered with plywood. The roof rafters are pinned to the wall studs with bolts, and the members are held together by tie rods every 13 feet to keep the sloped ceiling from spreading the walls.

INTERIORS
The interiors reveal natural wood shelving and an exposed ceiling and loft structure. Doors are painted a bright yellow; the irregularly shaped window at the top of the loft is painted purple; Sheetrock walls are painted white. Flooring is gray carpet. The interior is keynoted by careful detailing, such as the joints connecting the loft structure to the wall: steel support brackets attached to the wall within which the loft beams are bolted.

THERMAL COMFORT AND PLUMBING
No heating or air conditioning is provided. French doors permit through-ventilation.

LIGHTING
Two industrial fixtures are hung below the loft. Lighting is otherwise natural, with many windows on all sides.

MANAGEMENT AND DOCUMENTS
A conventional set of working drawings was produced. The architects served as general contractors for the owner during the 11-month construction period.

SPECIAL DESIGN TREATMENTS
The architects have manipulated scale and surprising elements to differentiate the inside space from exterior elevations. The change of materials works with false perspective to make the small structure look larger than it really is. The stair, for instance, is skew in plan, the lower risers being wider than the upper ones. The thickness of the garden wall and its overscaled scoring pattern make the small house seem as if it must be a part of a giant complex.

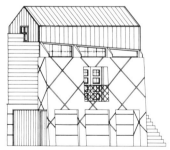
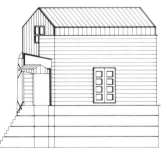
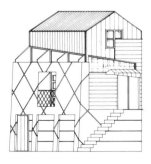

Top: The horizontal divisions consist of a plaster base scored diagonally, a middle band of horizontal siding, and a vertically ribbed metal cap.

Above: The window at the top is painted purple; the door is bright yellow.

Right: The false perspective of the stair and the thickness of the garden wall distort perception of the actual size.

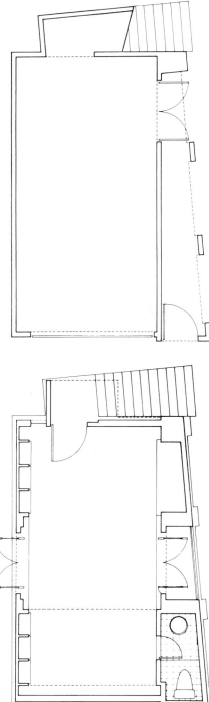

Left: The interior is distinguished by careful detailing, such as the steel brackets that connect the loft structure to the wall.

Above: The scale distortions can be seen in the plans: the gently narrowing stair to the second floor and the deep wall and arcade below that vary in depth.

FRANK O. GEHRY & ASSOCIATES, INC.
SANTA MONICA, CA

Inexpensive industrial materials, left unfinished, are applied to conventional construction

This architect noticed that most houses look more interesting before finishes are applied. From his interest in common rough materials and as a result of working with some tight budgets, Frank Gehry has evolved a technique of combining raw industrial materials such as corrugated metal, unfinished plywood, and chain-link fencing with unusual shapes and spaces.

The success of this unique approach depends on the designer's ability to juxtapose unfinished materials with windows and doors, mechanical equipment, and areas where finish is required or desirable. An important factor is the joining and fastening of materials. Exposed, unfinished construction is normally unacceptably rough because of the lack of care in nailed connections and run-of-the-mill structural members. It is possible, however, to use additional care with connections and material selection at very little premium in cost.

HOUSE 42
FRANK O. GEHRY & ASSOCIATES, INC.

Two-unit house on a narrow lot expands vertically

The site is a narrow interior lot near the beach, bounded on one side by a three-story brick apartment building and on the other by one-story residences. Costal Commission requirements set the program as a two-unit project with off-street parking for four cars. The owner, a single person, intended to live in one dwelling and rent the other. Each unit was designed to be self-contained and private, with outdoor terraces and decks.

The two units evolved into two compact boxes, separated by an open court in the center of the lot. A gate and walled passage on one side lead to the front unit, intended for rental, and open to a walled garden. The two-level, mostly open spaces are pierced in the center by a large angled skylight open to the ground floor. A roof terrace is shielded from the rear by a wall. The passage on the opposite side leads to the private central court and the owner's apartment. The rear unit rises higher, as a three-story, 50-foot tower relating to the mass of the apartment next door and providing ocean views from the roof terrace. Stacked one above the other are a garage, living area, and roof deck.

PROJECT: Spiller house, Los Angeles (Venice), CA
ARCHITECTS: Frank O. Gehry & Associates, Inc.; Santa Monica, CA
AREAS: 2,700 square feet on 30-x-90-foot lot, plus 200-square-foot garage and open on-site parking for three additional cars
DATE COMPLETED: 1980
COST: $200,000 for both units

SITE WORK

Connections to city utilities and paving for access were required. The building is set back within its own property lines; no site preparation along the lines was required.

GRIDS AND MODULES

None.

MATERIALS

The exterior wall material is primarily unpainted galvanized metal siding. Stud walls and roof framing have been exposed where appropriate: behind window glazing, at some wall and stair locations, and at skylights. Unpainted plywood is used on the bay that projects from the rear unit into the court. Above it, a skylight window extends vertically to enclose an open stair leading to the roof deck. Interior finishes are painted drywall; unpainted exposed wood ceilings; and plywood, carpet, or tile floors.

CONSTRUCTION TECHNIQUES

The structure is a concrete slab on grade with a conventional wood frame. Glazing is fixed, applied directly over the studs or operable and fitted between them. The corrugated metal siding was conventionally applied directly to the studs.

Skylights were installed directly on top of the exposed structure. Sheetrock finishes were brought up to the exposed structural frame around window, door, and skylight openings and finishes with J-bead corners. A good reason for this is the difficulty of fitting stock windows and doors within a conventional stud frame without an unsightly gap around the edges. Carpenters generally allow rough openings slightly larger than the actual window or door dimensions and shim around them to get a tight fit. Unclosed gaps would be unsightly and would permit air infiltration.

INTERIORS

Painted sheetrock contrasts with the exposed studs and floor joists. This combination of smooth finish and rough members accents the decorative quality of the structure. Light from unexpected sources enhances the quality of the space by casting shadows of the structure on finished walls.

These sections, taken from the working drawings, show the exposed studwork.

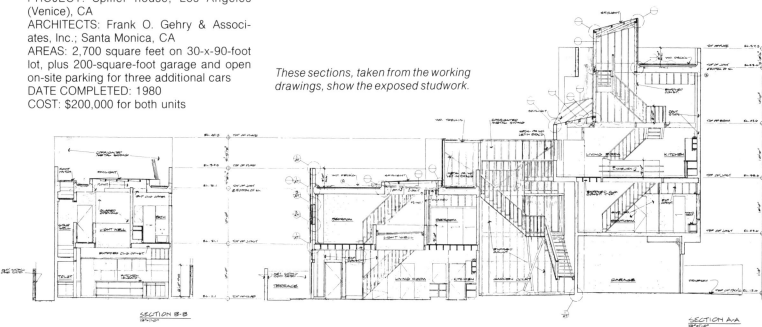

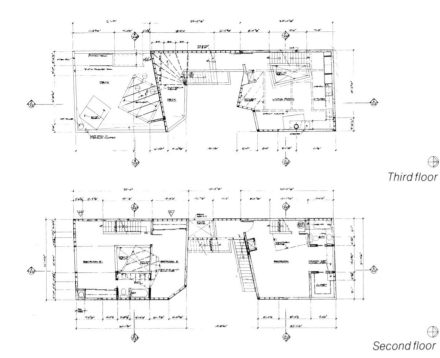

Third floor

Second floor

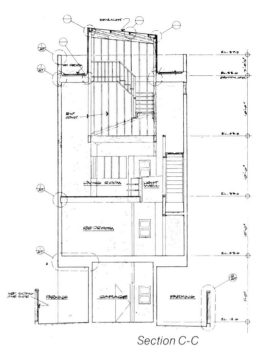

Section C-C

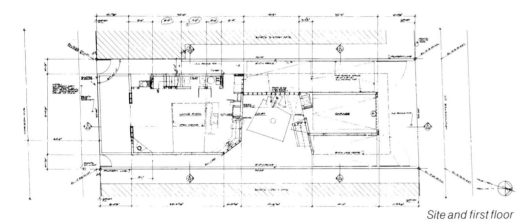

Site and first floor

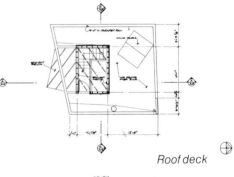

Roof deck

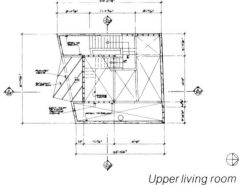

Upper living room

Other than the perimeter walls, which follow the lot lines, most of the interior walls are irregularly placed.

THERMAL COMFORT AND PLUMBING

Heating is with forced-air gas-fired units. Solar panels on the roof of each unit heat water.

LIGHTING

Artificial light is provided with an exposed outdoor spotlight mounted to junction boxes fed by an exposed rigid conduit.

MANAGEMENT AND DOCUMENTS

The building was constructed from a complete set of working drawings, which included ¼-inch scale plans, elevations, sections, details, and specifications. To keep architectural costs down, the client took on much of the coordination responsibility, working closely with the contractor and limiting the architectural supervision time to a minimum. The contractor was challenged by the unusual nature of the project, taking special care with the exposed studs and glass detailing.

SPECIAL DESIGN TREATMENTS

The corrugated metal exterior avoids looking industrial because of the location and sizes of windows and skew skylights. The interiors manage to look finished partly because of the placement of selected exposed structural details, mostly designed to be seen through windows and skylights. This layering of forms adding to the spatial illusions being set up.

Left: The exterior is clad with unpainted galvanized metal siding. The domestic hot-water collectors, facing the optimum direction for solar gain, provide a sculptural accent at the top of the building.

Above: On the rear elevation, the entire wall is skewed from the perpendicular.

Structural connections, such as the one seen here where the short beam butts into the two beams in the other direction, are accomplished with steel shoes, rather than normal joist hangers. Care was taken to avoid visible hammer dimples at nailed connections.

Finishes are stopped at points that make it clear that the arrangement of materials was the designer's intent.

HOUSE 43
FRANK O. GEHRY & ASSOCIATES, INC.

Three "for sale" artist's studios on narrow lots emphasize security

The program called for three inexpensive units on a 40-foot-wide lot in Venice, California, to be sold as condominium-artist's studios. The surrounding neighborhood is run-down, so security for the occupants was a prime consideration.

Three detached two-level "boxes" were lined up front to back within the long, narrow site, enclosed by a high-security fence. Two of the three units have direct access from garages; the third is entered from a walled access walkway. The two front spaces have two levels; the rear, one level over the garages.

PROJECT: Three artist's studios, Venice, CA
ARCHITECTS: Frank O. Gehry & Associates, Inc.; Santa Monica, CA
AREAS: Total 4,500 square feet for three units, plus 800 square feet for garages (six cars), on 1/5-acre sites
DATE COMPLETED: 1981
COST: $220,000 ($73,330 per unit)

The rain leaders are diagonal accents on the side walls.

SITE WORK
The state Costal Commission required off-street parking for two cars per unit. Sewer, electrical, and water connections were also required.

GRIDS AND MODULES
None.

MATERIALS
Exterior materials, different for each of the three boxes, are inexpensive asphalt shingles, unpainted plywood, and stucco. To keep costs down, interior spaces are unfinished shells; owners will finish and subdivide the interiors according to their own individual requirements.

CONSTRUCTION TECHNIQUES
Ceilings and Sheetrock walls were left unpainted, and no finish was applied to the plywood subfloors. The inside of the stepped form in one unit, originally to be covered with drywall, was kept exposed because during construction the architects saw it that way and liked it.

THERMAL COMFORT AND PLUMBING
Interiors contain only a minimum bathroom, stub-outs for kitchen equipment, wall heaters, and electrical outlets.

LIGHTING
Skylights and windows provide generous natural lighting, important to the artists who will be the owners. Occupants will provide artificial light.

MANAGEMENT AND DOCUMENTS
The building was constructed from drawings that included ¼-inch scale plans, elevations, sections, details, and specifications. The building was designed so that in only a few places (all on exterior) was careful workmanship required. The architects supervised the project. The same contractor built this project and the earlier residences shown on pages 213–215. Construction time was only four months.

SPECIAL DESIGN TREATMENTS
The units have a spacious character appropriate to their use as artist's lofts. The inexpensively finished and unfinished interiors are well suited to artists' desires to change their surroundings. The high ceilings, large windows, and skylights were designed to permit the construction of mezzanines and additional levels. Outside, the inexpensive asphalt shingles, stucco, and plywood finishes reflect the character of the neighborhood. The stucco colors pick up the shades used on adjacent buildings: pale green, blue, yellow, and even pink. The intent was to blend in rather than to upstage the surroundings.

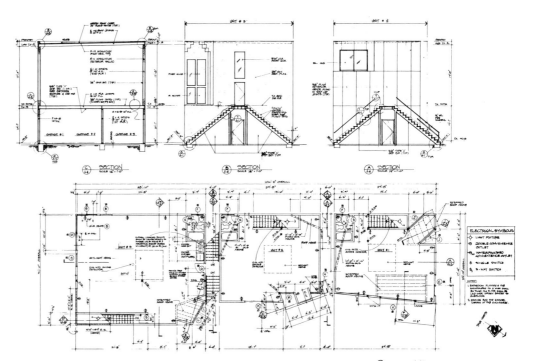

Second floor and sections

The architects pack their drawings with essential information.

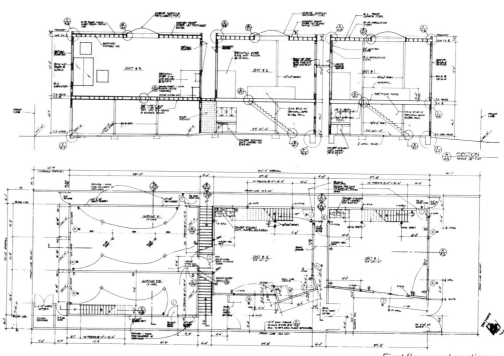

First floor and section

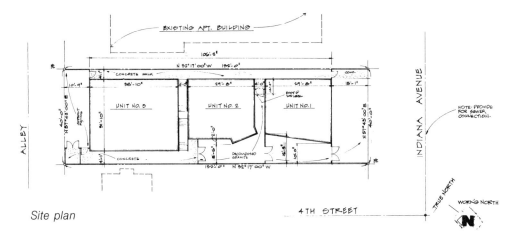

Site plan

Above left: The three units are separated from each other by the minimum fire clearances.

Left: Views are framed in unusual ways.

Top: Oiled plywood is the exterior finish material.

Above: Sheetrock within the units was spackled but unpainted, and floors were left unfinished, so that occupants could finish these areas themselves.

203

CHAPTER 4

HOW TO MAKE A PROFIT

The major question for architects who design houses is whether doing so can be profitable. Architects are underpaid in comparison with other professionals such as doctors, lawyers, and accountants. The reasons for this lie in the American tradition of architectural practice as an avocation rather than a legitimate business. During the early years of this country, architects were amateurs who derived their principal income from other business ventures or from the process of building itself—such as the seventeenth- and eighteenth-century carpenter-architects who constructed buildings based on pattern books from England. This tradition has led to some dilettantism and poor business practices, often among the small firms to whom most house design falls.

What is the remedy? The best path to profitability is to make the most of one of the talents that attracts architects to their profession in the first place: the ability to plan. The task of the architect is to plan buildings, starting with a blank piece of paper and working toward a solution that will satisfy clients' programs, fit their budgets, and fulfill everyone's aesthetic aims. The same sort of planning applied to the financial side of the business—analyzing how your office runs and then allocating time and money carefully—will enable you to make a profit.

HOW TO NEGOTIATE A FEE

The place to start improving your profitability is the negotiation of a fee. You must accept the proposition that your clients are entitled only to what they pay for; let them know this early in the game, as tactfully as possible. You must also decide that you are able to meet their needs adequately with a simple, direct design that will be handsome and efficient and that this design can be provided within your fee.

It is necessary first for you to determine what your clients want. In house design, some clients want a "statement" by a talented designer that will get published and win design awards. Others want no more than a simple, cost-effective, energy-efficient enclosure. Practically all clients who seek the expertise of architects want something out of the ordinary. Few, however, are wealthy enough or willing to subsidize the architect's efforts with a 25 percent fee in order to get it.

To tailor the fee to the clients' expectations, ask the following questions:

- Are the clients looking for in-depth service—design guidance for the smallest hardware and landscape decisions—or do they want the plans necessary for building-department requirements with perhaps an attractive facade as a bonus?
- What special services do the clients require? For instance, in energy-efficient houses, are they interested in a computer analysis of the annual energy use of the house, and are they willing to pay for it? Services of this sort, whether you provide them yourself or through consultants, may well justify a higher fee.
- Are the clients interested in an unusual arrangement such as a guaranteed price and a bonus if you come in at budget or even below it? Such approaches require a careful analysis of program and cost at the beginning of the job and are not recommended for architects who cannot say "no" to program expansions that force budget adjustments.
- Is the initial program on which the fee is based realistic? If you do not think so, a percentage arrangement will protect you from program expansion and contingent extra work.
- Whom have the clients interviewed among your colleagues? If you keep in touch with your peers, you can get an immediate idea of what the competition is asking.

Once you've determined what the clients are interested in and what you're competing with, you can ask for your fee in several ways:

1. A percentage of the total cost is one of the oldest and best ways. The main problem with it is that the clients may doubt your desire to hold costs down, because you will make more money by exceeding the budget.

2. A lump sum is an arrangement that all clients like once they accept it, but you'll have to watch your time carefully and explain that you've based the sum on a certain number of hours. Try to stipulate renegotiation of the fee if there are problems such as a design review board or an extended construction period that will require more of your time.

3. An hourly rate works well if you can negotiate it. Few clients like it, but some architects insist on it. It certainly makes the client aware of your time and more careful of wasting it. A ceiling on the maximum amount may be reasonable.

4. Some architects charge on a square-foot basis. They generally run "plan service" offices that make stock plans available to builders. Modifications to the plans are made on a time or negotiated lump-sum basis.

If you've presented the various fee options that you think will give you a fair profit and the client tries to negotiate a lower fee, you have two options:

1. Try to explain that your time on the job will cost something and you'd like to do the best possible job. If the client adamantly requests a lower fee, try to determine whether the services the client requires are of a lesser scope than you'd normally provide. If not, you should then decide whether you are prepared to cut the time required in your customary search for the best possible design and give the client what he or she is paying for.

2. Turn the job down. This is hard to do if you want or need the work, but you should carefully assess the clients and ask yourself if they are prepared to let you lose money. If you think so, it is far better to turn them down at this stage. If you do not, you may need a lawyer's assistance later on.

Many house designers get calls requesting a "set of plans." If you are set up to provide this service, you can quote your normal rates. If not, you can explain that their interests may be better served by spending more on the services of an architect to do a custom design that will fit their program and site.

The pitfalls of negotiating a fee are numerous. You will be well armed, however, if you have determined in advance what your lowest possible production costs are so that you can hold that as a nonnegotiable position.

HOW TO IMPROVE PRODUCTIVITY

Negotiating an adequate fee is only one side of the profitability question. Its partner is efficiency in the office, which increases productivity. Here are some ways to do that:

· Condense the drawings as much as possible. It is reasonable to expect that a good house builder will be able to understand standard wood or masonry construction. If you deviate from standard practice, however, you must be prepared to do more drawings, make more explanations, and participate in the building process. You should evaluate whether these departures from standard building practice are desirable; if not, reduce the time you spend drawing details that any builder would do by habit anyway.

· Improve your interoffice communications. Establishing a system or module that will enable staff members to understand one another will save time. For instance, a modular system on graph paper will enable everyone to interpret rough sketches.

· Better communications with clients will help. Find out early if they are able to visualize the design from plans, sections, and elevations. If not, build a model. The effort is frequently repaid because it averts later misunderstandings of what the design looks like. You should make model building an optional extra and charge for it separately from your fee, but recommend it when you think it is necessary.

· Although many house designers are unable to spend time writing letters, it is important to document design and budget decisions on paper. Try to get in the habit of writing letters or design memorandums that summarize design decisions and their effect on the budget. A photocopy of your notes with a typed transmittal is adequate.

· Builders are generally specific about their needs, and they do not need detailed drawings. Their main reason for coming to you is the realization that good design does not necessarily save money but will increase the salability of a house and justify the money spent on producing it. Most builders know their costs far better than architects; try to find out early what the builder regards as important in cost-saving measures. For example, many builders will try to eliminate unnecessary doors or pass them along as optional extras. Others want floor joists and rafters sized to eliminate cutting. When you find out these things, gear your efforts accordingly.

NONFEE APPROACHES

Approaches other than conventional ones of determining your compensation are worth considering. Here are some ideas:

· Design/build requires either equity capital or labor. In either case, you must have enough cash from other sources to survive; and you must be prepared to wait for the sale of the house to recoup money spent. If it is available, design/build can be profitable. The most common example of this arrangement is a speculative house—the architect buys a piece of land and builds a house on it, using his or her own capital, a partner's, or the bank's. This can work, provided that the lot and house are a suitable combination that will sell for more than the initial investment. The major pitfall is the architect's tendency to put more design effort and money into the house than will be recoverable in resale.

· Another kind of equity position is a partnership with a prefab manufacturer. The proposal from such manufacturers is usually a percentage of sales or a lump-sum fee on each sale. In general, you should turn down these deals, unless the manufacturer is well established and has strong financial backing. Most prefab outfits in the United States have failed because of poor marketing or overly large overhead costs. The companies that have prospered, such as the one illustrated in this book—and there haven't been many— have done so through a combination of astute marketing, careful cost control, and good design.

· Operating a plan-service office requires a large initial outlay of time to build up a variety of plans. You must also have a connection with plan publishers who will get your designs sufficient public exposure. It is also possible to publish your own catalog of plans, which you can advertise in the widely circulated housing magazines. Charges for plans are low, but architects who have wide exposure can do well financially with them.

SUGGESTED PLAN FOR BUDGETING FOR A PROFIT

Break your estimated fee down into the various components of services. Using the American Institute of Architects (AIA) format, 35 percent goes to preliminary design, 40 percent to construction documents, 5 percent to bidding, and 20 percent to construction observation. If you are more efficient in one of these phases, the proportions can be changed.

Using a fee of $12,500 as an example, you should first deduct 20 percent as your margin. This is a reasonable target of profitability and will also serve as your contingency. This leaves approximately $10,000 with which to produce the job. Thirty-five percent of this, or $3,500, is allocated to preliminary design, 40 percent ($4,000) to contract documents, and so on.

The next step is to analyze each phase in terms of man-hours, being careful to allow for office overhead and mandatory employee benefits, such as Social Security. Direct technical personnel expense is usually multiplied by 2.3 to allow for overhead and benefits. Charge separately for principal's time.

A typical breakdown might look like this:

Preliminary design	**$3,500**
Principal: 20 hours x $100	$2,000
Staff: 65 hours x $10 x 2.3	$1,500
	$3,500

Contract documents	**$4,000**
Principal: 15 hours x $100	$1,500
Staff: 65 x $10 x 2.3	$1,500
Consultants: direct expense + 15%	$1,000
	$4,000

Bidding	**$500**
Principal: 2 hours x $100	$ 200
Staff: 13 hours x $10 x 2.3	$ 300
	$ 500

Construction	**$2,000**
Principal: 5 hours x $100	$ 500
Staff: 65 hours x $10 x 2.3	$1,500
	$2,000

Profit and contingency	**$2,500**

This format is only one of many available. You should try to do a similar time and money breakdown for every project.

The main purposes of this chapter are to suggest a working plan for profitability and to describe the hazards that surround it. There are other approaches; the important idea is to learn to plan your finances.

DIRECTORY OF ARCHITECTS, CLIENTS, AND LOCATIONS

INDEX OF PHOTOGRAPHERS